BAUBLES OF BLASPHEMY

Edwin F. Kagin

BAUBLES OF BLASPHEMY

With a Foreword by Tom Flynn

Revised Second Edition

American Atheist Press
Cranford, New Jersey
2009

First edition ©2005 Edwin F. Kagin and the Atlanta Freethought Society, Inc., 1170 Grimes Bridge Road, Suite 500, Roswell, Georgia, 30075. www.atlantafreethought.org Editor: Edward M. Buckner. ISBN 1-887392-14-9 First printing January 2005. Second printing March 2009.

Second revised edition ©2009 Edwin F. Kagin. Published by American Atheist Press, P.O. Box 158, Cranford, New Jersey 07016. www.atheists.org Editor: Frank R. Zindler ISBN-13: 978-1-57884-004-5 ISBN-10: 1-57884-004-X

Library of Congress Cataloging-in-Publication Data

Kagin, Edwin F., 1940–
    Baubles of blasphemy / Edwin F. Kagin ; with a foreword by Tom Flynn.— Rev. 2nd ed.
        p. cm.
    Includes bibliographical references and index.
    ISBN-13: 978-1-57884-004-5 (alk. paper)
    ISBN-10: 1-57884-004-X (alk. paper)
    1. Religion—humor. 2. Creationism—Humor. 3. Religious right—Humor. I. Title.
    PN6231.R4K34 2009
    818'.607—dc22
                                200925243

Front cover designed by Kathryn Kagin Cohan, based on an idea by Helen Kagin.
Back cover designed by Ann Zindler and Kathryn Kagin Cohan.

***Blasphemy is the crime
of making fun of ridiculous beliefs
someone else holds sacred.***
—Edwin F. Kagin

Isaiah 37:3: *This day is a day of trouble,
and of rebuke, and of blasphemy ...*

Mark 14:64: *Ye have heard the blasphemy:
what think ye?*

Matthew 12:31: *Wherefore I say unto you, All manner
of sin and blasphemy shall be forgiven unto men:
but the blasphemy against the Holy Ghost
shall not be forgiven unto men*

Advance Praise for Edwin Kagin and
Baubles of Blasphemy

Edwin Kagin has penned a delightful book reflecting his views as freethinking satirical critic, humorist and, yes, a curmudgeon of sorts. Between the covers a reader (depending on his or her intellectual disposition) is sure to discover a gathering of essays and poetry that will inform and provoke, anger and elate, seduce— and in some cases surely outrage—and finally do what any book should do, namely, clamor for a place on the bookshelf of any thoughtful person, believer or infidel.

Admittedly, we've heard many of these thoughts before, whether from ancient critics of religion, or more recent titans like Joseph McCabe, Robert Ingersoll or even Madalyn O'Hair. The treasure of this book is how Edwin says what he says, how he turns a phrase, how he mints a title (I especially like "On Genital Based Morality") and the near storyteller quality his words convey. It is all friendly, upbeat, and fun. Edwin is a wag, an epigrammatist, a punster, jester, jokesmith and banterer. But his ideas are, well, serious and to the point. We have here a book that even some of the most religious can laugh at, and with, and even the most serious Atheist will find a lighthearted relief in an otherwise burdensome debate.

Open these pages, gentle reader. Be entertained, be taunted, but by all means be enlightened!

Ellen Johnson
President, American Atheists
January 11, 2005

Is Edwin Kagin another Mark Twain? Not really. Mark Twain would have considered these writings blasphemous. But then Twain never heard of Falwell, Robertson, or Ashcroft.

Will this book win Edwin Kagin a Nobel Prize for literature or poetry? Probably not. But we would be living in a much better world if it did.

Herb Silverman
Leader, Secular Humanists of the Low Country
Charleston SC

When I first met Edwin Kagin it was during a campaign in which the Creation Science [sic] crowd had attempted to run roughshod over county officials and local residents to establish a "museum" in Boone County Kentucky. As a pastor of a mainline Christian congregation I found myself happily on the same side with this witty and delightful person. I knew I would like Edwin when he tried a few one-liners on me which I found to be edgy and insightful. He saw me in my multicolored tie-dyed clergy robes and declared, "A chameleon could commit suicide on that thing." During a debate with a local fundamentalist clergy Edwin described Mary Magdalene's account of the resurrection of Christ as "the testimony of a deranged hooker." After attending one of our church services he straight facedly referred to the communion service as "swallow the leader." I do not always agree with some of the things this man says. But I know him to be a person of great integrity and thank God for him as the gadfly to my most cherished views. Edwin helps keep me honest and most definitely keeps me laughing.

The Reverend Mendle Adams
Senior Pastor, St. Peter's United Church of Christ
Cincinnati, Ohio

I've greatly enjoyed Edwin Kagin's humor, the ideal antidote against theistic fissiparousness.
As one who was an Atheist in an Omaha Beach foxhole in 1944, I particularly have been touched by his foxhole song. Holy Zeus, who better to be found in between the sheets with Franz Kafka and Frida Kahlo (actually, on page 604 of Who's Who in Hell) *than this inspired Kentucky attorney and son of a Presbyterian minister!*

Warren Allen Smith
Author, *Who's Who in Hell*

Acknowledgements

While it is perhaps trite to say that there are people who should be acknowledged for their perhaps unknowing help in influencing, inspiring, or providing good suggestions, whether wanted or not, on the works here presented, let me be trite and say there are more people to be acknowledged than can be remembered all at once. Those unmentioned are not unappreciated.

Of the greatest influence, inspirational and correctional, on the contents of this book have been my wife Helen (and yes, on occasion, her predecessors in title), my children Stephen, Eric, Heather, and Kathryn, my stepdaughter Caroline Good, and my sisters Roberta and Mary (together with their spouses and their children—both those ascertained and those which are, as of this writing, works in process). This is so whether these good people know it or not, and whether or not they approve of, much less agree with, many of these writings.

I am also indebted, beyond any attempt at evaluation, to the staff and campers of Camp Quest.

I gratefully acknowledge the help and encouragement of Atheist writers, leaders, and thinkers like Tom Flynn, Warren Allen Smith, Ellen Johnson, Conrad Goeringer, Frank Zindler, Herb Silverman, Bobbie Kirkhart, Bart Meltzer, and many others.

And to various professional Christian types, including a lot of good ones, like Rev. Mendel Adams. And I regretfully acknowledge the influence of a whole lot of bad Christians, and other religious types, past and present, ranging from harmless fools to dangerous lunatics. Without them, *Baubles of Blasphemy* would have been neither possible nor needed. If they are permitted to have their way, it will not long survive.

In the production of the physical reality of this book, I gratefully acknowledge the Atlanta Freethought Society, and the Freethought Press, who dared to accept the challenge of bringing *Baubles of Blasphemy* to the public. One printer actually refused to set these words on paper. And I acknowledge the able assistance and guidance (merciless tyrannical browbeating) of my editor Ed Buckner, who heartlessly drove this project, arranging my amorphous collection of rantings, establishing impossible deadlines, and, for reasons known only to editors, cutting words, works, etc., thought to be of the highest irreplaceable merit by the author. And I gratefully acknowledge the help of Leonard Zanger, Diane Buckner, and Helen Kagin, who all compulsively read the manuscript and suggested meaningful editorial changes to the text and format, including the cover.

Perhaps most importantly, I acknowledge with sadness and gratitude the contributions to freedom of thought and to the human condition of those martyrs who gave their lives that we might be free of the very concept of "blasphemy." I salute those who died for our right to explore, to discover, and to teach to others truth that defies dogma, to those heroes who stood, at the cost of their lives, for science over superstition, for inquiry over inquisition, for reality over revelation, for creativity over creed, for facts over faith. It is because of their sacrifices that you can legally own and read this book today.

No matter what some fool says, it is not today a crime of blasphemy for you to say (in most places at least), without fear of the gulag or the stake, truths that some in our barbaric past have not liked, and which some may not now like, such as that the earth is round, that the earth goes around the sun, and that humans evolved from other forms of life.

The future of your right to speak your own baubles of blasphemy is by no means certain. Whether or not you, or your children, can do so tomorrow is up to you.

Edwin F. Kagin
January 2005

Table of Contents

Foreword
Tom Flynn

Boy, would I hate to be sued by Edwin Kagin.

How to describe Edwin Kagin to a reader who is about to encounter him for the first time? (Yes, I could just scream, "Run for your life!," but that would be too easy.) Edwin Kagin is intransigent. Implacable. Irrefragable. And other big words. Florid language is fitting when the topic is Edwin, for more than anything else he resembles one of those early nineteenth century pioneer farmers who could deliver a calf of a morning and carry on a disputation in Latin and Greek that afternoon. His fiery combination of a backwoods manner, feral urbanity, and an absolutely ruthless search for truth makes him an unmistakable figure on the landscape of American irreligion.

Have I mentioned that he's unhesitating?

Edwin Kagin is a lawyer whose office (aptly marked by a logo of a pen covering a sword) adorns a hardscrabble Ohio River town in that great yahoo state of Kentucky. Unpromising ground for an Atheist activist, one might think; but in thinking that, one underestimates Kentucky, which has given the nation more than its share of visionaries, reformers, and muckrakers. And one underestimates Edwin, who would doubtless be his flinty, penetrating self no matter where life happened to set him down. (Though when Edwin walks into a humanist conference in a big-city hotel with his fishing vest, floppy-brimmed backwoods hat, two or three really top-of-the-line knives, and a six-foot walking stick, it's a pretty sure bet that he ain't from New Jersey.)

Did I say that he's obdurate?

I first encountered Edwin through Kagin's Column, a regular feature in *FIG Leaves,* the newsletter of FIG, the secular humanist group in Cincinnati. (I won't keep you in suspense; FIG stands for Free Inquiry Group.) You never knew what Kagin's Column would contain: whimsical poetry with claws, a satirical contemplation of some foolish specimen of popular belief, perhaps a clarion cry for readers to bound out of their easy chairs and meet some fundamentalist foe on the ideological battlefield. I never knew what Kagin's Column would contain, but each time I faced a pile of local group newsletters

1

Edwin F. Kagin: *Baubles of Blasphemy*

I tended to pluck up *FIG Leaves* first, and Kagin's Column was what I read first. Not a few of the works in this book started out as Kagin's Columns.

Before long, I met Edwin face to face on one of my frequent visits to Cincinnati. (I'm fond of Cincinnati, having gone to college there; I owe the Jesuits at Xavier University a great debt for making me the Atheist I am today, but that's another foreword.) Edwin was fervent, inexorable, sagacious. I met his wife Helen, immediately marking her as an exemplar of devotion and endurance, if not of taste in men—hey, I can say that: When Edwin introduces Helen to someone, he often creates the impression that her middle name is "I-don't-know-why-she-puts-up-with-me."

Did I mention that Edwin is shrewd and adamant?

Edwin is also a man who knows what he likes. The year my book *The Trouble with Christmas* came out, I made a speaking tour of humanist groups throughout the Midwest, my sleigh—oops, station wagon—loaded with copies to sell. Cincinnati was one of my early stops. My good friend Joe Levee, co-founder of the Free Inquiry Group, opened his delightful house for my talk. Edwin was in the audience as I traced the unedifying history of most people's favorite holiday and called for secular humanists to make themselves conspicuous by finding something else to do on December 25th. Afterwards, Edwin approached me and lauded my speech in immoderate terms. (Then again, Edwin does everything in immoderate terms.) With a conspiratorial urgency, he asked where I kept my stock of books for sale. I led him outside to my car ... where he bought them all. If memory serves, I had enough books to cover visits to eight more cities, and Edwin bought the caboodle. I had to have more books overnighted to my next destination. As for Edwin, he sent *The Trouble with Christmas* to everyone on his Christmas list. During the following year he spent some time considering my argument, wisely decided that I was right, and resolved thenceforward to live Yule free. When that year's "helladay" season drew nigh, Edwin sent a note to everyone to whom he had previously sent my book, advising them that he would no longer observe a holiday that wasn't the birthday of anyone he knew, so please don't send cards or gifts or expect any in return. I'm told that most recipients were ... unsurprised.

Foreword

Francis Church's "Yes, Virginia," the smarmy 1897 newspaper op-ed in which he mixed Emersonian transcendentalism, Victorian romanticism, and an unhealthful preoccupation with fairies in order to bamboozle a young girl's honest inquiry as to the reality of Santa Claus, seldom gets the abuse it deserves. (In fact, it seldom gets reprinted in full, as some of its later passages are so embarrassing.) Edwin's ruthless deconstruction of "Yes, Virginia," is one of this book's great pleasures.

Did I mention Edwin's passionate zeal?

Edwin Kagin is well known in the greater Cincinnati and northern Kentucky area as a fighter for church-state separation, the civil rights of unbelievers, and the independence of scientific inquiry. When evangelist Kenneth Ham of an outfit called Answers in Genesis came to the area and proposed to open a museum of young-earth creationism opposite the entrance of a Kentucky state park famed for its fossil deposits, Edwin leapt into action, mobilizing FIG and sundry members of greater Cincinnati's scientific and educational communities as he went. It turned into one of organized humanism's more colorful success stories: the campaign Edwin led blocked Kenneth Ham from opening his museum for several years. Ham finally got his museum built, but he had to settle for a far less conspicuous location. During this period Edwin frequently unleashed his pen in the general direction of the Reverend Ham, producing everything from vitriolic essays to hilarious doggerel. Not a few of the "baubles" in this book came out of the Battle of Big Bone Lick (which was the name of the state park).

By the way, Edwin is cunning and uncompromising, did I tell you that?

Sometimes Edwin Kagin can be as eloquent as a neglected laceration starting to plump up with pus. Not for a little while, either—he is often so *tenaciously.* Surely nothing bespeaks Edwin's tenacity better than a little thing called Camp Quest. For as long as I've known him, Edwin complained that secular humanists needed to provide some of the same developmental experiences for their children that religious parents provided for theirs. Over time this occasional topic of Edwin's became an obsession, then a mania.

Then he got really serious about it.

Edwin F. Kagin: *Baubles of Blasphemy*

The result was Camp Quest, America's first residential summer camp for humanist children. It's been running for almost a decade now at multiple locations in the United States and Canada. To call Edwin the father of Camp Quest is to understate, because to become a father one requires the cooperation of a prospective mother. Without minimizing the important contributions dozens of other people made to the Camp Quest phenomenon, it must be said that at the most fundamental level, Camp Quest is Edwin's creation and Edwin's alone. Without his ardent, unyielding advocacy over a period of several years, Camp Quest would never have happened.

I remember several visits to Cincinnati in the early 1990s, often in the company of then-*Free Inquiry* editor Timothy Madigan. On each visit Edwin would loquacify at progressively greater length on the hungry, aching *need* for a humanist summer camp, always enhancing the persuasiveness of his arguments, always dialing up the passion. He was not just convincing, he was overpowering. Uncontainable. Running a camp is not without risks—hey, a kid could fall out of a canoe and drown—and humanist organizations are not exactly known for their eagerness to take on risks of that sort. First Edwin had to convince the other members of FIG that a small organization that had heretofore published a newsletter, campaigned against creationists, and annually erected a "wall of separation" display on Cincinnati's municipal square should take on the temporary stewardship of other people's children. Of course, having resolved to hold a summer camp, one faces next the question what one will have those children *do* while they're there 24/7 for a week or two. But fear not, Edwin the former Eagle Scout and accomplished backwoodsman knew just what to have those children do, and he arm-twisted—I mean, networked—to assemble an astonishing range of genuine experts to give those kids rich side exposure to astronomy, geology, philosophy, critical thinking, you name it. Not just the idea of having a camp, but the day-by-day program that became Camp Quest bears the impress of Edwin Kagin's single-minded tenacity.

Edwin's years of campaigning for Camp Quest culminated in an astonishing, almost Ingersollian feat of oratory at the then-new Center for Inquiry in 1995. The last people Edwin needed to convince were Paul Kurtz, founder and chairman of what we then called the Council for Democratic and Secular Humanism, and members of the Council's board. The occasion was a meeting of humanist group leaders from around the country, and the agendas of such things tend to be rough-and-tumble affairs. When the topic of Camp Quest came up, Edwin had about fifteen seconds' notice that yes, Virginia, *now* was the moment to make his strongest case for the Council providing Camp Quest with some seed money and promoting it in *Free Inquiry* magazine. I think he talked nonstop for an hour and a quarter, maybe longer. He anticipated and disposed of every objection, and infected all present with his own firm conviction that this summer camp was something that *had* to happen. He left that meeting with the Council's endorsement, its seed money, and a commitment of magazine promotion—the final elements needed for Camp Quest to become a reality.

Once more Edwin's bulldoggedness would be required to save the project. By the time the above-mentioned decision was made, it was well into fall 1995. Would there be time to promote the camp and induce parents to make an early-spring decision to send their children? *Free Inquiry* was a quarterly then, and we had legitimate concerns that time was too short. Perhaps, we suggested, the first camp should be held in 1997, not 1996, allowing a full year to educate the humanist community about this unprecedented project. Edwin would have none of it. One final time he shouldered the craggy boulder that Camp Quest had become and bulled it toward his goal, shouldering aside all skeptics and nay-sayers as he went. The first Camp Quest was held in 1996, and despite a few rough edges (such as having to hold it in a campground rented from a Baptist organization) it was an enormous success.

I could say much more about Camp Quest—the saga of the Baptists' eventual decision not to rent their camp to goldurn atheists any more almost rates a book of its own—but suffice it to say that Camp Quest will long stand as the manifestation of Edwin Kagin's lone will and vision. Few human beings get to put their sole personal stamp on a creation in that way. And of course, being Edwin, he'll never stop telling us about it, as he does in some of the delightful works in this volume.

Did I mention that Edwin is artful, rigorous, and plain-spoken?

Edwin F. Kagin: *Baubles of Blasphemy*

He's been especially plain-spoken about the threat of Christian fundamentalism. For Edwin, fundamentalist Christianity doesn't just threaten to turn a few thousand churchgoers' brains to tapioca or infect young Americans with inaccurate ideas about the history of our planet. No, in Edwin's view it poses a fundamental threat to the foundations of our culture and our democracy. He's right, of course—most of us in the humanist community now recognize the importance and the urgency of the culture wars in which we are engaged. But Edwin saw it early. He was willing to speak and write about it with his trademark want of subtlety, even if many of his fellow humanists thought he was vastly overdrawing the threat. Perhaps the single purest dose of Kaginism in this volume is his relentless essay, "On the Coming American Religious Civil War." When he published it in 1995, quite a few who read it thought he radically overstated the ambitions, malevolence, and sheer power of our fundamentalist adversaries. Reading it today, with George W. Bush in the White House, billions of tax dollars flowing to religious organizations, and wars raging pretty much wherever the inhabitants are not white and Christian, one realizes that Edwin was only telling us the plausible parts.

If we are indeed headed for religious civil war in America, we can be grateful that Edwin Kagin is *our* weapon of mass destruction.

Oh, did I mention that he's intense?

Tom Flynn is editor of Free Inquiry *magazine, director of the Robert Green Ingersoll Birthplace Museum, and author of* The Trouble with Christmas *and the novels* Galactic Rapture *and* Nothing Sacred. *He is currently editing an all-new edition of Gordon Stein's 1985* Encyclopedia of Unbelief.

Editor's Note
Ed Buckner

I seek here to claim far more credit than I should. It was, I think and hope, I who first suggested to Mr. Kagin that his writings be organized into a book. It has been my pleasure to be the one who has organized his writings and acted as midwife to these his children in other ways as well. I can even claim that one piece found here was written at my request and to my specifications, some years back (the reader will have to guess which piece that is.) It is labor I'm very proud of, as I'm proud to have my name associated with this book. (That doesn't mean I agree with Mr. Kagin on all he says; surely no one does.)

Even those readers who think they know Edwin Kagin well may be surprised though delighted even as they are caught unprepared. His humor is sometimes subtle, sometimes broad, nearly always barbed with deeply serious intent. Most of his writing leads one to conclude that the one best word to describe him and what he has to say is "irreverent." But he also is a good poet, capable of making you see in new ways and inspiring awe at natural beauty and, especially, at life. If you are in any sense an orthodox thinker, his writing may piss you off—he may in fact have been eager to do so. [*Editor's note to the Editor's Note:* Pissed at seeing the word *piss* in print? If so, please see, in the King James Version of the Holy Bible, 2 Kings 18:27 or Isaiah 36:12, for an even less appetizing use of the fine Middle English/Old French word.] Kagin will, I promise, make you think as well as laugh, and he will stir your political passions, your outrage, maybe your fears, and certainly your love of life.

The book is divided into sections, but not into serious matters versus comic (the material simply cannot be so divided). Nor is the poetry segregated from the essays. The organizing principle, by subject matter, is somewhat arbitrary and somewhat unfair. (Kagin himself may sue me—and win.) He does not write in neatly compartmentalized subject areas, instead commenting on the broadest of themes, ridiculing or satirizing or glorifying an amazingly broad array of subjects. As I have cast them into sections, I have in many cases interpreted one aspect of a piece as the dominant one when the reader may see—and Kagin himself may have intended—some other view of it as the central one. I have also in some cases grouped pieces into one section rather than another on no doubt flimsy grounds. Kagin fans, and they are legion, can argue about my divisions—but don't. Read all the pieces and enjoy.

Preface

Edwin F. Kagin

(January 2005)

This book is no more about baubles, or about blasphemy, than a book on 'creation science' is about creation or about science. The book's title was to get you to buy it. Thanks. Hope you like it. If you are reading this for free in a store, go buy the damn book. If you like it, tell others and write nice letters about it. If you don't like it, you are encouraged to give it such a hard time that lots of others will want to buy it. You know, sort of like *The Catcher in the Rye*, or *The Satanic Verses*, or *Ulysses*. Might never have heard of any of these if some group with the temporary power to do so didn't ban one or more of them at various unhappy times. Anyone who thinks *Ulysses* is a dirty book has never read *Ulysses*. The same type people will probably buy a copy of *The Confessions of St. Augustine* off the rack at the bus station for titillation *en route*.

There is no such thing as 'blasphemy.' The word refers to some idea or statement you or anyone else can condemn as unholy, irreverent, or maximally distasteful if you or he doesn't like it. It also applies, depending on who is in power and what you say, to other ideas, whether political, scientific, literary, or anything else for that matter, which are not popular, are not generally accepted, or are not liked by whoever is calling them blasphemy. 'Dirty books' are usually ones dealing with some aspect of the amazingly popular subject of sex. The word *blasphemy* usually isn't applied to 'dirty books.' Such are more commonly seen as 'sinful.' Apart from perhaps having actual grime on them, books are not dirty. They are either well written or they are not well written.

The idea of blasphemy is most often applied to religious views that a person with power to state what is and what is not blasphemous doesn't like, or which makes fun of things the person with that power holds to be sacred. If such persons have the power to do so, they can make the stating, or the writing, of the thing they don't like against the law. Blasphemy has been, and in some places still is, a crime. Yeah, right now. That's why the book is named the way it is. It is part of the message. A bauble is a useless or worthless little thing. That's what blasphemy is. No harm to anyone. Words can't hurt you. Can they? Blasphemy is a remarkably plastic crime. At some times and in some places it was, and maybe in some places it still is, punished by a fine or by simply deciding you will go to hell when you die. At some times and in some places, including right now in some places, being convicted of the crime of blasphemy can get you executed (killed) for blasphemy.

Here's how it works. If you are a Christian, it is blasphemy to say that Jehovah didn't have a son, *i.e.* Jesus. People have gotten killed horribly for saying that that god was childless instead of acknowledging that he miraculously made a baby on the unwed body of an underage girl. Fine so far. But if you are a follower of Islam, it is blasphemy to say that Allah had a son or any child of any kind at all. So, pay your money and take your chance. No matter which side you come down on, someone will want to kill you for blasphemy. Some folks in the past, and maybe now, thought anyone should be killed who thought One-True-God was not three separate gods in one god. Others thought anyone who thought some god was more gods than one god should be killed. What for? For blasphemy, of course. In Christianity alone, people have been murdered for whether they believed converts should be baptized by being dunked in water or by having water sprinkled on their heads. And for many other things. And these are only two religions. There are lots more, most containing subgroups within them, each claiming the only truth, and each having their unique catalogue of what constitutes blasphemy.

It should be fairly clear by now that if someone is permitted to have the power to say what is blasphemy, and the power and desire to punish the person committing blasphemy (known as a blasphemer), then we can never make any kind of progress in anything. What if someone decides that the earth is flat, or that the earth is the center of the universe and that the sun goes around the earth? And what if the persons so believing could make it a crime for anyone to say otherwise?

Preface

Unless we like the idea of killing each other over contradictory beliefs, we are much better off without having any concept of blasphemy at all. At least not one enforced by the criminal laws. If you disagree with someone's religious belief, or lack thereof, fine. But please just be content with the knowledge that you are saved, that you believe correct things, and that your righteous person is going to go to Heaven when you are a dead hunk of meat, and that those persons you view as believing, and saying or writing, wrong things about religious beliefs are going to be punished forever in torment in whatever version of an afterlife you or your grandmother says is so. And let it go at that. Don't let anyone have power who thinks their views of religious truth should be made law universal. Someone might get the job who thinks you are a blasphemer.

This volume contains various works of poetry and prose whose variety of content and message is sufficiently diverse to offend or shock almost everyone at one time or another. There is history and fantasy, reporting and opinion, analysis and mocking. Some offerings are satire. Some are not. Some are even quite serious. Some are personal statements. Readers can decide which is what for themselves. When an author releases creative works for public consumption, the author loses control over what those works mean. *Baubles of Blasphemy* celebrates the right to enjoy and to exercise independence of intellectual thought and action. Sorry if you don't like that.

Some of my best friends are Christians. Some of these works have been quoted by real ministers in real sermons on real Sunday mornings. Occasionally, a minister will contact me and ask for a sermon idea. Thus was established my free service "Edwin's Secular Sermons; Compassionate Help for the Homiletically Challenged."

This book will be a success if it makes you laugh. Laughter is good for you. Humor, even corrosive humor, can heal.

On February 17, 1600, Giordano Bruno was burned to death (so that his blood would not be shed) by the Christian Inquisition for blasphemy. Before he was burned, his tongue was nailed to the roof of his mouth. He had written that the earth went around the sun. That was his bauble of blasphemy.

11

Edwin F. Kagin: *Baubles of Blasphemy*

If you are convinced that certain works in this collection of writings are true, or are not true, or if you think you know what the author was up to when any of those things were written, you are almost certainly wrong. If you agree with the author on any of these writings, or if you agree with any other writings anywhere for that matter, that's okay. If you think the author, or any author, is wrong about anything, that's fine, too. Write your own book.

Just don't rile up the villagers to go after the author, or any other authors, with pitchforks and torches.

This is a book about freedom.

THE AMERICAN RELIGIOUS CIVIL WAR (ARCW)

Keeping Government Out of the
Hands of Religion and Religionists

On the Coming
American Religious Civil War (ARCW)
(August 1995)

War is hell.
Little understood aphorism.

THIS MAY BE YOUR FIRST NOTICE OF THE COMING AMERICAN RELIGIOUS CIVIL WAR (ARCW). If so, you should date and preserve this warning. Then your distant descendants (maybe the "Daughters of the ARCW") can have something to be smug about—in the unlikely event that they, and this notice, survive the fires, and anybody can still read.

The ARCW has already been started by the superstitious. They call it a "civil war of values." The shooting has already started. They call that "protecting innocent life." The purpose of the war is to overthrow science and constitutional democracy and to replace them with the Bronze Age myths and laws of ancient Iraq that became preserved in a collection of writings known, in translation, as *The Holy Bible*. They regard this undertaking as "bringing America back to God." Loyal Americans should regard it as treason.

The effects of the stated ends of the traitors include: harming children by not teaching them about human sexuality; harming adults by irrationally circumscribing consensual sexual and reproductive freedom; harming democracy by imposing laws enforcing mythological interpretations of a supernatural being's will; harming civilization by preventing inquiry and suppressing evidence that disproves the myths; harming human development by teaching that humans have a duty to live for some superstitious spiritual world rather than for the world of flesh in which they happen to exist. The traitors do not view their teachings or methods as harmful, but neither did their pious ancestors who beat children and burned women alive for their own good.

The fanatics have declared war on reason and human progress. They have done this because they suffer from fundamental misunderstandings of the nature of American democracy and of the Bible.

15

Edwin F. Kagin: *Baubles of Blasphemy*

History tells lies. It is important to understand this to understand the ARCW. A particularly harmful lie is that the United States of America was founded as a Christian nation. The traitors truly believe this because it has been taught them since they colored pilgrims with crayons in church nursery school while their parents were in the sanctuary learning to be more judgmental. As the young bigots grew into adultery [*sic*], they accepted this teaching uncritically, just as they accepted that everything in the Bible is true, and that science is wrong, if not evil, when it proves that humans have evolved from non-human life forms. The traitors should, in fairness, be permitted to prove the intensity of this mental abuse in their defense at the ARCW war crimes trials.

America was not established as a Christian nation. To the contrary, it was intentionally set up as a godless nation. That's why no god or religion of any kind is mentioned in our Constitution. This was so important that it was memorialized in the first words of the first amendment to our Constitution, to wit, "Congress shall make no law respecting an establishment of religion, or prohibiting the free exercise thereof...." The people who started this country knew what religious war and holy terror was, and they wanted to be very clear that America was a democracy set up under human law, not religious authority or rule. This was made exquisitely clear when, in a treaty with Tripoli, signed by President John Adams on June 10, 1797, the United States Senate unanimously declared, "...the government of the United States of America is not in any sense founded on the Christian Religion." That's that, said the grammarian. People who don't like the American way, and think church and state should not be separated, really ought to move to Serbia where they can kill and rape non-believers with impunity.

The traitors who push the ARCW think they are doing their god's will by trying to force their sacred texts and prejudices on those who want to dance to other celestial music or simply stay home Sunday mornings and brush the cat. Before our Constitution, several states made criminals of people who didn't attend the right church, or, whisper the thought, did not attend holy services at all. Some very wise people made us a nation where it is legal to stay home with the cat. If we want to keep it that way, it is necessary to win the ARCW.

16

As the believers, who think the fault is in the stars and not in themselves, are waging the ARCW on many fronts, thus on many fronts must freedom be defended. Particularly valuable allies can be found among Christians who find attempts to force their foot into someone else's shoe offensive. After all, if the existence and will of any god were clearly known, there would be no need for faith or debate. No one seriously doubts that objects fall down if dropped, but there is murderous dispute over beliefs that cannot be proved as convincingly as gravity.

This is a wake up call. Don't press the snooze alarm. The barbarians are at the gates, and, because they encourage breeding beyond the ability of the breeders to house, feed, and educate the breedees, violence and social disorganization continue. As the most Christian nation on earth watches its civilization dissolve like a Dove bar fallen off of that ark, attempts to enforce irrational superstitious solutions will accelerate. That Branch Davidian thing was a sample. Lots of other messiahs are waiting. Maybe we can have court-ordered Branch Davidian Social Services counseling for people who won't share their wives with their god's anointed. Maybe courts can acquit murderers if they believe a god's finger was on their trigger. Maybe the barbarians will actually succeed in assuring that books, pictures, ideas, doctors, judges and military commanders share their vision. Then we will have a lot of interesting tribal warfare. One useful defense will be humanistic hermeneutics.

Hermeneutics is a fancy word for biblical interpretation. When religious types want to make something simple sound holy and mysterious, they often give it an important sounding high falutin' name. This practice contrasts sharply with the usage of secular humanists, who, in explaining their views, employ simple words, that fall trippingly from the tongue, like 'eupraxophy.'

Hermeneutics can be an important weapon to use against religious fanatics in the coming ARCW. The hard core nut cases—those who would control every aspect of our lives by forcing us to accept their understanding of the will of their god—tend to share certain operational assumptions. These include the belief that:

Edwin F. Kagin: *Baubles of Blasphemy*

(1) Every word of the Bible is true.

(2) The English translation of the Bible authorized by King James the First of England, completed in 1611, Common Era, is the only fully acceptable, authoritative, and inspired-by-god translation of holy scripture. This translation is accurate in every respect, including punctuation marks.

(3) The Bible is the basis of all morality. Without it there can be no morality.

(4) The United States of America was established, and should be governed, according to biblical principles.

(5) The Bible is without error.

(6) No part of the Bible is in conflict with, or contradictory to, any other part.

(7) Hermeneutics can be used to clarify and explain those truths of god in the Bible that might appear, to finite minds, to be in conflict. The goal of hermeneutics is to reconcile all portions of the 'Word of God' (the Bible) into a seamless, complete, infallible, and final statement of all past and future history (the latter is called *prophecy*), of divine law, and of how humans should behave and understand morality. The Bible, properly interpreted, is the final word on *everything*.

Ignorance, while regrettable, can lead to some interesting discussions. As an example of how hermeneutics works, one gospel tells us Judas hanged himself after betraying Jesus. The Book of Acts says Judas fell forward into a field and exploded. Proper interpretation, guided by the 'Holy Spirit,' reveals this to mean Judas hanged himself over a cliff. Then the rope, or branch, broke, and Judas fell down the cliff. If the author of the "Song of Solomon" in the Bible appears to drool over a woman's breasts, this is not to be understood in some sexual sense that would keep the Bible out of family-friendly libraries, but rather as a poetic metaphor of Christ's love for his church. See, it's really quite simple.

Fanatics feel that only the godless and the immoral could possibly understand the Bible as a collection of diverse literary myths, sexy stories, primitive laws, and biased histories, unconnected in their presentation, and unworthy of belief in their totality. Such true believers are quite satisfied with the famous refutation of reason of the early Christian church: "I believe it because it is absurd."

The problem is that they are not content to believe what they want and let others believe, or not believe, as they choose. The ARCW they have declared has the avowed purpose of making our democracy one nation under their idea of god. This is treason in its purest and most virulent form.

America was not founded on biblical principles. There is nothing in the Bible about democracy. Democracy was invented in Greece, some five hundred years before Jesus. It was overwhelmed for centuries in religious bloodbaths of kings and emperors, and, with minor exceptions, disappeared from human affairs until it was rediscovered and memorialized in the Constitution of the United States of America. To insure that dictators and priests would be kept forever at bay, after much debate, our Constitution was consciously created as a godless document that established a wholly secular state. Love it or leave it.

The religious fanatics who are traitors to our way of life must be stopped before their un-American attempts to replace our democracy with their mythology causes the ARCW to become a shooting war. Using their principles of hermeneutics, their own book can become a powerful weapon against them in ways reasonable people (including most Christians) can understand.

The Bible contains a relatively limited vocabulary when compared with the great contemporary literary works of Greek and Roman writers. The style is also awkward by comparison. One might argue that a work dictated by a god should be expected to be better than the writings of heathens, but, alas, it is not. There are no original ideas or thoughts in the Bible. Much of it is plagiarized from Egyptian and Babylonian sources. There is little that passes for morality as we understand it. Slavery is condoned, as is the murder of children of nonbelievers; a rebellious son should be stoned to death, and women are to be totally subjugated to men. A man could have many wives in the Old Testament. If it is argued that the New Testament created a 'New Covenant' wherein only one wife is permitted, we might wonder if the changeless god might have changed his mind. If so, how can every word of the Old Testament be taken as the will of the same god?

Edwin F. Kagin: *Baubles of Blasphemy*

From a search of the sacred text itself, using a computerized King James Bible, available in Christian bookstores, we discover that the following words do not appear in the Bible: cooperate; cooperation; moral; traditional values; rational; rights; morals; independence; congress; compromise; progress; republic; republican; democrat; democracy; insight; morality; jury; vote; test; due process; consequences; coincidence; parliament; majority; minority; constitution; achievement; aspire; human; invention; explore; discovery; humanity; humanism; university; universe; homosexual; fairness; harmony; treaty; logic; sexuality; abort; abortion; fetus; poet; poetry; artist; creativity. [*Editor's note:* As a matter of fact, the word 'brain' also is not to be found there either!]

If the Bible is the foundation of morality and our way of life, we are in serious trouble indeed. If the ARCW is lost, we will have no need for those omitted words.

On Genital Based Morality (GBM)

Morals are manners, and manners are subject to change.
—Mrs. Carolyn Benton Cockefaire

As this blasphemy is written in early February 1999, the next to the last year of this millennium, a sideshow skirmish in the American Religious Civil War (ARCW) whimpers to an end. This fanatic digression from reason (fortunately doomed to failure—for now at least) was flamed by attempts of the storm troopers of the religiocencratic forces to kick out the President of the United States because they deem him immoral and unfit to govern because of what he and a human of female persuasion did with his and her genitals, and that he then allegedly lied concerning the doing thereof.

Voluntarily, with the consent of the victims, our nation has managed to become a joke among nations because the piously powerful refuse to recognize or admit that human beings are sexual beings — and not necessarily monogamous ones. In furtherance of this fool's folly, they ground their understanding of morality on a vain attempt to define humans as somehow outside of the natural world (the only one we know) and apart from other living creatures with whom it is imperfectly shared. If humans were monogamous, they would behave in monogamous ways, as do monogamous animals. To cope with not being monogamously made, rules have been invented requiring monogamous behavior from non-monogamous creatures. These made up rules, that human nature deplores, are defined and presented as the unchangeable moral law of the god of the entire universe. In consequence, pretentiously pious persons lie about sex and delude themselves about morality by genitally defining goodness, and damning, as morally defective, all who dissent, detract, or disobey— including our head of state who also just happens to champion a variety of humanistic causes his detractors undauntedly damn.

Incredibly, the miserable monolithic moronic moral code of those ethical paupers who would destroy us and our democracy in the ARCW is based on genitals (not to be confused with gentiles). This is indeed curious in that sex (not gender—gender is a term of grammar), would be hard pressed to get along without genitals. Where

21

there is sex, there are genitals. It's Yahweh's plan; "male and female created he them." The god the stories say ordained procreation wisely gave created creatures the tools with which to procreate. These tools of that god's plan are the very genitals conjugally challenged sufferers of moralist madness abhor. Rejection of dreaded essential genitals is the center, the very essence, of their nutty notions of moral law. This idiotic and evil short-circuiting of reason, this delusional deduction of dunces, may be understood as Genital Based Morality (GBM).

GBM is an infantile system of primitive simplistic thinking, involving magical make-believe, and is thus quite easy to understand. Abortion, homosexuality, pornography, prostitution, unmarried sex, oral sex, sodomy (maybe Gomorra), non-monogamous sex, 'adult' videos, nudist clubs, nude beaches, nude dancing—anything that touches upon, views, uses, or has anything whatsoever to do with genitals, is immoral and bad. See how easy it is? Further inquiry, reasoning, or evidence is superfluous and irrelevant. If it is genital, it is bad. Barbie and Ken must not have genitals lest they display the ultimate reality of being human, and thereby educate, confuse and corrupt little children who should be taught to believe the world works in ways other than it does. Legislatures and judges should let a religiocrazy kill their kid by denying medical treatment, yet prosecute nudist clubs for permitting people to walk around in the uniform of the day of Eden. Steal from widows and orphans if you must, so long as you don't do the dirty in forbidden ways, or watch others do it, or pay for it, or, Zeus help us all, enjoy it. Rather think of England and canning apricots than be damned by those damned genitals causing forbidden thoughts or, in cases of extreme sin, actually giving their owner(s) forbidden pleasure. GBM subordinates every other consideration regarding personal and group thought and behavior to this prime (not primal) directive.

How did we come to this unhappy state? Scene shifts to downtown Baghdad, Iraq. Where the Tigris and Euphrates rivers meet. Garden of Eden. Year the first. Setting of a Bronze-Age myth that has done much mischief whenever and wherever believed. Adam and Eve were set up by Yahweh. They were naked. They didn't know this was bad because Yahweh didn't tell them. Yahweh knew it was bad, but they didn't. So there they were, the first nudists, as innocently unclothed as the heathen participants in the first Olympic Games, put naked in paradise by a voyeuristic god in a place where snakes talked and had legs and told the truth about knowledge not killing people. Then Eve got Adam, per snake advice, to eat of the tree of knowledge of good and evil, of which a god had told them not to eat. And he did, and she did, and women have been blamed for this ever since, for a god was displeased that they had disobeyed, listened to that snake, and acquired the nasty knowledge that the only human genitals on earth were shamefully exposed. Yahweh then killed some innocent animals to clothe our first parents so they would not be in a state of shame with their genitals showing. Some believed this story and taught others to believe it. Some believe it today. Thus was Genital Based Morality (GBM) born. We don't know what the god wore.

It is unclear just how A & E could have been expected to know it was wrong not to obey that god before they had knowledge of good and evil. But religion need not be rational. The lesson is that knowledge is bad, and that nakedness is shameful. With full knowledge of their shameful state of genital visibility, Adam and Eve were booted out of Eden by a loving and all-knowing god, a god without whose knowledge and approval no sparrow falls. Ever since, those predestined to sin by this same all-merciful god have been damned to eternal suffering for sinning. GBM has never claimed to be logical or fair. Neither has its god. Actually he/she *has*, but this claim is not supported by the record.

Secular humanists, and others who think an ethical system should extend beyond the groin, are condemned by those who see themselves as righteous and saved. The self-righteous contend nonbelievers cannot be good people, for such sinners lack a proper sense of shame and guilt derived from an alleged moral base. This fantasizes an objective, defined, findable, and absolute moral authority that tells good people what is right and what is wrong, a moral compass without which there can be no values. In this understanding, it is a lack of belief in 'natural law' (a misunderstood term) that has spread from godless humanism to science, to classroom, to generate the corrosive moral rot that is wrecking our society, denying us the intervention of a displeased god, whom we offend with abortion, homosexuality, unwed sex, pornography and, Huitzilopotchtli help us all, evolution. Oddly, all of these but the evolution thing seem to have something to do with sex. Come to think on it, the evolution stuff does too. The bottom line says if you aren't guilted out by GBM you are a bad person who is going to spend eternity in Hell.

GBM is a relatively recent religious repression. Apart from the Eden tradition, religious teachings of the past (including lots of really sexy Bible stories they don't tell you about in Sunday school) haven't made anything like this much of a fuss over genitals. Indeed, they seem to have been rather favored—both kinds (genitals, not religions—there are lots more than two kinds of religions). The ancient Greeks made much larger than life models of them (genitals) and put them (the models) on display at public theatres. Such a display in modern moral middle America would get you sent to the cooler in seats of learning like Cincinnati. Genitals probably haven't changed much, but attitudes toward them have. The fault is neither generic nor genital. It is the miasmal moral morass of garbled, glib, guilt-gilded gibberish packaged, proclaimed, and peddled as the 'Will of God' given unto lesser mortals by those who interpret the truths of natural law. You know, people like Dr. Laura, Henry Hyde, and the bigots who run 'Right to Life,' claim to be "family friendly," seek "answers in Genesis" (not genitals) and, because of the GBM that guides their petty lives, want to kick our President out of the White House, as the naked A & E were kicked out of Paradise (not to be confused with Club Paradise) because they acquired knowledge and an awareness of being attached to their genitals.

Those waging the ARCW claim our head of state lied under oath about his private conduct with his privates. Ah, wonder if they know of the manner of swearing when one swore a mighty oath before the holy Patriarchs of the Bible? Abraham and Jacob's method of swearing required the placing of "his hand under the thigh" (Genesis 22:4–9). This involved, I swear, the person giving the oath putting his hand on the genitals of the one to whom he swore. This practice gave weight to the oath. Don't know why this method was adopted, or when it was abandoned (am just glad it was). At least GBM had a real, if different, meaning back then. Maybe the President was attempting the reintroduction of this ancient practice. Don't know how women took oaths, or if such was even permitted. After all, who could trust any woman after Eve? My Helen has a bumper sticker that says, "Eve was framed."

Genitals were so important in the Bible that trimming the male version via circumcision was a religious requirement. And it is written in the 'Word of God' that one who has had his "stones crushed," *i.e.*, had his testicles smashed, "shall not come nigh [*to the altar*] to offer the offerings of the Lord" (Leviticus 21:20*ff*]. Doesn't seem right or fair somehow, but it does show how much genitals meant to those who penned those bronze-age writings. Jesus later suggested that it would be better if a man cut off his genitals (Matthew 19:12). Some early church fathers, like Origen, did just that. Don't know if the "crushed stones" rule applied and kept him out of heaven. That would have been a shame indeed. After Jesus, genitals did not seem so highly regarded, but they were made even more important by being used to define all aspects of the moral law—by becoming the basis of good and evil. Maybe Jesus started GBM. Whoever did was probably scared of women.

The pre-GBM Bible book, the Song of Songs, sometimes erroneously called the Song of Solomon, has quite a bit to say about genitals. It is Jewish and pre-Christian. Puritans, not daring to recognize it for what it is, say this Bible story is an allegory touching on Christ's love for his church. It is actually an erotic work (seems Egyptian, really) about a man's lust for his sister, touching on his desire to climb her branches and, like a young roe, graze about her breasts and genitals. Christ's love for the church, indeed! How much in general genital denial these clever clerics be — especially those proudly proclaiming the cults of celibacy and cloister!

Consider as an alternate approach, one in marked contrast to modern GBM, the ancient Egyptian creation myth. It was a bit different from the one taught in Christian Sunday schools. The great god Rah ejaculated (yes, from his genitals) the stars and all that is—sort of a climactic cosmology. The Egyptian version of the Holy of Holies held a statue of the god with erect phallus. Priestesses and priests held sacred ceremonies reenacting, with the pharaoh, the living god, the cosmic climax. Now how's *that* for a religion? Gives a whole new meaning to the idea of handmaidens. Archeological evidence of these religious beliefs and practices were suppressed by modern puritans who displayed some of the sacred religious art of the Egyptians with an informational museum type sign placed, like a fig leaf, over the essence of the religious symbolism of the pictorial depiction of the turgid pharaoh, the living god. Only by moving the sign could the true meaning of the mysteries of Egyptian religion be revealed, truths once commonly accepted and viewed openly by all, including little children who were not taught to be embarrassed or shamed by genitals. After all, reasoned our unsaved predecessors, where would we be without them?

Then there was sacred prostitution. And there were seasonal approved-by-prevailing-local-religions orgies to teach the crops and herds to reproduce and grow and to encourage the gods to let them do so. The great men of the Bible had many wives, with no complaint from their god. When king David was old, they put two young women in bed with him to keep him warm (1 Kings 1:1*ff*). Lot's daughters got him drunk and seduced him (Genesis 19:30–38). If a king could not get an erection, it was felt he could no longer rule. No impeachment-plot nonsense over sex then. Genital shame is a modern Christian phenomenon. GBM has replaced ethics. Denial has become duty and holiness has been traded for honor. Repression has pushed reason from the banquet table of life. Moralists who think everyone should follow their GBM are generally good persons in the worst sense of the word. If they tell you they are "born again Christians," thank them for the warning. They are usually more tedious and venal the second time around.

Do you find all the moralizing and genital ranting going on these days just a little silly? Good. It is. GBM denies the realities of the world. The preacher doesn't tell on the deacon when they meet in the whorehouse. Everybody lies about sex. Under oath, too. Ask any divorce lawyer. This is because of GBM and the failure to admit that we, who some say are made in the image of god, are not all monogamous creatures, and monogamous or not, we tend to like sex (the exceptions to this are beyond the scope of this discourse). This causes problems when a moral code is imposed and accepted that denies our mortal nature. Our kind would have become extinct long ago if we had followed such a moral law and actually repudiated the idea of deflowering virgins. Enforcement of rules that try to cancel out the very chemistry of life will be about as successful as attempting to plow the sea or baptize a cat.

So we laugh when moralists like Dr. Laura get caught with their pants down in indiscreet photos—from a less famous time—posted on the Internet, or when those who accuse the President are found to have themselves tasted forbidden fruit. Hate and hypocrisy are the twin tyrannies that fuel GBM. Surely there is more to living a good life than making ethical judgments based on genital repression. Consider, dear reader, if you would care to spend eternity in the company of those who do.

If history teaches anything, it is that moral judgments change. This applies to everything from sexual behavior to smoking in public (some say they smoke after sex—others say they never noticed). Today's customs can become tomorrow's perversions, as we make taboo the thrills of our fathers or heap honor on persons and ideas they hated. Things change. That's the one universal truth.

And there are, to be sure, decent monogamous (not to be confused with monotonous) humanistic humans. There are also humans who can eat spaghetti with chopsticks. This does not mean we should outlaw forks.

July 4th, 2004: A Call to Patriotism
Lake Hypatia, Alabama

On this Independence Day
Hard won rights are being lost.
How can we let them slip away,
Are they worth less than what they cost?
Shall pious lies and greed replace
Freedoms traitors now disgrace?

While we pause and hesitate,
While we with whining anguish cry,
The wall that holds back Church from State
Crumbles as our freedoms die.
Shall we stand frozen in our tears
With no resistance but our fears?

Again inspire our nation's rage,
Again hold back a barbarous age!
Become those patriots we prize
To wake our nation from its daze
And freedom's promise realize!
Expel those criminal fools and knaves
Who dare defile our martyrs' graves!

From: Edwin Kagin
Sent: Wednesday, October 03, 2001
To: editor@usatoday.com
Subject: Atheists in Foxholes

Dear Editor of *USA Today*,

Hello from another Atheist in a foxhole.

I have attached four photos taken at the dedication of the only known monument to "Atheists in Foxholes," erected by the Freedom From Religion Foundation at Lake Hypatia, Alabama. Thought you should know before you get the Inquisitorial fires going against patriotic Atheists.

Kathleen Parker thinks these veterans are not good Americans, even though many have risked their lives to protect her Constitutional rights to believe as she wishes and to protect the Constitutional rights of Atheists not to believe as she wishes.

I am proud to have served in the U.S. Air Force to help defend our basic American freedoms. Freedoms like the absolute right to believe in many gods or no gods, without some traitors trying to force American citizens to play in their religious sandbox—you know, like those fanatics who attacked our country.

So yes, Kathleen, there are Atheists in foxholes, no matter what you may think or have heard. They helped found our country, and they have been helping to protect it against people who think there are no Atheists in foxholes ever since.

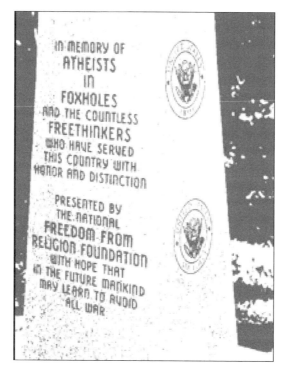

Photo by Hank Shiver

Atheists in Foxholes Song
(May be sung to the tune of
the Marine Corps Hymn)

For the Bill of Rights of our free land
For the Treaty of Tripoli
Many Atheists have fought and died
In the air, on land and sea.
Atheists in many foxholes served
With no task too hard to try
Give the Atheists the thanks deserved
Don't dismiss them with a lie.

Remarks in Opposition to the Northern Kentucky Board of Health's Proposal to Replace Sex Education in the Public Schools with Abstinence and Morals Training
(March 28, 2001)

Members of the Board:

My name is Edwin Kagin. I am an attorney in Union, Kentucky, the father of four children, and a former college instructor who has taught students training to be teachers in the public schools.

I speak tonight, while one still can, against the proposal to educate students in human sexuality by not educating them in human sexuality and by substituting for factual information religious views regarding proper moral behavior that are not shared by all citizens whose children attend our public schools.

The proposal must be rejected because it is patently unlawful and because it is profoundly immoral.

It is patently unlawful because it is yet another attempt by zealots to mandate that their religious opinions become required teachings in public schools, funded by the taxes of all. It is unlawful because it is a violation of Section 5 of the Constitution of Kentucky, which forbids the state from funding any religion, or enlarging or diminishing the rights of any person "...on account of his belief or disbelief of any religious tenet, dogma or teaching." It is a violation of the First Amendment to the Constitution of the United States, which, in the first words of our Bill of Rights, prohibits the state from establishing a religion or from preferring one religion over another religion, or of giving preference to religion over non-religion. The proposed scheme rejects the very system that has kept us a free people. It mocks the opinion of the U.S. Supreme Court that, "...we have staked the very existence of our country on the faith that complete separation between the state and religion is best for the state and best for religion."

The proposal is profoundly immoral because it denies our children, who are our only future, necessary information about the nature and functioning of their own bodies. It would deny them knowledge of that which makes us human. It seeks to substitute rules for knowledge. Lack of information can be deadly. Ignorance can kill you. Don't handicap our children with your hang-ups. Curb your dogma.

Under the moronically flawed reasoning of your "Human Sexuality Committee Report," a pooling of nonsense and religious babble, if young people are just taught moral rules, and schools eliminate health-based, medically factual, sexuality education programs in favor of abstinence-until-marriage programs, then we can prevent sexually transmitted disease and pregnancy. Right! Simple; straightforward; stupid. Under this brave new educational reasoning, we should similarly abolish Driver's Education in our schools. Then our young people won't have automobile accidents.

Members of the Board, you cannot do this. We the People will not tolerate it. We have met and crushed this serpent before. We intend to seek the promises of the future, not the errors of our authoritarian past.

Let this latest threatened inquisition hear free people say, "You shall not press down upon the brow of education this crown of thorns. You shall not crucify our children on this cross of control."

Separation of Church and State
Lecture given at Marshall University,
October 22, 1996

I am a secular humanist. I got that way primarily by reading this book, The Holy Bible. This is the one put out by the Gideons. It's the 1611 edition known as the King James Version. Fundamentalists believe that this is the only authorized gospel, the only Word of God. It was written in 1611 under the auspices of King James the First of England, a homosexual, and is used as the authority for the fundamentalist church. My father was a Presbyterian minister and I was raised deeply into this book. I understand it: if you want to talk the Bible, we can talk the Bible. If you want to debate the Bible, we can debate the Bible.

I have also studied the Constitution of the United States of America and the principles upon which the republic was founded. I understand the laws upon which this country was founded. One of the reasons that secular humanist alliances have sprung up on various college campuses recently is that there is a new and very dramatic movement in this country toward getting away from some very important things on which America was founded. There are people today who are trying to impose upon America, upon a free democracy, their ideas that America is a Christian nation. Not only that it is a Christian nation, but that it is their *kind* of Christian nation. And to that end, we are to have prayers in public schools, mandated by law. We are to teach creationism, not evolution. We are to go backwards to the days of the theocracy.

Some years before the authoring of the American Constitution, there were witch trials in Salem, Massachusetts. By the way, there were no witches burned in America—that's a myth. Witches were *hanged*—they hanged quite a few, too, several dozen. And primary among the evidence was what was known as spectral evidence. That's where someone would come and say an angel or a demon appeared to me and told me Mary So-and-So is having an affair with the Devil. And based upon this evidence, they were hanged. So, ultimately, the governor of Massachusetts prohibited that kind of evidence in a trial.

Prior to the development of our Constitution, many states, including Virginia and Connecticut and other states, had language in their constitutions saying that the governments of those states were based upon Christian principles. Sounds good, doesn't it? Well, if you didn't go to the right church, and the right church was a Congregationalist church, they'd find you and come and talk to you. You could be accused and convicted of a crime called Sabbath-breaking. If you did it again, you could go to jail. You'd be put in the public stocks. There were many people who didn't want to attend a Congregationalist church—there were some Catholics, there were some Baptists, there were some Anabaptists. There were all sorts of different religions that had different views.

We get the impression in history, especially around Thanksgiving time, that the Puritans were a bunch of righteous people who came to America seeking religious freedom. In point of fact, the Puritans came from England after their regime was overthrown in what was known as the Restoration. They chopped off the head of their king, Charles the First. Then a very strict religious theocracy under Oliver Cromwell was set up in England. They closed the theaters. The Puritans were in complete control. It was said that a Puritan was someone who suspected somewhere, somehow, there might be someone who was still happy. So a very rigid system of belief was imposed upon the people. After a while, the English got tired of it, and they brought back Charles the First's son Charles the Second from France. He opened the theaters, and things got happy again. The Puritans, not content with this, left and sailed on the Mayflower to the New World. While off the shores of America, they formed what is known as "The Mayflower Compact." You will hear fundamentalists say this was how our country was set up—not so. This was the articles of faith of this one religious group. They didn't come here to escape religious persecution, they came here because they couldn't persecute everybody else anymore. And they have been trying to do it ever since. We are the heirs of the Puritans in the New World.

Thomas Jefferson, Benjamin Franklin, and Thomas Paine accepted the prevailing belief of that time: a philosophical doctrine

34

known as Deism. This was not Christian: it said that there was a god, but that this god had made the world and then gone on to other things—sort of forgot about it. He had put things into motion and then went on to other places in the universe. Thomas Jefferson was very well aware that many of the state constitutions said that they were set up on the basis of "Our Lord and Savior Jesus Christ" and he didn't want anything to do with it. So after much debate, the Constitution of the United States was set up as a totally godless document. The word 'God' is not mentioned in the Constitution of the United States. You can win bets on this point. These people who say that America is a Christian nation are simply wrong. Sometimes they will quote to you in support of their argument the Declaration of Independence: "We hold these truths to be self-evident that all men are created equal, that they are endowed by their Creator with certain inalienable rights, and among these are life, liberty, and the pursuit of happiness." In the first place, the Declaration of Independence forms no part of the law of the United States. It was a document that was used to severe ties with England, and when Thomas Jefferson is speaking of the "Creator" and of "Nature" and "Nature's God," he is not talking in the same sense as Jerry Falwell or the religious right when they talk about America being a Christian nation.

In the Constitution of the United States, the founders wanted to be very clear that no particular religion was going to be given precedence over any other. If we're going to have prayer in the public school, whose prayer is it going to be? Catholic prayer, Jewish prayer, Branch Davidian, perhaps Mormon, Christian Science, Native American? Whose prayer will we have? I got written up by a Seventh Day Adventist awhile back. I had sued all of the judges in Northern Kentucky. They had entered an ordinance saying that anyone in a divorce who had children had to attend Catholic social services. *Liberty Magazine* of the Seventh Day Adventists sent a fellow who had a doctorate in theology degree to interview me. He was Christian, but I knew where he was coming from, and he knew where I was coming from. We got along just fine. I said to him, "I know why you want to do this. You know that if an official religion is ever set up in the United States, it ain't gonna be Seventh Day Adventism." And he said that he did know that.

Edwin F. Kagin: *Baubles of Blasphemy*

So what religion will be our official religion? Here's what the Constitution says: "No religious test shall ever be required as a qualification to any office or public trust under the United States." No religious test at all: not whether you believe in 'God,' much less whether you believe in a specific religion—no religious test at all. For you scholars, that is Article 6, Section 3. Once the Constitution was written, various states refused to ratify it until a certain Bill of Rights was added. Ten Amendments to the Constitution—not the Ten *Command*-ments—Ten *Amendments*. The very first amendment in the Bill of Rights—the same Bill of Rights that the thirteen colonies *insisted* be there before they would sign—reads as follows: "Congress shall make no law respecting an establishment of religion, or prohibiting the free exercise thereof." Those are the first words of the Bill of Rights. "Congress shall make no law respecting an establishment of religion, or prohibiting the free exercise thereof." Well, the fundamentalists say, "You're prohibiting the free exercise of religion by not letting us teach creationism and having prayers in the public schools." Ridiculous. You can practice all the religion you want in your homes, in your churches, in your synagogues, any place you want.

In fact, if you want to really get biblical on them, Jesus Christ in the Sermon on the Mount specifically forbade public prayer. Matthew chapter 6, verse 6: "When thou prayest, enter into thy closet, and when thou hast shut thy door, pray to thy Father which is in secret; and thy Father which seeth in secret shall reward thee openly." He then goes on in the Sermon on the Mount to tell what will happen to those who disobey: "And every one that heareth these sayings of mine, and doeth them not, shall be likened unto a foolish man, which built his house upon the sand: And the rain descended, and the floods came, and the winds blew, and beat upon that house; and it fell: and great was the fall of it" [Matthew 7:26–27]. So maybe the problems of America are not caused by lack of public prayer, but because of it.

Consider the Netherlands, which is perhaps the most secular nation on earth. In the Netherlands, birth control is freely given, homosexuality is tolerated, and many drugs are legal. You can get a marijuana cigarette after dinner. Pornography is legal. Euthanasia for people who are in intractable pain is permitted. And guess what?

36

They have a lower crime rate, they have fewer teenage pregnancies, they have less drug abuse, and fewer abortions than the most religious nation on earth, the United States of America. There may be a lesson to be learned here. America is by far the most religious nation on the face of the earth. More people are professing Christians here than any place else in the world. And yet a country like the Netherlands, where this is not true, does not have the kind of problems we have, because it is a rational society, where morality is based on the consequences of behavior. Moral choices have consequences. If you drive drunk, you are liable to get killed. You behave morally because of *reason*, not because some book told you to.

To the Eastern mind, Christianity is an incredible religion, because it calls on something outside of ourselves to tell us what to do. Christianity claims that without its god we are nothing, that we must look to some authority to tell us what to do, rather than be able to figure it out by moral choice. Hitler remained a loyal Catholic for his entire life. He was never excommunicated. Hitler made abortion illegal—it was a crime in Germany. Think about it. How much true good are the Mother Teresas of the world doing by going and helping these starving children that their philosophy helped to produce? Is this moral, or would it be more moral to have birth control universally available?

In the course of what I call the American Religious Civil War, the ARCW, the fundamentalists have declared war on reason and are trying to convince people in universities, on the radio, through tapes, TV, and other media, that America is a Christian nation set up on Christian principles. I wish to show you how to refute this overwhelmingly. You may have heard of Thomas Jefferson's letter to the Danbury Baptists. Oddly enough, the Baptists of a few hundred years ago were very much in favor of separation of church and state, because they were being persecuted by the Anabaptists. There were bloody wars fought over how you got baptized—whether you got sprinkled on your head as a child or whether you got dunked as an adult in a pool of water. And people died over this nonsense. The Danbury Baptists wrote to Thomas Jefferson to see what the First Amendment really meant. Thomas Jefferson spent a lot of time on his response and even cleared it with the Secretary of State. Here is what he said: " I contemplate with sovereign reverence that act of the whole American people which declared that their legislature should make no law respecting an establishment of religion, or prohibit the free exercise thereof, thus building a wall of separation between church and state." Here is church, here is state, and there is a constitutional wall between them and that is the principle of our democracy.

To give you an example of how some people can attack truth, we have in the fundamentalist camp a fellow by the name of David Barton. In an article from the *Freedom Writer,* "The Religious Right's Master of Myth and Misinformation," we learn that Barton is consciously and deliberately changing history in basic American documents. He has added a line to Jefferson's letter to the Danbury Baptists that I just read to you. According to Barton, Jefferson went on to add that the wall was meant to be one-directional, protecting the church from the state, but not the other way around. And furthermore, it was intended to keep Christian principles in government. That's what David Barton is saying, and it is a damned lie! It is a knowing lie. He *knows* it's not true, because he can look at the text and see what it says. It is not an accident, it is a "damn cussed lie." Telling lies for God! "Let the words of my mouth, and the meditation of my heart, be acceptable in thy sight, O LORD, my strength, and my redeemer" [Psalms 19:14]. He is damned by his own rules!

Let me give you just a few other examples of the principle of separation of church and state. Thomas Jefferson also said, "I am for freedom of religion and against all maneuvers to bring about a legal ascendancy of one sect over another." The only way any religion can be free is if they are all free and if there is no state religion. Let's suppose you have some little religious movement that nobody likes. Do you want to go to jail for it? Or do you want to have the right to free exercise? You can go build a church any place you want to. Nobody's going to stop you. But you can't come to Marshall University and have a Christian Center on campus, because that's illegal. That's preferring one religion over another. I have been to see your Christian chapel, and I understand it's paid for by private funds and is on private property. But they've got a sign that looks deceptively like a Marshall University sign, it doesn't have the "M.U." on it, but it looks just like it apart from that. Then further I note on the campus map that is paid for by taxpayers' dollars that the Christian Center is shown there. And I have also seen the Student Handbook where the Christian Center is listed as one of the services provided by Marshall University. That's the establishment of religion. That's preferring religion over nonreligion.

The fundamentalists want to give the impression that those who disagree with them are bad people, that they are somehow immoral, that they are responsible for all the sins of the world. I believe in killing the hummingbird with a cannon on this one: we are talking about the survival of our freedoms, we are talking about democracy. Thomas Jefferson said this: "The legitimate powers of government extend to such acts only as are injurious to others. But it does me no injury for my neighbor to say there are twenty gods or no God. It neither picks my pocket nor breaks my leg." "It is error alone which needs the support of government. Truth can stand by itself." Whose foot should we measure all shoes by? What religion shall be our official religion? Who here can define Christianity? If it was so clear and easy to define, then why are there so many sects, why so many different creeds? Even within the denominations, Baptists, Presbyterians splintering off. Do we believe that the Eucharist actually turns into the body and blood of Christ, as the Catholics say, or is it merely symbolic as the Protestants claim? How do we know? And if there is a god, why is it not perfectly obvious to everyone? Why are there some people who are rational, who otherwise seem to lead fairly decent and moral lives who say, "No, I don't see any evidence for it." And further, would a just god condemn creatures he made with the faculties of reason who use this power of reason to say, "I don't see the evidence"? Why doesn't the Blessed Virgin Mary appear simultaneously on all TV and radio stations in the languages of all the people announcing the truths of this god? Why not a message on the moon, clearly visible to all? Something that nobody could doubt. Why have visions only been appearing to schizophrenic children? Why so much misinterpretation about something so important as this?

Again, Thomas Jefferson says, "I will never by any word or act, bow to the shrine of intolerance or admit a right of inquiry into the religious opinions of others." "The clergy, by getting themselves established by law, and ingrafted into the machine of government, have been a very formidable engine against the civil and religious rights of man." James Madison spoke similarly, in a 1774 letter to William Bradford: "Religious bondage shackles and debilitates the mind and unfits it for every noble enterprize [*sic*], every expanded prospect." Our ancestors spoke out a lot more than we do. Why are we so afraid of these abysmal little tyrannical minds who are trying to commit treason against the government of the United States?! Why are we letting them get away with it? "The religion, then, of every man must be left to the conviction and conscience of every man, and it is the right of every man to exercise it as days may dictate. This right is in its nature an inalienable right."

On June 10, 1797, the President of the United States John Adams signed a treaty with the nation of Tripoli, a Muslim country. In the order of hierarchy of laws, the Constitution of the United States is at the top, underneath that are treaties between sovereign governments, then the various federal laws and the laws of the states. Under the Constitution, treaties (except maybe some with the Indians) have the highest force of law in our country. The treaty with Tripoli, signed by the President, and unanimously ratified by the United States Senate, reads, "The government of the United States of America is not in any sense founded on the Christian religion." I didn't make this up. This was widely circulated in the newspapers of the time; it was widely debated. The Constitution of the United States and the Bill of Rights were condemned by fundamentalist ministers all over the country as being godless documents. The people knew what these documents meant. Once again, we are witnessing this treasonous, un-American attitude arising, trying to claim that what the founding fathers said, what the Constitution said, and what the treaties between sovereign countries said, don't mean that. We're having people like this Barton fellow, who is trying to add lines to Thomas Jefferson's letter to the Danbury Baptists to try to make it say what he wants it to say and not what it says. Love it or leave. If you don't like the American system, go set up your theocracy on an island; get out of town. But don't mess with American freedom.

There is a wonderful little pamphlet, called a "nontract," put out by the Freedom From Religion Foundation entitled "Is America a Christian Nation?" Dan Barker of the Freedom From Religion Foundation was a fundamentalist minister. He converted a lot of people. And finally he started thinking, and he became an Atheist. He wrote a book called *Losing Faith in Faith: From Preacher to Atheist* (Freedom From Religion Foundation, 1992). He tells why he came to this conclusion and why he left the fold. He found that there was no proof for the claims of Christianity and that the people who were claiming to be religious were doing bad things.

Case in point: in Northern Kentucky right now, there is a state park called Big Bone Lick State Park. It is a park devoted to archaeological finds. An Australian fundamentalist group called "Answers in Genesis" has come to Northern Kentucky and is trying to establish a creationist theme park near Big Bone Lick to teach children and others that evolution is wrong and that creation science is right. If you ever wanted an example of an oxymoron, 'Creation Science' is it. What they are trying to say is that evolution is a religious belief system of the secular humanists and that creationism is a true science. They also believe that this humanistic belief in evolution is responsible for all the bad things that are happening in the world. They see it as a war. Here's one of their cartoons. We have two fortresses. Over here we have evolution at the base of this one, and there are flags that say, "Humanism, divorce, racism, euthanasia, homosexuality." All these things are caused by belief in evolution. And over here we have creation that has a flag of Christianity, blowing holes into the towers of evolution. I didn't invent the idea of the American Religious Civil War. They're the ones who declared the war on reason.

Let me give you some examples of how the religious right is trying to take over. A handout from the "Genesis Theme Park" in Northern Kentucky says, " Virtually all science museums, zoos, and other similar attractions indoctrinate guests with evolutionary and anti-biblical propaganda." Notice how they juxtapose neatly those concepts. That evolution is necessarily anti-biblical—you either believe one or the other. A classic logical fallacy is called the "either/or" fallacy. "It must be the Bible, or it must be evolution." The handout continues: "A major family park and learning center proclaiming the glories of God's creation and the authority of His Word is desperately needed to counter the anti-God philosophy so prevalent in today's world." They have declared war against reason.

Edwin F. Kagin: *Baubles of Blasphemy*

Here is a wonderful little comic book put out by *Mother Jones*. It's called "Holy War: The religious right's secret campaign to take over my daughter's public school." All over the country, stealth candidates are arising. That sounds paranoid, but these are real enemies. They are getting into the school boards, and they want to teach creationism. Right now in one of our counties in Kentucky, a school superintendent has glued pages of the science textbooks together which talk about the Big Bang theory, because that's wrong and he doesn't want anybody to learn it. They are trying to go back to the time before Copernicus. If we are really going to follow the truths of Genesis and the Bible, we must believe the earth is flat. You ought to read the Bible and see if you really can accept it as true. If you read it literally, the earth is flat. It speaks of the four corners of the earth, the pillars of the earth. Jesus was taken by Satan to a high mountain and shown all the kingdoms of the earth. You can't do that on a round earth. Clearly the people who wrote the Bible, like other people of the time, thought the earth was flat. There is even a religious organization called the "Flat Earth Society" that advocates that belief. They are dedicated to the biblical proposition that the earth is in fact flat.

Have you ever heard of "family-friendly libraries"? That's another thing the fundamentalists are trying to do. They think that only they can define a family. They've got a program called "Focus on the Family." There's a neat bumper sticker that says, "Focus on your own damn family. Leave my family alone." The "family-friendly libraries" are trying to censor books. Here's a wonderful little volume called the *X-Rated Book: Sex and Obscenity in the Bible*. It has enough gleaned from the Holy Word to make it banned in any fundamentalist library. That's why you ought to read the Bible. There is a wonderful story about Lot—the one who was saved from Sodom. His two daughters get him drunk and seduce him in order to get pregnant. These terrible stories just go on and on.

This [*holding up book*] is the field manual of the Free Militia. This book will scare the wits out of you. You know about the militia movements? These are people who believe that America was founded as a Christian nation and that it is their duty by force of arms if need be to preserve that. Anybody who disagrees with them is an enemy of God. Onward Christian soldiers! This is their field manual, telling what kind of guns to get, how to organize teams of eight people to attack the homes of nonbelievers. It is extremely scary.

As we get closer and closer to the year 2000, more and more of this nonsense is going to come up. There is right now a millennialist fever in the United States. There are many people who believe that Jesus will be returning at the millennium. I will note that many people thought that Jesus would return in the year 1000 as well. He didn't. In the first place, and this may come as a shock to you, the year 2000 is not the first year of the millennium. The year 2000 is the last year of this millennium. The first year of the next millennium is 2001, and that's why Arthur C. Clarke named his book *2001*. Arthur C. Clarke, by the way, is an Atheist. Our calendar dating the birth of Jesus is wrong. This is 1996 AD, which means *Anno Domini*, or, 'in the year of our Lord.' It is supposed to be 1996 years after the birth of Jesus. But it really isn't, because if we take the Bible literally, we know that Jesus was born during the reign of Herod the Great. We know from very accurate and numerous historic sources that Herod the Great died in the year 4 BC. So if Jesus was born during the reign of Herod the Great, he would have been born at least as early as 4 BC. So if that's the case, then the millennium has come and gone, and nothing happened. So don't worry about the millennium.

We have discussed prayer in the public schools, the creationist movement, and the attack on the libraries. My voice is getting a little stale, and I'm ready to answer some questions....

The State of Kentucky's Laws
in the Year of Our Lord 2000

Kentucky lawmakers have turned a mineral
Into Kentucky's own official state rock
And they've made a rock our official mineral
And offered even more nonsense to mock

They want schools to teach the history of religion
And compare religions in tales and in song
So long as teachers made it very clear
That every religion but one is wrong

Female public nipples are to be covered
But a newly sought law will impale you
If you are a man who is seen out in public
While concealing discernibly turgid genitalia

Proffered law will let schools teach evolution
So long as teachers do not postulate
That humans came from something not living
Or evolved from animals into human state

Laws are sought to protect the civil rights
Of those who would have us publicly pray
And would let church and state discriminate
Against the godless and the gay

It's desired we protect as fully human
Every fertilized egg and every fetus
Perhaps we need laws protecting humankind
To ban coitus incompletus

So see wisdom perish in Kentucky
Watch the retreat of common sense with awe
As these fools and their proposals
Create self-righteous stupid law.

On Why the Lights Went Out
or
The Necessity for a Psychics
Patriotic Participation Act
(August 2003)

Take from the church the miraculous, the supernatural, the unreasonable, the impossible, the unknowable, and the absurd, and nothing but a vacuum remains…. Religion has not civilized man—man has civilized religion.

—Robert G. Ingersoll

On August 14, 2003, there was added to our history the largest power outage in the history in the United States and Canada. At least fifty million (50,000,000) people were without power, and some nine nuclear power plants shut down. At first, the United States blamed Canada. The mayor of Toronto said the United States has never admitted responsibility for anything.

At the moment the blackout occurred, I, while driving in my car, was monitoring a Fundangelical (yeah, I made that up) radio station. I do that a lot; it is important to keep up with their ever-increasing rate of mental degradation. The immediate reaction of the commentator was to blame the blackout on a lack of deregulation of energy providers. Before they get around to claiming it was god's punishment visited upon America for the TV show "Sex and the City" or for taking god out of the classrooms or for any of that variety of stupid, uncritical, destructive, and harmful childish nonsense, it seems meet and proper to look at this blackout, to explain why it happened, and to suggest ways to prevent a repetition of such a thing in the future.

For the sake of this exercise, let us use the method of logic of the Fundangelicals. In their system, everything is caused, or permitted, by a supernatural imaginary friend known only as "God." That is basically their model for cause and effect. If something happens that is good, from their point of view, it is because their god loves them, favors them, and is looking out for their welfare. If something happens that is bad, from their point of view, it is because their god is punishing

45

them, or warning them, or because they chose evil rather than good, or a similar explanation grounded in some related ill-defined logical flaw. This particular type of mental speed bump, thus employed by brains the believers think were created by their "Intelligent Designer," is known in formal philosophy as the *post hoc ergo propter hoc* logical fallacy. If asked just why the god of love often seems to do bad things to good people, Fundangelicals are likely to refer the questioner to the book of Job in the Bible. Job is the ultimate loser's guide to religion.

So, let us analyze, in conformity with the egregious defect of thought that compels reliance on the whims of an imaginary supernatural world, just why this god permitted the power blackout on August 14, 2003.

Maybe it was because we continue to violate the Third Commandment (Second, if you are a Roman Catholic). That, of course, is the one forbidding taking the Bible-god's name in vain. So what do we do? We put the name 'God' on our money, when the Christian god had expressly stated that "ye cannot serve God and mammon" (money). Furthermore, we take the name of that god in vain when we place it in our Pledge of Allegiance without his divine permission. What makes us think this god likes that? Consider that, prior to doing these things, our country had great success in war. Only after our country's Third Commandment violation, above described, did we lose our first war. We will not even consider herein the effect it must have on Jehovah when we violate the Fourth Commandment (Third if you are a Roman Catholic) by attending holy worship on the First day of the week rather than on the Seventh, as he commanded, or that we pray in public, instead of in our closet as the son of that god commanded. Apparently, 9/11 was not warning enough.

Then, within the scope of our exercise, to add fuel to the divine ire, on the very day of the blackout, August 14, 2003, Judge Roy Moore, Chief Justice of the Supreme Court of the State of Alabama, one of the fifty States of the United States of America, announced that he would not obey the law he had sworn an oath to his god to uphold (despite the son of his god's prohibition against swearing at all and the Third *Command*-ment, *supra*) and that he would not obey an order from lawfully established authority to remove a 5,200-pound monument he had produced and installed in the Alabama Supreme

Court building, in violation of the Second Commandment, the one against making graven images (N/A if you are a Roman Catholic, because Roman Catholics like to make graven images, no matter what their god says), containing eleven statements Judge Moore claims are the laws of his god and that such are therefore somehow the basis for all American laws, America being unknown at the time this god selected the Hebrews as his only chosen people.

So, the very afternoon of that defiance of a god's laws, the blackout happened. Never has the will of Divine Providence blazed so darkly.

Now that we know and understand exactly why this massive power failure happened, how can we prevent once again arousing some god's righteous wrath? How can we perhaps prevent inspiring the god, out of his love for us, to send a yet stronger message? Obviously, the blasphemous and treasonous Judge Moore must be dealt with. The penalties called for in what he considers his god's holy writ are offensive to Atheist sensitivities and will not be herein discussed. Such measures could only be employed by the righteously saved. Beyond dealing with the offender, what can we do to protect ourselves? Clearly, we must bring within the ambit and under the control of our civil laws those practicing psychics who know when such things are to occur. Such clairvoyants are of course biblically prohibited anyway.

Consider that these persons, condemned in the "Word of God," had full and complete advance knowledge of the blackout, just as they had complete advanced knowledge of 9/11. They did, didn't they? Of course they did. Every one of them! Otherwise, they would be frauds! And not a one of them had the patriotism, or even the common decency, to give us any advanced warning whatsoever. What kind of Americanism is that? Why should they, just because of their more intimate relationship with the non-material world, have immunity from the loyalty requirements that bind all other of their countrypersons? Why should they be excused for not reporting that which would be required and expected to be reported by one not favored with their god-given (if not him, who?) prescience?

Clearly, we need, and must adopt forthwith, the hereby proposed federal "Psychics Patriotic Participation Act," or the PPPA.

Edwin F. Kagin: *Baubles of Blasphemy*

Here is a working draft:

Any person having psychic abilities, which include prescience, shall have an absolute duty to report in writing, with time and date of said reporting memorialized thereon, that person's knowledge of events that will happen in the future which will, or may, impact negatively on the homeland security of the United States. Such future events shall be understood to include, but are not to be understood as being limited to, acts of terrorism by any individuals or groups against the United States, and any natural disasters, or technological failures, which may tend to diminish the security of the United States. Any person or persons having psychic abilities, which include prescience, failing to so report as required herein shall be guilty of the felony of Treason against the United States, and shall be punished in a place and in a manner to be prescribed by law.

That ought to do it. The law maybe shouldn't cover certain specific "acts of God," because, if discovered in the law by the deity, such might cause the deity to deal even more harshly with us than has heretofore been experienced.

But then again, from a more cynical viewpoint, this whole matter could perhaps be analyzed differently—such analysis being derived from the faith-challenged viewpoint of those godless Atheists. The blackout could be considered through the *Weltanschauung* of those who deliberately disavow the very existence of any supernatural world at all—from the mindset of those who look for explanations of absolutely everything miraculous and mysterious and spooky only within the confines of their own limited and boring naturalistic existence un-enlivened by angels, demons, witches, and other imaginary good or evil out-of-this-world pretend creatures. You know, the kind of stuff one might find in the Harry Potter books that the religiocrazies are burning and want banned.

In this manner of thinking about things, Judge Moore's indifferent disobedience to, and disregard of, his oath to his otherworldly god would probably have had nothing to do with the blackout of August 14, 2003, unless said Judge Moore has far more friends in low places than has been heretofore known. Indeed, the logic that might be employed by our hypothetical Hell-bound Atheist misfits would probably include the suggestion that the blackout might have occurred because overpopulating groups of humans were hubristically using an excessive and wasteful amount of energy, and that the available resources for producing such energy had not been properly encumbered with reasonable safeguards designed to protect human beings against a power failure, even if such safeguards were employed at the expense of the profit-making of the owners of the power production devices, and that those regulations that had managed to be lodged had been unenforced and were, in consequence thereof, ignored.

And as to the most reasonable Psychics Patriotic Participation Act, those unable to feel the pull of the divine, those who deny the reality of things made true by sincere childlike faith in the reality of the unseen and the hoped for, those Atheists who cause problems for the children of the Most High—why they would probably oppose such a law as the PPPA for no other reason than that they think there are no real psychics who can foretell things yet to come, that there are no seers who have the ability to see that which has not yet happened but which is yet to be.

So, now you know why the blackout happened and what can be done to prevent such things from happening in the future uncertain. Make those psychics warn us! We shouldn't have to take responsibility for our own lives and destinies when there is a magical world at work just beyond our sight that can cause problems in our own drab plane of existence and when there are those among us whose future sight can tell those at the power stations which switches to pull today to avoid a power failure tomorrow. And once the god-defying Judge Moore has been given a comfort blanket in a warm safe room where he can be content in the knowledge that he tried his very best to give humankind his god's instructions, but that they hardened their hearts against the strivings of the messenger of the Lamb, and that he will get to go to Heaven, while all who disagreed with him will be smoking in Hell forever, then we can get on with other fronts in the American Religious Civil War (ARCW).

There are, after all, many other skirmishes in the ARCW to be dealt with, and there is a world to save from faith for the freedom of our children. And all of us have much too much to do to continue having to expend our limited power resources on repeatedly winning the Battle of Alabama.

Edwin F. Kagin: *Baubles of Blasphemy*

On the Fractionalization
of the
Recent Experiment in Government Known as
"One Nation, Under God, Indivisible…"

"A Republic, Madam—If you can keep it."

—*Attributed to Benjamin Franklin, in response to a question a woman is said to have asked him, in the late 18th Century CE, regarding what kind of government the Constitutional Convention had established for their newly created nation, The United States of America.*

There are lots of different methods available to operate nations. Democracy is one of them. And democracy is a rather recent and highly unreliable form of government. Democracy is an upstart newcomer in the pantheon of national gods. The oldest, and most reliable, form of government is that of an absolute dictatorship run by one person, usually male, with the necessary backing of a loyal priesthood. This priesthood, if not forcing the common folk to worship the ruler as a god, represents the ruler to the people of the nation as either the living embodiment of a god or as one whose authority to rule over all others of the nation comes directly from a god. King by the Grace of God.

This is the method of government set up, recognized, endorsed, and encouraged by that grouping of legal and literary writings and myths collectively known as The Holy Bible. Keep this in mind when chatting with those—sadly growing in number—who would have it that our land of freedom, our America, be "restored" to "biblical values."

But we just might not be all that happy with these biblical values. Democracy is not mentioned in the Bible. The concept was unknown. The very idea of it would have been rejected. It would have been thought to be a notion as absurd as permitting women to make laws or to rule over men. The practice of voting had not evolved in those times, when there was no air conditioning or computers, when people thought dreams foretold the future and believed the only way humans

50

could know right from wrong was if some god gave them the rules and the priesthood of the god explained the rules to them. The closest thing to voting was choosing a thing, or someone to do something, by lot. This was a form of gambling, where each candidate might, for example, put the name of a thing, or their name on an object, like a stone or piece of wood, and one object, with the thing or the name on it, would be selected in some manner by chance alone. God was credited with providing the outcome, a result every bit as reliable as predicting the future by looking at the guts ripped with a knife out of the belly of a sheep. The idea of a jury is not found in the Bible either. Nor is that of 'due process of law.' Neither 'compromise' nor 'humanity' appear in the King James Version of the Bible—the only Bible used by Fundangelicals until recently, when they discovered that their beloved good King James was, in life, a homosexual.

But I digress, and my editors are stern. [*Damned right.—editor.*]

A totalitarian form of government works because of the Golden Rule. The one with the gold makes the rules. And that person has absolute power over everyone else. If one disagrees, one can be killed. Simple, effective, and stable. Our American democracy has thus far survived a little more than two hundred years. And in that short time has seen a Civil War that all but destroyed its delicate fabric. And we now face another crisis of division that could destroy us. More of this in a moment. By contrast, consider that the ancient Pharaonical government of Egypt was measured, not in hundreds, but in thousands of years. There was as much time between the first king of Egypt and Pharaoh Ramses II as there has been time between Ramses II, who died in 1314 BCE, and the November 2000 Presidential Election. This fact should cause us to pause. For the latter event threatens to put our infant democracy as inexorably into the category of history past as other little understood events consigned to memory the kingdoms of those who prayed to Ra rather than to Jehovah for those fortuitous events of history they were pleased, when random chance operated in their favor, to call "miracles."

Government by decree requires only that the one doing the decreeing have the ability—make that the power—to enforce the decree on those who might disagree with the decree, and if need be, to see to the elimination of those who disagree with or disregard the decree. Safety comes from obedience. Just as one can know what is right and what is wrong by relying on the safety of the certainly of obeying the law of the god. Obey or die. Simple, effective, easily enforced, and easily understood. To be free, you see, you need to obey the decree. As the church song puts it, "Trust and obey / For there's no other way / To be happy in Jesus / Than to trust and obey."

Democracy puts a bit of a kink in this straight and true path to the way citizens conduct their lives. This is something the Fundangelicals of our free land have never understood. Their biblically endorsed forms of government simply cannot be reconciled with the idea of democracy that is foreign to their scripture. They cannot both obey authority and chart their own way. This is why, no matter what they think or teach, religious authoritarians really don't believe in the concept of separation of state and church that was, and is, so central to the American experiment.

Democracy requires that those who participate in it be, to a degree at least, of one mind. The citizens of a democracy must all accept certain ill-defined basics if this new experiment in human affairs of governing one's self has any chance at all of working. Happily, much of the time this is so. Thus, we have been free of the revolutions and civil conflicts that too often attend the transfer of power in lesser countries. By the processes of democracy and the democratic vote and by accepting the will of the majority, we have become, in our short history, both great and unique among the parliament of nations.

But there are dangers; there have been, and are, fearful portents and omens. The Liberty Bell did crack into ruin when first it was rung. We did have a great Civil War. This bloodiest and most disastrous conflict in our nation's brief history occurred when we were but "four score and seven" years old. Now that we are not yet seven score years distant from that national disaster and shame, we are again threatened. And the threat is now, as the threat was then, a dagger aimed at the very beating heart of our democracy.

We have accepted a working illusion, an operational definition that has kept our republic afloat longer than expected by its detractors. This is because we as a nation attempted to live by our motto, *E pluribus unum*, "Out of many, one." Sadly, in the 1950s, the unworkable "In God We Trust" replaced this motto and things haven't been right since. Our Ship of State may, like other crafts that lacked the wit to survive, be destroyed while attempting to pass safely between the Scylla and Charybdis of our divided land's oppositional perceptions of the world. These worldviews may be understood as a conflict between those who profess humanism and those who do not. Our democracy thus far, and not unproblematically, has been able to accommodate those who truly value democratic principles and those who really, whether they know it or not, want us to be ruled by authority, by gods and kings of their choosing.

This was what our Civil War was really all about. We were then, and we are now, two countries. Two nations, divided by a common language, forced by our democracy to live in unhappy harmony under the loosely stitched together tents of two very different ideologies. This is true despite the seeming need of each side to mouth much the same god talk. During our Civil War, both sides claimed the same god was on their side. Lincoln then observed that both sides may be, and one side must be, wrong. Deep down, these two sides truly hate each other. Somehow, with the exception of our Civil War, that is still not over, that is still far from resolved, we have managed to keep safe from one another with the mutual acceptance of an uneasy peace. Until now.

The American Religious Civil War (ARCW), that was foretold and has been reported upon in these pages [*see p. 15*] now threatens to destroy us, in consequence of an election so close that the voters of our democracy cannot agree on who won. This time the winners were not so clear that the losers could with honor fain the patriotism of acceptance and the humility of acquiescence to the public will. As we fractionate, each faction increasingly fears and distrusts the honor and motives of the other. Each side believes the opposition has cheated them of their rightful votes in an attempt to steal the election of our president and to pervert their democracy. At this writing, each side is in the courts, invoking the rule of law, our secular god, on behalf of their position. The only certainty is that without this rule of law, that we all have agreed and must continue to agree to accept, there will be nothing left to save. Should the judgement, the final decision, of the rule of law not be accepted by all sides....

Apart from the clear and present danger of such a situation, it is truly high humor. Aristophanes would have loved it.

Edwin F. Kagin: *Baubles of Blasphemy*

The ancient tensions and hatreds are straining at the tethers of civilization. And, as of this report, we do not know what end will come. There is little sign of compromise or restraint. There is mass confusion concerning just how the casting and counting of votes really operates. People are seeing defects that have been forever present, but, until now, not generally known. And moronic legal interpretations and opinions are creating a great pooling of shouting ignorance. Fanned by the public press, much shrill talk is shoving aside reason and legal knowledge. The ordinary citizens (peasantry in an earlier age) are already in the streets with signs. Soon they may come with pitchforks and torches.

That which could happen is too fearful to contemplate.

If it does not happen, which is likely, that which did not destroy us may strengthen us.

If it does happen, we will become a footnote to history. We will be one with Ramses.

It may be that we really do need two countries. Then we of like mind can live in peace and harmony, and those others will have to get passports to come in. Relocating everyone should be easier than straightening out this voting mess. Surely we will be happier. After all, those on our side get along with each other, for we understand things in much the same ways. I think our country should be in the mountains, with woods, ponds, streams, and cool mornings. My Helen, for some reason, thinks it should be by the ocean, where it is hot, salty, barren, sandy, and full of sand fleas. Can you believe such irrationality?

Just hope the rule of law holds.

Post the Ten Commandments

Let us post the Ten Commandments so everyone can see
That we all love and worship our Lord G_d our Deity.

Haul those statues from our courthouse, those paintings from
    our museum
Burn all photos in our albums so no forbidden likeness causes
    sin.

Break up those Virgin Marys, those icons our G_d has banned
Take G_d's name from off our money, good Christians take a
    stand.

Post those Ten Commandments, but do not let them be
    engraved
For such would be an idol that's forbidden to the saved.

Do not strive for filthy money or yearn for good things work
    can give
For one should never covet and, as birds and lilies, simply live.

Abolish social workers for they Heaven's G_d disgrace
When they prosecute those parents who beat their children in
    the face.

Children must honor parents, no matter how perverse
Even if they only leave their home inside a hearse.

Punish those who will not place our G_d who made these rules
Beside, or before, all other gods and call nonbelievers fools.

Edwin F. Kagin: *Baubles of Blasphemy*

You must not abuse G_d's Holy Name and only against
strangers may you lie
Even if a spoken truth might cause the innocent to die.

The Seventh Day, the Sabbath, is hallowed by Commandment
number Four
So Saturday sports and shopping must now be banned for
evermore.

Be certain these Commandments are in every small child's
school
Teach children about adultery and about how one might break
this rule.

No matter what the motive or the reason or the end
Stealing for every purpose has been made by G_d a sin.

How can we learn to behave if G_d doesn't tell us so?
No matter what the situation, G_d's rules apply we know.

If those we love are starving at the hand of enemies we dread
We must not profane the law of G_d by stealing them some
bread.

Because of the Ten Commandments we do not each other kill
Unless G_d makes exceptions in accordance with G_d's will.

So let us post this moral code, this basis for all law
And if we do not know them, still worship them with awe.

They are the very laws of G_d given by our G_d above
They show how much he loves us and we know that G_d is
love.

Punish those who break them, by their actions or their breath
Every violator should receive a slow and painful death.

On Displaying the Ten Commandments
in
Public Places as Another Satanic Strategy
for
Destroying American Democratic Freedoms

It is as I have said: every statute in the Bible and in the law books is an attempt to defeat a law of God—in other words an unalterable and indestructible law of nature. These peoples' God has shown them by a million acts that he respects none of the Bible's statutes. He breaks every one of them himself, adultery and all.
　　　　　　　　　—Mark Twain, *Letters From the Earth*

As everyone knows, the United States of America was perfect until the 1950s. Things started falling apart in the 1960s, just after "In God We Trust" was stuck on our money, and "under God" was added to our Pledge of Allegiance.

We had gone through a Revolutionary War, a Civil War, two World Wars, the Great Depression, and various other dramatic, but easily solved national problems, like slavery and women wanting to vote, without any need for a statement of reliance on a deity being placed on the cash or an unnamed god being added to our secular expression of loyalty to flag and country.

And Satan rejoiced. He saw the insecurity and the fear. He knew that people's need for public religiosity and for revealed rules meant private personal ethics had been replaced by public show and by dictated declarations of forced faith of the sort condemned in the Sermon on the Mount. The U.S. of A. had fallen into Satan's hands, and he has been pretty much in control ever since. The worse things have gotten, the more his maniacal merciless minions, wrapped in reeking robes of hypocritical righteousness, have caused the unsuspecting faithful to fall into the waiting clutches of that fallen angel.

Edwin F. Kagin: *Baubles of Blasphemy*

Lucifer, that Great Serpent, deceiver of Eve, author of evil, nightmare enemy of all that is right and good, remains tirelessly at work in other ways, deceiving even the faithful, verily as he deceived our first parents. He has, for example, in his attempt to destroy our democratic freedoms and bring about our ruin as a free nation, laid it falsely upon the hearts of some, who are weak of faith and easily misled, that abortion is a sin prohibited by Holy Writ. It is not, of course. Satan knows full well that little souls not yet tempted to sin go straight unto their Heavenly Father, who in his greater wisdom and for his own purpose and pleasure, hath predestined them from all eternity to come early home and be in communion with him forever (it should be here noted that the Roman Catholic Church, a self-styled infallible only true church, had for centuries said that these wee souls went to Limbo—but now they have announced that there is no such place).

Satan can't stand it, for he wants to create chaos and destroy our hard-won liberties and take away the personal choices that are only available to free people. He wants these children to be born unto sin and to commit crimes, and to grow unto profane vice, and to fall from their innocent state of grace, so they can be his, so they can be denied the beatific vision and the heaven of the sinless that was planned for them. Satan has raised up 'pro-life' a.k.a. 'right-to-life' groups, composed of persons misled and misguided, so innocent souls can be profaned by sin and required, under the very "laws of God" that are flaunted, to burn in hell for all eternity (for a more complete analysis of this particular line of blasphemy, please consult "On the Mythology of Abortion," in the "Life Cycles" section of this book or find it on the Web, if you can secure the assistance of an eight-year-old to help you work a computer—a device negligently not mentioned in the Bible).

Satan has also successfully inspired support for forbidden-by-Jesus public prayer in public places. This has helped the Prince of Darkness to hasten the establishment of an unholy profane theocracy and to further damage and diminish personal freedoms so that democracy can be more easily eliminated. Misguided demonically influenced school officials and elected law makers have actually wanted people to risk their immortal souls by engaging in public praying—when the son of god has specifically forbidden such activity (Matthew 6: 5–6, Holy Bible), and said that those who disobeyed would be as imperiled as fools who build their houses upon sand. (See "On Public Prayer"—in the "Religion: Insanity?" section of this book). What are children to think or do when they read in their school required Bible readings that their school-required public prayers are in direct violation of the word of god? Fortunately, this particular slippery slide to perdition has not been implemented in all that many places. In those venues where public prayer is actually regularly and heretically practiced, like in the Congress of the United States, the deleterious consequences are so obvious that reasonable persons cannot dispute the dire truth of the Savior's warnings.

Then there is the Satanist plot called "creation science." This movement oxymoronically tries to replace scientific fact and proof with the pre-scientific biblical mythology of origins. If he can get us to accept this stuff and repudiate evidence, Satan will have made much progress in destroying what our society has achieved with science and democracy.

But that ancient terror is even cleverer than previously understood. We note with horror that there is emerging a far greater Satanic threat—an attempted direct fatal blow aimed at the very heart of democracy. He wants the gullible faithful, those who should know better but don't, to make laws requiring that the so called Ten Commandments be posted in public places—places like public schools, courtrooms, and government buildings. Imagine! Satan has gotten public servants to actually give official endorsement to a set of primitive rules written in Hebrew for a Bronze-Age community of nomadic Jews. He knows that the fighting and the bloodletting certain to result over the meaning, the enforcement, and even the correct translation, of these Hebrew rules will put democracy on the ropes for sure.

He has laid upon certain of our elected elect the fanciful fear that without these dictated declarations of forced fealty, the faint of faith must needs wallow in sin. He has persuaded some uncertain souls that we all need certainty and a fixed moral law that should be interpreted for us by those in power over us. And since the rules are unclear and impossible, like not coveting (there goes capitalism, the stock market, achievement awards, financial rewards, aspirations to succeed and acquire—in short, the American Dream that we had until a god got put on the mammon), citizens are expected to constantly reaffirm their belief in the deity and his rules. Like quoting the Nicene Creed for example. This is not required if something is clearly so. We do not chant together, "I believe in gravity; I believe if I drop a thing it will fall down; it will not fall up as the unbelievers say." A ritual for facts is so unnecessary it seems foolish. Religious ritual is so foolish it seems necessary. Try believing in the Holy Trinity without faith. If a thing can be shown to be so, one does not need a religion in order to believe in that thing, and believing in a thing does not make it so.

Now it would indeed be nice if there existed on our earth ten rules, precepts, laws, or anything for that matter that everyone agreed were absolute rules of law and life that were so clear and so correct in their expression, application, and understanding that all people at all times would unanimously agree those rules should be followed as presented. Then we could post them in public places. And not a person would object, because everyone would agree with them and follow them as a matter of course. Sort of like the rule requiring breathing. Everyone follows it, and no one objects to the requirement that they breathe. Of course, in such circumstances, posting the Ten Commandments would be quite superfluous. We don't really need publicly posted signs commanding unto breathing people, "Thou shalt breathe" (some religious types command "Thou shalt breed," but that's a different type of thing and is another generally unnecessary directive).

Most people who think there is nothing wrong with displaying the Big 10 in public forums really don't know just what they are. So here are the Ten Commandments—in unnumbered Edwinian paraphrase:

I am the same god who brought you out of bondage in Egypt. There are many other gods, but you are not to prefer any of them over me, for I am a jealous god. You are not to make images of anything, worship any images, nor take my name in vain or I will punish your descendents unto the fourth generation. Because I created everything in six days, and rested on the seventh day, you are not to work on Saturday, nor is anyone in your house to work on Saturday, not even your slaves. If you want to live long in the land I have given you, you must honor your father and mother. You are not to steal, kill, commit adultery, lie about your neighbor, nor covet anything your neighbor owns, like his wife, his livestock, or his slaves.

60

As a public service, and in the interests of promoting greater biblical literacy, especially among those satanically inspired to and treasonably intent on imposing the Bible into all aspects of public life, your narrator additionally and thoughtfully now provides our readers with the actual words (King James Version, of course) of the so called Ten Commandments. The sacred text says:

EX 20:1 And God spake all these words, saying, [2] I am the LORD thy God, which have brought thee out of the land of Egypt, out of the house of bondage. [3] Thou shalt have no other gods before me. [4] Thou shalt not make unto thee any graven image, or any likeness of any thing that is in heaven above, or that is in the earth beneath, or that is in the water under the earth: [5] Thou shalt not bow down thyself to them, nor serve them: for I the LORD thy God am a jealous God, visiting the iniquity of the fathers upon the children unto the third and fourth generation of them that hate me; [6] And showing mercy unto thousands of them that love me, and keep my commandments. [7] Thou shalt not take the name of the LORD thy God in vain; for the LORD will not hold him guiltless that taketh his name in vain. [8] Remember the sabbath day, to keep it holy. [9] Six days shalt thou labour, and do all thy work: [10] But the seventh day is the sabbath of the LORD thy God: in it thou shalt not do any work, thou, nor thy son, nor thy daughter, thy manservant, nor thy maidservant, nor thy cattle, nor thy stranger that is within thy gates: [11] For in six days the LORD made heaven and earth, the sea, and all that in them is, and rested the seventh day: wherefore the LORD blessed the sabbath day, and hallowed it.

EX 20:12 Honour thy father and thy mother: that thy days may be long upon the land which the LORD thy God giveth thee. [13] Thou shalt not kill. [14] Thou shalt not commit adultery. [15] Thou shalt not steal. [16] Thou shalt not bear false witness against thy neighbour. [17] Thou shalt not covet thy neighbour's house, thou shalt not covet thy neighbour's wife, nor his manservant, nor his maidservant, nor his ox, nor his ass, nor any thing that is thy neighbour's.

Edwin F. Kagin: *Baubles of Blasphemy*

That's them. The rules the proposers say underpin our civilization and laws. Note there is nothing in them about democracy, due process of law, compassion, or being kind to your children so they just might honor you without a direct order from god.

God seems kinda insecure, too. Why need a god command worship if he is so clearly the better god? Why should he care? Does it bother you if an ant doesn't believe in you?

Despite current claims that they have nothing to do with religion, the first four commandments are religious rules (the secular basis for our culture indeed!), and the remaining six prohibit behavior that most societies address in laws that are usually much clearer about informing citizens of just what is in fact prohibited. Those who say the commandments they want to publicly post are not religious should note that the first four have over twice as many words as the six that follow.

The commandments are subject to all kinds of interpretations and exceptions that can lead and have led to unpleasantness and even bloodshed. This is why Satan wants us to do away with the notion of keeping church and state separate. Forcing religion into public life is the very best way to destroy democracy. What priesthood shall prevail?

Who is to say what the "law of God" *means*? For example, "Thou shalt not kill" sounds reasonably clear. One might naïvely think this law prohibits killing. Not so. It is okay to kill animals and okay to kill humans in war, in self-defense, and in capital punishment. God endorses these (depending on whom you ask) and other killings, but one learns this in Sunday School, not from the simple statement of the commandment itself.

People don't agree on how, or whether, to follow the Ten Commandments with anything like the unanimity with which they agree on the not-needed law requiring breathing. Roman Catholics, for example, don't have the second commandment as listed by the Jews and Protestants. That's the one about not making any graven images or worshipping any images. That's what it says, and it still says it even if one doesn't like it. The Catholics don't like it, so they leave it out and get their version of the ten commandments by making two commandments out of the last one. The practice of accepting as holy only those rules of god one likes and ignoring the rest is so common among different religious groups that they may be understood collectively as cafeteria Christians. That's why various Christians have public prayer, while others handle snakes, have women preachers, let kids die by withholding medical attention, think a god really created the world in six days, believe the earth is flat, and so forth.

The fourth commandment (all references hereinafter are to the Jewish/Protestant Decalogue—that's the one the public posting promoters are talking about—certainly not the *other* set of Ten Commandments in the Old Testament (Exodus 34:14–26) that prohibits, *inter alia*, the boiling of a kid in its mother's milk) says to worship on the seventh day of the week, Saturday, as the Jews, Seventh Day Adventists, and others do. It doesn't say to worship on the first day of the week, Sunday—as most Christians do, with no biblical authority whatsoever for so doing.

There is not a single commandment that is not subject to wildly different interpretations. And therein lies the problem. In matters of faith, whose understanding should control? How do we know they are right? Shall we, as in the past, have religious wars to decide?

But these matters are minor. Satan's true evil genius in selecting this issue to destroy democracy is seen when those who are both Theists and Satanists (if you believe there is a god, you are a Theist; if you believe there is a Satan, you are a Satanist) cannot even agree on which translation of the Bible to use, much less on the meaning of the disputed text. Catholics use a different Bible than do those Protestants they denounce as heretics. Jews read it in Hebrew, and they read it backwards.

If we really want to destroy American democracy by declaring that the Ten Commandments are really secular and that the rules contained therein regarding which god to believe in, and how to worship this god, and when to go to church, and so on, are not religious, then we should take care that we use the right translation of the Bible when posting these nonreligious principles to use for controlling the lives of others, for those who want them posted in public tend not to read Hebrew, and those who do read Hebrew tend to understand all too well how religious doctrines can be called something else when employed to harm others.

Edwin F. Kagin: *Baubles of Blasphemy*

Since its translation into English in 1611, the King James Version has been the Bible of choice of Protestants. It was the Bible brought to our shores by our Puritan forefathers. It is the Bible people know and quote. It is the Bible that, for well over three hundred years, has been to many the only divinely inspired true translation. It is the Bible most quoted when the Ten Commandments are posted. It is the Bible quoted above.

Yet other fundamentalists have recently condemned it, and denounced it as unfit for Christians to read. This is because they have finally discovered that King James I of England, who authorized the translation, was a homosexual—a fact historians have known for all those years during which the King James Bible has been "the inerrant word of God." This fundamentalist attack on the fundamentalist's Bible has been led, say the reports, by the Christian Coalition, the Americans for Truth about Homosexuality, and the Family Research Council (FRC). Gary Bauer, of the FRC, is said (falsely, by the way—the quote was satire—but it does seem the right tune) to have said "Anything that has been commissioned by a homosexual has been tainted in some way." And Christian Coalition leader, Pat Robertson is quoted as saying, "It's very important that we stand up to the homosexual wherever and whenever he appears." Satan must be happy indeed.

How can this possibly be resolved to satisfy everyone? Maybe we should just keep church and state separate and keep our democracy. Maybe we should make public display of our American Bill of Rights. There are ten of them after all, and they were written in English.

Unless, of course, we don't really believe in them.

Rock of Moore

(May be sung to the tune of "Rock of Ages")
(If you don't know it, ask a Christian)

Rock of Moore I say to thee
Don't impose thyself on me.
Rock of Moore I will be free
From your treasonous piety.
Rock of Roy Moore cleft for me
I don't accept your tyranny.

Judge Roy Moore I say to thee
Don't impose your god on me.
Take your rock and holy case
Take them far, far from my face.
Rock of Moore far from me flee
Get thee out of sight of me.

Rock of Moore go find some place
You will not Freedom's laws replace.
The majesty of human law
And of nature hold me in awe.
Superstition is disgrace
Remove your idol from my face.

Take away your cold stone creed
Your rules are not what humans need.
Remove your myths, don't leave a trace
In any free and public place.
Rock of Moore I say to thee
Don't impose thyself on me.

Address to
Godless Americans March on Washington
(November 2, 2002)

My name is Edwin Kagin. I am Director of Camp Quest, the first residential summer camp in the history of the United States for the children of the godless. I am honored to be an Eagle Scout. The concept of Camp Quest was inspired by the outraged awareness that the Boy Scouts of America had somehow become so un-American that its leadership had started denying admission to those "dirty little atheists," to those American boys who did not share the supernatural world view of those now making the rules. Camp Quest was founded in 1996 in response to this exclusion, and, for its seven years of continuous operation, has been a night light in a scary room for our children. Our campers and all-volunteer unpaid staff become, for eight days, an international secular community. Camp Quest is a unique and unqualified success in the battle for the minds of our children in what I call "The American Religious Civil War."

The American Religious Civil War, treasonously declared and waged against our Constitution by those who do not understand, or do not like, our American system of separation of government and religion, has already produced a frightening body count, and more casualties are yet to come. We must strengthen our children in their quest to live meaningful lives in a society where many wrongfully and incorrectly characterize them, marginalize them, and then reject them—where they are made taboo because they do not believe the 'right' way or in the 'right' things, as those traitors who would have our free land governed by their ideas of religious 'truth' want them to believe. At Camp Quest, our children learn they are important human beings with a right to believe, or not, as they choose; that they have a right not to be defined by others. Our motto is, "Camp Quest. It's Beyond Belief." *Quest* stands for: "Question; Understand; Explore; Search; Test."

When asked what she had learned at Camp Quest, one little girl replied, "I have learned it is okay not to believe in god." Please note she didn't say she had learned not to believe in god. We never teach that there is no god. She said she had learned it was okay not to believe in god. She didn't know that before coming to Camp Quest. At Camp Quest, our children are taught the principles of reason, critical thinking, logical fallacy, ethical behavior, and the methods of science and evidence. We teach our campers there is a difference between Righteousness and Self-Righteousness. They learn that the invisible and the non-existent look much the same. At Camp Quest we have two invisible unicorns, and there is a prize, as yet unclaimed, of a godless $100 bill for any camper who can prove that the invisible unicorns aren't there.

We teach them the difference between belief and proof; between faith and fact; that they are part of a great historic tradition of bringing light unto darkness; that there is a difference between that which is ethical and that which is expedient; a difference between being truly moral and being a follower of religious rules. Our children learn that science is based on facts, not on fairy tales. That evolution is a fact and that Creationism is a fairy tale. That there is a difference between coincidence and causation. A difference between potential and actual. That an egg is not a chicken and that an acorn is not an oak tree.

At Camp Quest, while enjoying all the childhood fun of any summer camp, our children who are our future learn that what happens to each of us and to our world is based on cause and effect—not on faith and miracles. They learn that behavior has consequences. If you run on a wet trail you can slip and be hurt. If you let fools be your rulers, then you will be ruled by fools. We teach them to live— not for life after death, but for life *before* death. They learn we all share the mystery of having been born human. We teach our children there are many races and religions and the meaning of our nation's historic motto, *E Pluribus Unum*, and that we Americans are truly 'Out of Many, One.' For their own safety's sake, we try to help them to learn to distinguish between logic and fallacy, between science and superstition, between real and pretend, between the wonder of discovery and magical thinking. We want them to grow up knowing the difference between doing and dogma, between imagination and mythology. Most importantly, we try to teach our children to be competent. They will be competent when they can survive, thrive,

Edwin F. Kagin: *Baubles of Blasphemy*

create, empathize, and interact justly with others, free of pain, fear, and guilt—without gods, without religion, and without us. If they can be thus brought to self-reliant adulthood, they will not need the gods or the religion, and they will not miss them. If we have done it right, they will not need us either. But they will miss us.

All we want, and all our children want, and all we want for ourselves and for our children, is to live as Americans in an America where it is "okay not to believe in god." To do otherwise is to defile the graves of our martyrs. All we want for ourselves and for our children is to live as free people in a free America, where all Americans can join together, in the words of our patriot ancestors, in pledging our allegiance to "One nation indivisible with liberty and justice for all."

THE LIFE CYCLE:
and,
IS RECYCLING IT POSSIBLE?

Don't take life too seriously;
you won't get out of it alive anyway.

—Edwin Kagin

An Observation on the Existentialism of an Anonymous Lemming

An old man caught a lemming once
That was trying hard to die;
Before it finished its last plan,
He took it home to fry.

He flicked its little head right off,
Prepared it for the pan;
"Now his meat can serve some use,"
Thought the little man.

"He'd aimed to end up his own way,
But that don't matter now;
This knife of mine worked just as good;
Besides he'll do for chow."

"No matter how you die, you're dead;
There ain't no doubt to that.
He chose to go; I helped him out."
And he popped it in the fat.

In Re: Cutting Edwin's Throat
(March 2000)

To all Edwinophiles, Edwinophobics, and to all those otherwise interested or merely morbid, greetings:

As you may or may not know, for I have tried not to make a fuss over it, I have been having a pain in the neck (the possible puns available will not be herein explored) for well over a year.

As the pain became progressively worse, I had X-rays and two MRIs (amazing devices) done that conclusively revealed that my fourth cervical neck bone (a.k.a. C-4) has moved backward (subluxated, for the medically literate or curious) about half of its width. This is what is causing the increasing pain, and it is now pressing on the spinal cord. The doctor says the vertebra is "unstable." That means it could slip further and injure or cut the spinal cord, a happening that could cause death or paralysis from the neck down. Neither condition is desirable.

Given this set of facts, it seems best to have an operation to fix the problem. So that is what is to happen, and that is why I am writing to advise you why I will not be seen or heard from (if ever) for a while.

The operation is to take place on Friday, March 17, 2000 C.E. at The Christ Hospital (ain't that something!) in Cincinnati, Ohio, at 2:00 PM.

The surgery is relatively straightforward. It initially involves the same general procedure as that used in giving a lethal injection. Drugs will be employed (injected) to put me to sleep (make that render me unconscious) and to stop all reflexes, breathing, *etc.*, that generally go with being alive. Then a machine will be employed to breathe for me (the difference between this procedure and a lethal injection is that the latter omits the breathing for you part) until the operation is over and the death drugs withdrawn. Then the surgeon (Dr. William Tobler) will cut my throat from the side, and take out C-4 in pieces. Another cut will be made over my hip, and a piece of my right pelvic bone will be sawed off and carved into something similar to the shape of the to-be-discarded C-4. My unconscious head and torso will then be pulled slightly away from each other to permit the newly whittled part to be snapped into place between neck bones C-3 and C-5. Next, a titanium plate will be fastened by four screws to said C-3 and C-5, to make a solid bond for the replacement part. My now bionic and unresponsive body will then be sewn up, put in a neck collar (to remain for three months, more or less), taken off the lethal injection type drugs, and then wheeled into a 'recovery' room to see if I does or doesn't recover.

One or the other is certain to happen, each option requiring a somewhat different analysis.

As you can see, it is really quite simple, and the whole thing will only take about two hours.

The chances for survival seem quite good. However, should I not, you can find appropriate suggestions in another essay I've written on disposing of human remains. [*Editor's note—see later in this section.*]

But I do think the whole thing will go just fine, and that I will be fully healed and ready in time for Camp Quest 2000.

I even have a new song for the event, "Neck Bone Connected to the Pelvic Bone."

Catch you later,

Edwin

In Re: **Cutting Edwin's Throat: The Sequel**
(a few days later in March 2000)

On March 14, 2000, I sent to a list of undisclosed e-mail recipients an e-mail message styled "*In Re*: Cutting Edwin's Throat."

The responses to this confession of mortality were surprising and quite touching. I did not know how many folks would have such an intense interest in the details of my throat being cut. But they did, and calls and e-mails were received from lots of diverse people and places. All were most appreciated. Most shared the commonality of thinking the whole thing was hysterically funny.

And so it was. And you have a right to know. On Friday afternoon, on schedule, I underwent the near-death-like procedure that consumed 3-½ hours from cut to close. I have no memory whatsoever of anything that I don't remember.

Edwin F. Kagin: *Baubles of Blasphemy*

I do remember seeing some eight to ten quite serious looking people in the operating room. Many were friends of my Helen, who served there (The Christ Hospital) as an anesthesiologist for some 30 years, before retiring to be registrar of Camp Quest and to do lethal injections as an income supplement. I have a T–shirt that says, "Sleep Better With An Anesthesiologist." Dr. Rich Stilz, anesthesiologist, and nurse anesthetist Patty Hornak, whom I have known for better than 15 years, were in charge of the lethal injection part.

They also know me, so it came as no surprise to them when, upon seeing TV monitors in the O.R. ("Operating Room" for those who don't do television), I asked if it would be possible to have a video made of the procedure. Well, it was, and was, and you can now get your very own copy of "Cutting Edwin's Throat: The Video" for a modest contribution to Camp Quest. This Edwinian request did come as a surprise to the very nice young Dutch doctor doing a Fellowship at The Christ Hospital in Neurosurgery. His name is Dr. Rashid Janjua, and he is a Muslim. It is a long story. Anyway, I was reminded later he had politely and innocently introduced himself to me in the O.R., told me he would be assisting my surgeon, Dr. William Tobler, and asked me what I did for a living. I told him I sued neurosurgeons and anesthesiologists.

Rashid became my primary informant thereafter for what happened. He even checked out my Web-site, and asked my Helen that most commonly asked Helen question, "How do you put up with him?" He speaks very good English, is 30, unmarried, and his e-mail is available upon request. He was unaware until later that when Nurse Hornak spoke unto me the first angel-like first words in the recovery room to advise that I had in fact lived, I asked her if Akhenaten was still pharaoh. But Patty is used to it. She has been reading "Kagin's Column" for years. The original e-mail on Cutting Edwin's Throat has been posted in the Department of Anesthesiology and is being read throughout the hospital. Perhaps this will be added to keep it company.

I learned that Dr. Janjua carved from the outside right of my throat until he got to the narrow lifeline that had to be worked around with much skill if I hoped to walk or speak again, or even to make morning roll call. Here the more experienced Dr. Tobler took over and, using microscopic surgery, cut away the body of the 4th cervical vertebra, and removed the discs above and below the bad vertebra. He next sawed living bone from the right iliac crest of my pelvic bone, from which he fashioned a new C-4, and then snapped it into place.

Next, a titanium plate was installed in me with four screws that expanded into C-3 & C-5 to create a bionic and bony bond for C-4. The manufactured plate and the new osseous artifact are now a part of me until death do me part. This plate alone will cost the insurance company some $2000. So I guess I will never be broke. This plate is about 3 mm thick and goes in from the front. I have confirmed that, after my body is one day cremated (hopefully being dead first, rather than being mined by fortune hunters), this plate will survive and remain, perhaps to be made into an amulet for one of my children to wear, labeled "Dad." I have seen this plate installed in my body on X-Ray, and it is quite attractive. How it will react in high magnetic fields is not fully known. For all I know, under the right conditions, it will pick up NPR.

Thinking about that plate, the general theory could be quite useful for a more permanent dog tag for soldiers, bearing important engraved information. The benefits for identifying random remains seem obvious, but this may be an idea presented before its time. Leathernecks could be known as.... You get the idea. Remember, you heard it here first.

So, as you have doubtless gathered from the foregoing, I am at home, in good shape, and at computer. I am quite relieved the whole thing is over, and the pain has been dramatically less from the moment I returned to life in the presence of the angels of the recovery room. I am healing quite rapidly, a fact that can no doubt be attributed to my being a superb human physical specimen and to the (so far as I know) absence of prayer. The fact that my doctors were as good as they come had quite a bit to do with it as well. The religious significance of a Dutch Muslim on my surgical team is important in exact proportion to his obvious surgical skills.

From the moment the anesthetic was injected, until I woke up some 3-½ hours later, there was no sense of growing tired, of drifting off to sleep, of seeing tunnels of light, or indeed of anything whatsoever. I experienced an instantaneous, seamless transition from being in the Operating Room to being in the Recovery Room. The only thing 'faith' had to do with it was the confidence I had in those who gave me the anesthesia, confidence that my surgeons could do an operation that would have been impossible during the crusades or the inquisition, confidence in my own physical condition, and confidence that I had made a rational decision by my acceptance, based on all evidence known to me, of the high likelihood that this would work. Frankly, it worked better than I hoped. It might not have. It was worth the risk.

If the procedure had been done at a time in our history when some medicine man might have stuck bones in the eye sockets of a cave bear and a knife in my neck to cut out the evil spirit he thought was causing the pain, all the while chanting nonsense to the believing sheep, I probably would not now be sending you this sequel, and my failure to survive would have been ascribed to a lack of faith. "What did you think would happen? Didn't he write all those Kagin's Columns?" Even if I had, by virtue of random chance operating in my favor, lived, you can bet I would not be telling you of it on a miracle of electronics that will put these words on your computer screens before you can look up the Ten Commandments in a Kentucky legislative bill. This miracle on which I write was invented by human minds. It was not in use on the Ark. Imagine if Moses could have had a laptop, with Internet access.

The fact that I went into the death-like state on Friday afternoon, and arose from my bed and came unto my home early on the first day of the week is a fact that seems oddly familiar — like I've heard it somewhere before.

Thank you for your many good wishes. I also thank the doctors and the staff who fixed me up and prevented my death or paralysis. I will try to reward you with humorous things.

Lifelines

I raced my young sons down the beach
And barefoot first the ocean reached.
Time and time again I won,
A father stronger than each son.
I knew one day those two must win
And dash on past where I had been.
Summer following summer they gained on me
As I deterred what had to be.

One day in time at last I lost
And knew our lines of life had crossed.
We cast in other plays that day,
Each set to race a different way.
Toward that sea of fame and name
Where lifelines start and end the same.

On the Mythology of Abortion

Beware the man whose god is in the skies.

—George Bernard Shaw

There is a movement afoot in America to prevent pregnant women from deciding whether or not to have a baby. The control freaks who advocate this view characterize their beliefs as 'pro-life' or 'right to life.' Those who hold that they, and not the woman, should decide whether to let a fertilized egg develop into a living child share a common mythology. It goes roughly thus: all life comes from the deity. The deity gives life, and every zygote is imbued by the creator deity with an 'immortal soul' (a concept found nowhere in the Bible). Microscopic products of conception are perceived to be persons vested by the deity with the right to be born. The exercise of rational reproductive choice in obtaining an abortion is viewed as the murder of a person.

The mythology is powerful enough that its advocates think they can ignore the laws of nations and impose their will on those who disagree. Basically, they have initiated a holy war—us against them, good *versus* evil, we are right and you are wrong—the same primitive absolutism and lust for power over others that produced the Crusades. Moralists have declared war on reason. With aborted fetuses emblazoned on their shields and chastity belts secured, the armies of the Christian god, like ancient pestilence, are marching to stop forbidden sex and to ensure all products of ill-advised copulation be born. The births proclaim the truth that the only reason sex is lawful at all is to make babies for that god.

According to the theocratic understanding of biology of the anti-choice movement, at the moment the sperm penetrates the egg, the mythical 'soul' is placed in the zygote, presumably whether it is in a uterus or a petri dish. That which God has infused with soul may not be removed by the mere mortal choice of not wanting a baby. This notion of a soul inhabiting a collection of cells that may, barring accident, abortion, or whatever, become a child is rather new in mythological thought and bears analysis.

78

There must be a soul bank somewhere for the almighty to draw from to implant the soul moments after male orgasm (female orgasm is unnecessary for this or any other reproductive function, and is therefore discouraged), or the heavenly power must create new souls in a soul shop for all of the fertilizations. This would cause the creator to work after midnight most Friday and Saturday nights and thus violate the day of rest established by 'God' for the Sabbath. Even a large soul bank would need replenishing, because surely no rational god would have planned for sufficient souls to overrun the resources of his creation like maggots on a dead possum. And people do die, and new souls are needed. The anti-choice forces reject the idea of recycling the souls through reincarnation. It is really quite confusing, until, upon reflection, the answer becomes clear: the anti-abortion movement is a tool of Satan.

Consider that Satan wants to create as much chaos on Earth among humans as possible, to make people unhappy and to grab souls for himself. The Satanic solution is to prohibit abortion. Force the heavenly powers to work Sabbaths and all to crank out souls for crack babies and AIDS babies, incest and rape conceptions, souls for babies who aren't wanted, aren't cared for, aren't educated, babies who can create crime, war, disease, poverty, famine and all of the evil and sin Satan needs to destroy the beauty of the Earth and shatter human aspirations for peace, love, and contentment. As further proof, remember that an innocent soul not tempted to sin goes directly to his creator god (perhaps after a period of dry cleaning), a better place than prison, hospital, or hell. A soul aborted is a soul lost to Satan, but one unwanted and forced to be born can produce unspeakable evil, to do glory to Satan and mock a caring, benevolent god.

This mythical interpretation is obviously correct. Consider that all of the Satanic anti-choice fetus people prayed that an American president not be elected who believed a woman has a right to reproductive freedom. They abraded their knees and polished their prayer beads to beseech God to elect a bigot president. The very heavens rang with the noise of their prayers and rantings. God either did not listen or disagreed with their position. Their candidates were defeated, and pro-choice was affirmed as the law of the land. Never has the will of a god been so clearly seen. God saw through Satan's motives and rejected the prayers of those who would let Satan get his paws on those little souls.

Totally undaunted by this most obvious expression of the divine will, the unwitting forces of darkness have increased their efforts to control those who disagree with them. Indifferent to the laws of their god and man and the rules of basic humanity and courtesy, they have engaged in a reign of terror against doctors, facilities, and personnel dedicated to following the law and assisting women who don't want a conception to become a child. The tactics have included bombings, threats, harassment, intimidation, assaults, and now, finally and predictably, cold-blooded murder. A gentle healer was shot in the back by one of Satan's converts who wanted to stop the doctor from helping women. The murderer's fellow travelers have raised funds for him and have implied, and sometimes stated, that the murder was morally correct. There was despair in heaven and rejoicing in hell. Satan had succeeded in making evil appear to be good.

But "God is not mocked." He who sits in the heavens will laugh them to scorn. Satan's siege against dignity and humanity will be long, but reason will prevail. If it does not, these demonically possessed people will kill everyone who disagrees with them on abortion and then turn their efforts to those who believe in evolution, who read forbidden books, to all of those who do not want to be ruled by evil people purporting to speak for a god.

Defend our constitution. Speak out against wrong misguided mythology. You must. For your own safety's sake.

Don't tell them about the I.U.D. It has been sluffing fertilized eggs for years and has thus far escaped their notice.

Study

Outlined by the window

She sits with face of Gothic cast

In two dimensional form

(A water-wash of pastel tint

Covering gesso's hardened white).

But knowing time, as time will do,

Can even oil and cloth wear out,

She, within her parlor room,

Puts chiseled lip to china cup

To drink her portion that she brews

Fresh each lonely afternoon.

And then she slowly blends again

Into the prison of her frame

A still life of the soul.

The Case of the Frozen Embryo

Bye baby banting;
Soon you'll need decanting.
—Aldous Huxley, *Brave New World*

A biology student named Delf
Scientifically played with himself
And when he was done
He labeled it "Son"
And filed it away on the shelf.

—Anon

Nonsense struck another blow

In the case of the frozen embryo

A Judge has ruled it's human life

And awarded custody to the wife.

In the divorce it was her wish

To get the goo from the petri dish

Where the little ones were conceived

Where marital passion was relieved.

The children went to a frozen tomb

To await resurrection in some womb

There will have to be child support

Ordered by paternity court

To keep the frozen kids alive

Until it's time they should revive.

But it really must be nice
To keep your babies' lives on ice,
Frozen solid until you say
You are ready to let them play.
But there must be other fears
For those who wipe their icy tears.
If they should be flushed away
Or allowed to thaw and rot one day,
Would a murder charge obtain
For those who dumped them down the drain?
And what day should their birthday be,
Those who were conceived *in petri* ?
Do the cold days of gestation count
For little souls who just want out
Of a limbo that won't start
The beating of a little heart?
Of course there is no heart to beat
Or even tiny fetus feet.
There are no bitsy toes on embryos
And what the sex is no one knows
So you cannot even name
Those cells that all look just the same.
Ah, the problems that occur
When rational thought and reason err.

Sonnet To . . .

You knocked at doors where none had knocked before
To enter in my dungeon of dark days;
In faint response to your entreating ways
With tiny taper lit I crossed the floor,
And nerves numb nude could be concealed no more.
Moving as one fresh waked, by sleep still dazed,
I, to your ceaseless knocking, slowly raised
The portcullis that guards the inner door.
Now in, press on! I may your love betray
And foolish foils may parry at your thrust;
But best each guard as you approach the whole
Until feeling then what now I cannot say,
I yield, and, hot with fear, give you full trust

To move the rusty hinges of my soul.

The Rights of the Unconceived

Let's add to irrationality
To nonsense unbelieved
And urge, against free human choice,
The rights of the unconceived.

The unborn, however unwanted,
Have protestors who defend
Who will not take their misery home
But make sure their paths begin.

The maimed, the pained, the hopeless
Have rights of tragedy unrelieved
Yet we ignore a great moral sore
The plight of the unconceived.

We must have laws with iron-braced jaws
To insure new lives are received
It should be a crime at any time
To deny life to the unconceived.

Should fertile lad and fertile lass
Henceforth with any passion pass
Consummation must be achieved
To insure the rights of the unconceived.

Conceived Again

I understood I was conceived,
And born, in original sin;
And preachers said, and I believed,
I must be born again.

But I really sought to know,
And hoped to clarify,
Just what I must do to go
To Heaven when I die.

I'd heard baptism and rebirth
Would start my life anew,
So when I left this sinful earth
I'd join the righteous few.

But knowing all of that, from God
There came unto me this perception:
Being born again is very odd
If life starts at conception.

If I became me when first conceived,
I was already me at birth;
So what has second birth achieved?
What's being born again worth?

We sinners must be reconceived
So Heaven we can win!
This is the great truth I've received,
We all must be conceived again!

I know not how this can be done—
Our creeds will need revision.
But there's a Heaven to be won,
So make a reconceived decision!

Come all, and be again conceived;
Be reconceived to be reprieved;
Don't be born again deceived;
Second birth hath not thy sin relieved;
Ye must instead be reconceived!

So consider theology as a whole
And make thee thy selection—
To elevate thy immortal soul
By election or erection.

Edwin F. Kagin: *Baubles of Blasphemy*

On the Disposal of Human Remains

Here lies an Atheist, all dressed up and no place to go.
—Humorous tombstone

Today's cheery topic treats what to do with your carcass when you are dead. Like it or not, one day you will have to be disposed of. Animals don't make a fuss of this fact; they go off and die. Humans, believing they are better than animals, invent religions. The prime motive of most religions is to create a myth about some kind of individual continuance after all electrical activity in the brain stops and the organism starts to rot. As the old preacher put it, "Brothers and sisters, this is only the shell; the poor nut has gone." Where the nut has gone is a matter of much debate, as is the problem of what to do with the shell. Some religions believe the body must be buried, others hold it must be burned. Take your choice.

Traditional Christian human remains disposal involves burying the corpse in a box in the ground. Bodies were to be laid east to west, so the dead flesh could rise to great Christ who is coming from the East. No kidding. Christianity teaches a bodily resurrection and an ascent of the reanimated cadaver to heaven. The Bible says nothing about humans possessing an immortal soul. You can win bets with believers on this point. Them bones are to rise again. The ghoulish, and those who have witnessed autopsies, may wonder how those who slept in the graves will get by with the brain, heart, lungs, intestines and other really important stuff removed and thrown away. And mystical indeed will be the rebirth of the decapitated—say a saint like Sir Thomas More whose body is in one place and whose head was stuck on Traitor's Gate. Ah, the mysteries of faith. What of those who died in Christ in explosions or carnage that converted living flesh to mangled roadkill? What of the woman whose murderer husband ran her dismembered body through the wood chipper? Will those whose bodies are cremated to ashes in a fiery furnace "yet in the flesh see God"? So goes the belief. The Book of "Job" says yes, even if the carcass is eaten up by worms, you will see Jehovah in your bodily form. The age you will be isn't revealed. Maybe you get to choose.

The Life Cycle

Persons planning to be buried should understand that no grave on earth is anything other than a present or future crime scene or archaeological site. Eventually, someone will dig you up for saleable goodies or for information your burial stuff and postmortem analysis can reveal about your time. Or your grave can be scooped away to make room for a subdivision to house the children of the life-what-a-beautiful-choice movement. The greatest tombs of the greatest kings, designed to be secure for eternity, were magnets for thieves who weren't fooled by myths of curses. You can stroll through the burial chamber of a pharaoh, stripped by tomb robbers centuries before archaeologists put the living god's remains in a glass case in a museum. Native American sacred burial grounds, and even Civil War graves, are being plundered by the irreverent, who sell the honored dead's tools and belt buckles at flea markets. There are more people alive on earth today than have ever been alive on earth together at any one time in the past. If everyone is buried, eventually there will not be space available for both the living and the dead. Guess who wins that argument.

You could donate your body to a medical school for dissection by students, but there are usually more than enough dead incompetents to satisfy this need. The best way to get rid of your burdensome dead body is to burn it up. Crematorium ashes are sterile and far easier to dispose of than decaying meat and bone. The ashes can be scattered somewhere, cast into a bust of yourself (to be sold at some future garage sale), put in a decorative vase, or used to plaster the wall or provide variety in the cat box. Your then heirs can be creative. It doesn't matter—for you won't be there. The Bible says, "For to him that is joined to all the living there is hope; for a living dog is better than a dead lion. For the living know that they shall die: but the dead know not any thing, neither have they any more a reward; for the memory of them is forgotten." Ecclesiastes 9:4-5, by God. How the foregoing can be reconciled with the notion of life after death is another of those mysteries of faith.

If you have lived in such a manner that anyone will miss you or lament your absence, there are rational ways for them to celebrate your existence, share and purge grief, and then get on with their lives. Those tending to your disposal should cremate your corpse privately and quickly, after permitting family, if they wish, to see how your dead body looks. It may help them appreciate you are really not going to be seen or heard from again. After a suitable number of days or weeks, depending on how your survivors feel, they can have a party in your memory. Photos and videos could accompany anecdotes of your presence on earth, and artifacts of your life's journey could be displayed as, amid feasting and merriment, you, in your diversities (if any), are remembered.

Before you return to wherever you were before you were born, it might be a good idea to so live that people remember you fondly. This is not a dress rehearsal. Life ends / Tao flows.

Don't take life too seriously; you won't get out of it alive anyway.

RELIGION: INSANITY
or
ONLY INANITY?

Religion is not the answer—it is the problem. Everything considered, we would be better off without it.

—Edwin Kagin

Dear Intelligent Designer

Creator God of Everything, I hope Thou'lt not decline
To answer me my questionings of Intelligent Design.

I know that every living thing came from Thy mighty mind
That Thou created perfectly every life form that we find.

Some pious people tell me they have, through Thee, resolved
That Eden spawned all living things and that life has not
    evolved.

That each kind of Thy created works Thou did to finest form
    refine,
And human perfection clearly shows the intelligence of Thy
    design.

Creator God, please do explain the truths of I.D. unto me
And why some flaw-free eyes Thou mad'st need glass to
    clearly see.

Tell me God of Everything, for I know Thou cannot lie,
Why every perfect thing Thou mad'st must one day age and die.

And why are joints, and backs, and bones subject to ruin and
    pain?
Why must heads ache, and kidneys leak, and blood vessels
    burst from strain?

Why do we jettison out our waste so near the port of birth?
Why should any of Thy organs quit? Were we designed just for
    Thy mirth?

Edwin F. Kagin: *Baubles of Blasphemy*

Barely can we walk upright; most teeth will rot or fail.
And what does our appendix do? Did we once have a tail?

Why is our trachea, through which we breathe, placed to
    nearly meet
Our esophagus, so we inhale the things we'd rather eat?

Why do some bodies attack themselves, when from disease we
    might be free?
Tell me truly, God of Truth, were all our afflictions made by
    Thee?

Why does Intelligent Design make so many people fat
Why have we not the grace or ease designed into the cat?

I have other questions Deity, and I really don't know how
A moment ago I knew them, but cannot recall them now.

On the Visit of the Blessed Virgin Mary
(September 2, 1992)

P.T. Barnum, the great showman, supposedly said, "A sucker is born every minute." As proof, and for profit, Mr. Barnum reportedly filled a large fish tank with water, added some castles, shells and such, and posted a sign, "Amazing, Invisible Fish From Afghanistan." Folks paid their fee, pushed their noses against the glass, and announced "There's one," "I see one," "Yea, honey, I see it now," "Sure enough, there one is," and "Ain't that something?"

The Virgin Mary is a mythical construct of Christianity. Mary, a Jewish girl of questionable virtue, gave birth to Jesus, the god figure who gives salvation if one believes he was martyred as a sacrifice for sin and then came to life again and was taken alive by the chief god, Yahweh, his father, into a supernatural place called Heaven. While in Christian belief, Yahweh is the only god, clearly Jesus, and Mary his mother, are prayed to and treated, if not like gods, like demigods, who can get to Yahweh for them. Hence, the chants, "Holy Mary, mother of God, pray for us sinners, now and at the hour of our death" or "in Jesus' name we pray, Amen."

The reverence for Mary is because of the belief that Mary had conceived Jesus without sex, a motif popular at the time for the birth of gods. The earliest Christian writing, the letters of Paul, do not mention the conception of Jesus by divine fiat, or that his mother was asexual prior to his birth. The belief grew later, probably to compete politically with myths of other religions.

Some Christian subdivisions give more importance to Mary than others. There are even divisions of theology known as Mariology. According to the 'Catholic' division of Christianity, Mary remained a virgin forever (a basis for an anti-sex platform that still does great mischief) and, like Jesus, was transported bodily alive to Heaven. What one does with a body in a place otherwise peopled with bodiless souls, angels, and such is not explained. Mary is venerated and worshipped, and has, from time to time been reported to have appeared one way or another to earthbound believers. These visits have been in obscure places, to children, or to other limited audiences. Never, to my knowledge, has she or any other Christian god figure who seeks belief as a condition of salvation given their message by interrupting every radio and television program on the earth simultaneously, in the language of every hearer. Such a happening could end much debate and save many a hell-bound skeptic's soul. In any case, alleged divine wisdom greater than mine has limited the appearances to forums smaller than Times Square on New Year's Eve.

Now we have been treated to a special appearance of the Blessed Virgin Mary (hereinafter BVM) in our area. An unnamed visionary in Greater Cincinnati revealed that the BVM would appear Monday, August 31, 1992, at 12:00 midnight in St. Joseph's Church, Cold Spring, Kentucky. (The city name is appropriate for a virgin). The vision was widely reported in the press, and, while doubted by many, was believed by many. Thousands made the pilgrimage to Cold Spring. Vendors sold BVM statues and medallions.

But the important part of this story is that while my Helen and I were on vacation in Canada this August, as I sat by a lovely lake, the BVM appeared to me. I knew it was she. She looked just like her pictures: a blond, blue-eyed Jewish girl dressed in blue, red and white. She spoke softly and said unto me, in English, "Arise, Edwin and go unto Northern Kentucky and its suburb Cincinnati. Go and say unto them that I have visited thee, and have told thee this telling of my visit to Cold Spring is not true, but is verily the work of Satan to deceive the faithful. For I do not make scheduled visits, for only the Father Yahweh makes my schedule, and of this I know naught until it is accomplished. Warn that those who believe and attend this Satanic visitation are surely damned," and then she vanished in soft peace from my view.

When we returned home, I contacted friends in the media and proclaimed this vision and message. But they did not print it. Here was I, recipient of a private revelation of the BVM and the press ignored it. I was willing to go public, yet they chose to print the Satanic message of an anonymous oracle. I could only guess at the fate awaiting those who planned to attend. Why wouldn't they listen? How could anyone not believe a lawyer?

Helpless, I turned to other things. Perhaps a BVM world tour tee-shirt, listing various stops, Lourdes, Fatima, Guadalupe, Medjugorje, Cold Spring (with a question mark after the latter). I was told such an idea would be blasphemous and that my revelation was blasphemous. Blasphemy is the crime of making fun of ridiculous beliefs someone else holds sacred.

The appointed time came and passed. Some said they saw the BVM in the trees. Some took photos of the sun (never look at the sun, especially through optics) and said a door in the sun opened and the BVM started toward Kentucky Highway 27. These folks can probably pass polygraphs on their revelations, as can their fellow travelers who have hitched rides on UFOs. Most people didn't see anything. The Bishop of Covington said nothing happened.

Thus, my vision of the BVM (which is a lie) was true and that of the "visionary" was false. That's how it is with private revelations. The press reported the whole thing as an actual, possible happening, sounding like it was a jump ball whether the BVM would appear or not. The press did not report it as a hoax or delusion. They didn't say there is no BVM to appear, or that Jesus' mother, if any, has been dead going on 2,000 years.

Those who saw her will believe, as did their grandparents who saw P.T. Barnum's fish. And these people are permitted to vote and sit on juries. They also want to tell us what our morals should be.

This whole problem would never have happened if only people had listened and printed my vision of the Satanic nature of the event.

Too bad if you went.

On Miracles and Microchips

It's a miracle!

—Overworked monastic scrivener in TV commercial,
upon introduction to Xerox electronic copier.

The Reverend Gilder Smelt, of the Mail Me Magic Money Miracle Missions Movement, had been blessed with the gifts of miracle healing and of prophecy, but, regrettably and inexplicably, he had been denied the gift of correct grammar. He was held a prophet of God by his followers when he spoke on the 7Ms Club's vast radio and television network. He had succeeded the movement's founder, Dr. Ducworth Bliss, after the latter had been, according to Rev. Smelt, translated directly into heaven like Elijah and the BVM.

Secular authorities held the less metaphysical view that Dr. Duck, as they termed him, had faked his death in a plane crash in Brazil, where he then proceeded to reside, safe from secular extradition, among fellow travelers of Nazi persuasion. Authorities also cynically believed that Bliss had taken with him a large quantity of mailed miracle money, sent him by the gullible who accepted the teaching that the last dollar of the starving, if sent as magic seed money in cash to 7Ms, would be multiplied and returned by God to the sinning sender seven times seventy fold. Because 7Ms was an officially recognized church, it paid no taxes and could not be made to disclose how much money it received, or how much was missing, assuming anyone really knew.

Dr. Duck's disappearance permitted the grammatically challenged Smelt to expand upon the mendacity of his mentor, and added a certain irony to 7Ms' theme song, "More More Money Makes Miracle Missions Move." Previously satisfied with receiving the last mites of the hopeless, whose faith usually proved inadequate, after the transfer of funds, to achieve the miracles sought, the 7Ms Club, under Smelt, tooled up for serious electronic chautauqua.

With the compensated aid of shills, and the uncomprehending cooperation of the habitually hysterical and hypochondriacal, 7Ms' fortune and fame flourished. The only real problem Rev. Smelt encountered was deciding whether to condition members of his audience—of the soon to be miraculously cured—to fall backwards or forwards following his heavenly healing touch. He settled on forwards. Some of the fallees seeking the strong arms of salvation were attractive, full bosomed young women.

None of Brother Smelt's miracles, whether calling on the power of his god to produce healings or to prevent hauntings, were ever verified by competent skeptics. Why permit the damned to question the ordained? What, Smelt unartfully argued, could science, or logic, or reason hope to provide the human spirit that could possibly compare or compete with faith, with the promise that all things hoped for would be provided, if not immediately, then in an invisible future world where you don't get hurt if you fall on your face. When asked by a godless cynic why so many people sent so much money they didn't have for miracles that didn't happen, Gilder Smelt replied, "We done it for God." And, as predictably as a Harvard graduate telling you he is one, the insecure and the frightened lined up to fall down.

7Ms' miracle mania swept the world. Audio tapes, videos, CDs, interactive CD-ROMs, tee shirts, bumper stickers, mugs, and every conceivable sort of bizarre religious kitsch was sent out for free to believers who sent in love gifts of magic miracle seed money. One popular item, the Ye-are-the-salt-of-the-earth, glow-in-the-dark, seashell salt shaker, formed in the image of the translated to heaven Ducworth Bliss, was sent without charge to those who made heroic love gift payments on their eternal life insurance policies. Often this variegated shaker became the centerpiece on altars of families whose polluted water supply would prematurely merge them with The Eternal Bliss.

Sufficient funds were received to permit Miracle Missions to expand into world-wide real estate holdings. Miracle theme parks, hotels, office buildings, campgrounds, and even Miracle Meals fast food restaurants became common throughout America and most foreign countries. Gilder's favorite dish, grilled Spam and Velveeta cheese with onion, lettuce, mayonnaise and ketchup on white bread, was sold by the billions as the Miracle Smelt Melt. 7Ms was ready to control the world.

Almost as fast as a priest on a choirboy, individual religions lost their identities. When a denomination discovered 7Ms suddenly owned even its church properties, rather than be evicted, the elders usually agreed to change their signs. Eventually, and not altogether bloodlessly, 7Ms came to hold solid supernatural superiority on earth. When only the conventicles and those pesky secular humanists seemed beyond their reach, 7Ms decided to change some laws.

The previously shepherdless sheep, who now consumed Smelt Melts, willingly elected religious bigots and scientific illiterates to all public offices. School teachers taught children the More More Money song, and all learning became dedicated to the proposition that one lived only for 7Ms, so that one could live blissfully after death. All knowledge was held electronically and dispensed electronically, by video while awake, and by audio while asleep. Creationism and faith classes replaced the teachings of outlawed scientific heresies that had claimed it was possible to find out how the world really worked, or where humans really came from. The libraries of the older learning were destroyed.

Years passed. Everywhere was seen the fixed smile and thousand yard stare of the fanatically faithful. There was the occasional stoning of someone who claimed the fixed earth moved, and every so often children were reassigned, and their parents re-educated, if their traditional family was found to be practicing home schooling in science, or sex education, or teaching the heresy of reason. But, in general, life was good. For a while.

Suddenly, things fell apart. Viruses evolved that didn't know there was no evolution, nor that they could be stopped by faith. Almost simultaneously, the equipment that directed electrons to become images and voices failed. Secular scientists and science had been outlawed. Anyone who remembered and practiced the old ways, who knew how to repair or create a computer or a microchip, was in hiding or dead. 7Ms could neither deal with the plague, nor get their messages on line. Everyone was sick or dying; no miracle worked, and the voice of god in the machine was silent. *A fortiori,* faith failed.

Blame for these happenings was imputed to the secular humanists. The Blissful Judgement was upon the faithful, because they had been meek and gentle with those who had sought to control nature and deny their god's plan.

Darkness and death covered the land. The dead were left to bury the dead. No invisible electron could be controlled. Faith was swallowed up in viruses. The unseen world had triumphed over the seen.

Some time passed before the first of the secular humanists emerged. He was an ancient, gaunt man; his hand held the hand of a beautiful young woman. They had received inoculations, from their people, before their own computers had fallen silent in their secret places. All electronic information in the world was now forever lost. The destruction was as complete as that of the righteous fires that once consumed the collected knowledge of the Maya. This time, religion had destroyed itself in its own temple, using its own rules.

"Hypatia," the old man said, "I want to show you something." They walked in silence, until they reached an outdoor Altar of Bliss. He swept away the salt shaker, and shells and salt splattered as the icon smashed on the marble. He withdrew a package from his bag, and placed it on the altar. When the tattered, watertight wrappings were removed, he stood back and let the child gaze in wonder at the treasure. After some moments she said, "Grandfather, it's beautiful. What is it?"

He looked deeply into the health, and strength, and creativity, and intelligence, and curiosity of her human eyes, unglazed by grace, and said, "It's a book."

Edwin F. Kagin: *Baubles of Blasphemy*

On Arming for Armageddon
(December 1999)

What you don't know won't hurt you—it will kill you.
—Sign in U.S. Air Force training facility.

Then said he unto them...he that hath no sword, let him sell his garment, and buy one.
—Jesus, the Christ. Luke 22:36.

If, on December 31, 1999, at the very stroke of Midnight that heralds the dawn of the year 2000 C.E., the world ends, the Messiah comes or returns, the Apocalypse happens, the Battle of Armageddon begins, the saved are raptured from moving cars that careen on into busloads of godless, unbelieving, Camp Quest-type little children, believers ascend up into the air to meet Jesus who is on his way down to Earth to establish his Kingdom—if the trumpet shall sound and the dead shall be raised, and if the Revelation to Saint John the Divine prove true and one third of the stars fall to the Earth, and the Four Horsemen of the Apocalypse ride, and the sheep be separated from the goats, and the believing good be lifted up unto the highest Heaven to take their reserved seat at the Wedding Feast of the Lamb, whilst the unbelieving bad are dragged to their well-deserved eternal torment awaiting them in the deepest pits of fiery Hell as Gounod's *Faust* plays in the background—then, Gentle Reader, you should know that you are now holding your very last ever "Kagin's Column," because your narrator is going to repent, be saved, and be out of here, leaving you condemned remaining sinners with only this final heresy. That should make it quite a collector's item—if anyone there be left around to collect it.

But, bless you, the world should go on as before, and there should be more Kagin's Columns, because none of these dire things will happen. They won't happen because such beliefs are superstitious nonsense. They are primitive myths. The only way they can be harmful is if they are believed. Contemplate, if you will, just what would really happen if one third of the stars "fell" to Earth.

102

Religion

Webster defines 'superstition' thus: *any belief, based on fear or ignorance, that is inconsistent with the known laws of science or with what is generally considered in the particular society as true and rational; esp., such a belief in charms, omens, the supernatural, etc.* The myths are not the danger. Those who *believe* in the myths are the danger. A related problem is that there is very poor agreement in our "particular society" regarding what is "true and rational." Some think the world is only ten thousand years old and that animals and people were created from nothing in six days. No evidence to the contrary makes any difference. They want their myth taught in schools. Others want their myths taught instead. For the past two thousand years, we have had a lot of wars over what myths should be taught in school.

The feared 'Y2K bug' is somewhat different. For future researchers, reading this in the far future, Y2K (standing for 'Year 2000') is a code given for the unpredictable problems inherent in the unfortunate fact that lots of the computers that order our lives have not been taught to understand that time might go past the year 1999. Until the clock strikes 2000, we just won't know how big a problem that little training defect really is.

Anyhow, a seemingly growing population of irrational humans are preparing for the disasters they are certain will flow from their end-of-the-world delusions that mingle the non-existent with the fixable, as they set about to bring upon themselves and us the chaos that is feared. People are hording food, water, and weapons to await the end of civilization, the end of the world, the coming of Jesus, Judgement Day, and Lord knows what else. And they are prepared to waste other believers whose eschatology (look it up) is only slightly different from theirs. Guess what they will do to people like those secular humanists, who they think really caused all the problems of the world in the first place by teaching evolution, and by taking the Ten Commandments out of public courthouses, and by prohibiting prayers in public places like Jesus ordered on his last visit.

Let's say Jesus really did 'return' to Earth. How well received do you reckon he would be, considering that the many different Christian denominations appear incapable of agreeing on even the smallest points of theological doctrine? Do you suppose His Holiness the Pope will step aside and let Jesus have his chair? Do you guess the TV

103

preachers will leave their bully pulpits and, on bended knee, hand over to their Messiah their microphones and their diamond mines? Does one even wildly imagine that the many religious leaders of the world will be disposed to permit the god they have awaited to resolve for them the disputed points of their several faiths?

To survive the madness that seems certain to befall us, we need to understand that the feared coming millennium is not a real thing. There is no *real* millennium, just as there is no *real* line on the ground between the states of Kentucky and Tennessee such as one might see on service station road maps. A millennium, like all measurements of time, is something humans made up and then forgot that they made up. We can measure time any way we like. It makes no difference, so long as all agree on the rules. But even the rules are unclear. China, the Maya, and lots of other countries and peoples all have very different dates, based on different origin myths, for what we call 1999.

The year 2000 is not the beginning of a new third millennium. It is the last year of the second millennium. 2001 is the first year of the third millennium. Here's why. When a baby is less than one year old, her age is cooed out something like, 'five days old,' 'nine weeks old,' 'three months old'—that sort of thing. She is not said to be zero years old. When said child has lived a full year, she is then said to be 'one year old,' and has her 'first birthday,' surrounded by adoring relations. At one year old, the child starts her second year of life. For all of that second year she is said to be one year old. The second year of life, when finished, is celebrated as the child's 'second birthday.' And so it goes throughout life. One is always from one day to three-hundred-sixty-four days older than one's stated age.

If our numbering of years worked like birthdays, then 2000 would indeed be the first year of the third millennium. Like the aging baby, the 2000th birthday would mark the completion of the 2000th year of living and the start of the 2001st year of living, and 2001 would come at the end of the 2001st year of living. But it doesn't work like that with dates. There is no dating of 'three days,' 'seven months' or such, during the first year of this imaginary calendar, as there is in the dating of the lives of babies. The first year of the calendar would have been the year one the entire year, from New Year's Day on — not the year zero or some fraction of time less than one year. At the end of that first year, the year one was finished, and the year two began on New Year's Day. The tenth year of the calendar means that nine previous years have been completed, and that one is living in a true tenth year, not working toward the end of the eleventh year, as would be the case if we were talking about birthdays rather than calendars.

For birthdays, the start of year 2000 would mean you have actually started the 2001st year of living. For calendars, the start of year 2000 means you are starting the final year of that millennium. 1000 was the last year of the first millennium, just as 100 is the 100th year of a 100-year period of time. 101 is the first year of the second set of 100. 2000 is the last year of this millennium. 2001 is the first year of the next millennium. Most people don't understand this and think a new thousand-year period starts at midnight on December 31, 1999. This is particularly true of the crazies who ascribe cosmic meaning to that event, as did their predecessors in religious madness in the year 1000. The world didn't end then. The world won't end now.

The whole idea of the importance of the coming millennium is that it is believed to be two thousand years after the birth of Jesus. But this is incorrect. If the Bible is to be believed, Jesus was born during the reign of Herod the Great of Judea. It is a well-known fact of history that Herod died in the year 4 BCE. Therefore, Jesus could not have been born later than that date. Therefore, sadly, the real millennium occurred on or before 1996, and we missed it.

Chances are that, if you are reading this, you are a naïvely innocent liberal who thinks people are inherently good and well intentioned, and that religiously, or otherwise demented, fanatics won't really shoot you in the face for no sane reason if, with tolerance and caring, you simply understand and accept them. People who hold this view are frequently identified only as 'victims.' It has been said that a conservative is a liberal who has been mugged. Please accept, for your own safety's sake, the truth that there really are dangerous people about who will kill you for the fun of watching you die, and please further accept that millennium madness will bring these types out around New Year 2000 like earthworms after a summer rain. There are Christian militia groups, often commanded by ministers, trained in the use of military firearms, committed to "regaining" America for Christ. They have trained home invasion units to deal with the

Edwin F. Kagin: *Baubles of Blasphemy*

enemies of God—you know, those who practice the "religion of evolution," promote the "murder of the unborn," want "special rights" for homosexuals, want "God" out of the classrooms, and so forth. Do you know the type? You better, because they know you.

Your narrator has been denounced by them in churches, as have other identified individuals who disagree with them. Well, they are making straight the way for the return of Christ to lead them against the Antichrist, believed by some to be already among us, and revealed by the "mark of the beast" in such things as the bar codes used in food stores. Yeah, no kidding! They really are that nuts, and they are armed and extremely dangerous.

If you don't have enough respect for the value and importance of your own life, and the lives of those you love, to acquire and learn the safe and disciplined use of appropriate tools for self protection and home defense, then at least try to acquire a working knowledge of the belief systems of those committed to harming you. Defending one's life is a moral obligation. Knowledge is indeed power, and you may learn enough to avoid a deadly confrontation. Jews in Germany tried to avoid confrontation. Ask someone in Israel today how they feel about the liberal's dream of making their family safer by not having a gun in the house.

Here's a crash course in just what, in broad overview, those looking for something supernatural to happen around New Year's Eve or Day believe:

Chapter One. Yahweh, a god of the Bible, for uncertain reasons, decided to make everything from nothing, including our universe, our planet, and ourselves. Yahweh then made people, and they disobeyed the god by gaining knowledge of good and evil. Although they could not have fairly been held to know it was wrong to disobey a god before gaining knowledge of good and evil, Yahweh punished them for not being the kind of created beings he wanted them to be.

Chapter Two. The numerous descendents of the two created people who had disappointed Yahweh also disappointed him, so Yahweh killed all of them in a flood. Only eight adult people survived, by living for a year in a large floating box that was 450 feet long, by 75

106

feet wide, by 45 feet high, that also contained samples of every kind of animal, bird, and bug of the inundated planet. Every living child on earth was killed by Yahweh's flood, as was every pregnant woman and every fetus. That god's views on the murder of children could not have been made more clear. Yahweh promised not to do it again.

Chapter Three. The Earth is repopulated by the eight people and the animals that survived the flood in the box. Yahweh was still disappointed by the behavior of the descendents of the people he had saved from drowning. Yahweh then supernaturally produced a son from the body of an unwed teenage girl, so that the boy could grow up and be killed as a sacrifice to Yahweh for the sins of everyone else. After the son was killed, Yahweh brought him back to life and took him to Heaven. All people have to do to go to Heaven when they are dead is to believe that Yahweh let his son be killed, as a child sacrifice for their sins, and then brought him back to life. Before he went back to Heaven, the reanimated dead son said that he would return shortly to Earth to take believers back with him to be with him and Yahweh.

Chapter Four. For nearly two thousand years, the faithful have waited for the son Yahweh made, permitted to be killed, and then brought back to life, to come to Earth and get them as he promised he would do. For some reason, this is thought more likely to occur on thousand-year, round-numbered years. So, despite the Bible's assertion that no one can know the day or the hour it will occur, the crazies prepare for the return of the son of the god, with wildly differing versions of what will happen upon his return. Some, but far from all, of the possible events and outcomes predicted are set forth in the opening paragraph of this blasphemy. As in most matters of faith, you can take your choice.

Naturally, nothing supernatural will happen, because there is no supernatural to happen. That is not the concern. What *is* of concern is the possible actions of those who believe something end-of-the-world like will happen and *who are committed to helping it along.* Some such have already emerged, and they have worked much mischief. We can be certain more wait the fast closing end of the year 1999. It is these living persons set upon harming others and achieving self-fulfilling prophecies that we should fear and guard against, not the fears and fairy tales that drive them. They are the darkness we need fear.

Here are some of your narrator's prophecies for the future, drawn far more specifically than any of those of the Bible or of any of the 900-telephone-line psychics. The year 2000, the last year of this millennium, will come. The Messiah will not come. The world will not end. Neither Jesus nor Satan will appear. Nor will the Antichrist. There will be no Rapture. There will be no apocalypse. There will be no battle of Armageddon. The failure of these events to occur will strengthen the faith of some, as the people continue to imagine a vain thing. There will be more Kagin's Columns.

The final year of this millennium, that will so quickly come, should be for us a time of reflection. The dating of our years, the structure of our centuries, and the very idea of a millennium, are, to be sure, artificial. But so are most of the many signposts that mark our roads and measure our days. Symbols are powerful. They are of great importance and value, so long as we don't mistake the symbol for what it is meant to symbolize. We can find meaning in the final year of this arbitrary thousand-year period that is a slice of how we measure time. The past one thousand years has been filled with war and with superstition, the latter often giving birth to the former. The next thousand years can see our kind populate the stars, or it can see us regress to the worst of the past darkness from which our evolved human minds have delivered us.

Consider, as a benediction for our age, the words of Thaddaeus, said to have been from the first century of the first millennium:

* * *

May that measure of peace, justice, harmony and understanding denied religion and its deities be attained by mortals through the use of their minds, and may reason, science, curiosity, and discovery replace the fear, the guilt, the pain, and the ignorance of trembling in terror before capricious gods. Ecce homo.

On the Transubstantiation of the World: The Revelation to Edwin
(January 2000)

This is the way the world ends
This is the way the world ends
This is the way the world ends
Not with a bang but a whimper.
—T.S. Eliot

Edwin, unto those who yet remain for the eternity to come, to all those left behind who, though damned, yet know it not, greetings. Little of comfort can be said or given unto you, save the assurance that truth, however dire, should be valued of more worth than the vanity of false belief and the futile imagining of a vain thing.

I erred when last I wrote, in false strayed prophecy, that the world would not end and that the rapture would not come. On the midnight stroke that called in the 2000th year of our Lord, this, our world, ended. The saved saints, living and dead, were raptured into Heaven. We, and all of us who remain—who you must now know are the eternally damned—were left behind. Left behind, forever, without hope, in a world that has been utterly destroyed. Left in a world beyond repair. Left in a world that is, with no hope of redemption, ruined.

That which had been prophesied, this horror foretold, was not at once known to have been so fully and so finally fulfilled. There were only small things to be seen as signs. The weather was too warm, and cats seemed less opaque than usual. Cats, we note too late, are not mentioned in the Bible. Dogs are mentioned eight and thirty times. Now know we why. Cats know why too. Cats have always known.

The truth, the horror, of what had happened was made known to me, for reasons I neither know nor understand, in a mighty vision. Whether in the body or out of it, whether asleep or not, I can in no wise truly say. I only know it was revealed unto me that our world is now past and forever gone. And that I am charged to tell you.

Edwin F. Kagin: *Baubles of Blasphemy*

Hope of supernatural salvation for any who remain is likewise gone, for the blessed of the almighty power, all of the chosen elect, have been raptured away. We who are left are left unto eternity, denied forever and forever the beatific vision, denied the fulfillment of the blessed hope. There will never be offered another chance to gain that heavenly world beyond the natural world. We are all alone, with our fallible human reasoning, in our world that lack of faith destroyed. The only world we have ever had. No supernatural power will ever visit us again. We are alone for all time, with only ourselves to guide and save us.

How, might one ask, as I asked, can our world have ended, yet seem so solidly to continue and appear so plainly to remain? So asked I in my vision, and the answer as a mystery came. With the mystery of that answer came the charge to publish the truth abroad—to assure the anguish of all of us who are fellow travelers on this orb that was first created and lately then destroyed.

There appeared before me a book, the edges of which were blackened and burned, as in a refiner's fire, and the seals of which book, wherewithal it had been sealed, had been broken asunder. And the book was open unto a page. And the words upon that charred and tattered page could still be plainly seen and clearly read. And these were the words that were thereupon writ:

Know thou, doomed mortal, that thy world hath ended. It ended in the first moments of the first day of the first month of the year you call 2000. The Rapture hath come. It came as the world ended, and those who were chosen to be saved have been taken away unto a new Heaven and a new Earth. All who are ever to be raptured have been raptured, and all those not then raptured are never to be raptured. Those not raptured are left behind, by Divine Design, to live out their mortal lives in a world that hath now ended, a world in which they, the not saved and the not raptured, must henceforth forever remain.

Then asked I, through terror and tears, unto the unknown darkness about me, how our wrecked and ruined and wretched world could still so sentient seem.

And a voice, likened unto a voice of doom, sounding as the taste of wormwood and gall, answered from out a whirlwind unto me, with directions to tell the answer unto you, my fellow mortals, who along with me alike to death are damned:

110

Hear, Oh fool, thou who would not see the supernatural or on faith believe that which was unseen. Know thee, in this final answer—for no further answer shall ever come—that thy world has been transubstantiated, with all of its substance forever changed, with only the accidents of its appearance as land, sea and sky remaining, that cause it to seem, in each of its particulars, to those of undiscerning hearts, immutable and unchanged. As it was in the days of Noah, so has it now been finally fulfilled as it had been formerly forever of old foretold.

As it was in the time of Noah! The flood, the ark, the animals, the drowned children. Only eight adult humans spared. Only four breeding pairs of humans left alive when finally dried the heavenly waters that had choked the life from all other adults and from all children, both in and out of the womb, from those who, in person or by the hands of their doomed mothers, scratched and screamed, as their lives slowly ended, against the splintery sides of the ark of salvation, as it floated above their weakened forms that finally sank beneath the righteous waves. Seven pairs of every clean animal were mercifully spared. Those not saved then died. Their fate was to be preferred to that of those not saved this time, to the fate of those condemned to live where faith has failed.

I then understood this vision granted me. Those awaiting the rapture of the blessed were as foolish virgins awaiting their bridegrooms while despising their coming. Few were chosen, and few were taken. It was not written how many would be saved, only that it would be as in the time of Noah, and surely it was so. The religiously pious, the self-righteous, those assured unto themselves of their goodness and of their salvation, all are as fully denied as are those who, through the use of reason, reject untestable faith as folly.

Heed not the much speaking yet to come from false preachers, for such fools are as sure to die as you. Laugh at pretenders who claim knowledge, at those who dare presume upon eternal truth, for they are here with all of us, un-raptured and alone in a transubstantiated world, in a world wherein their faith has failed.

My charge is now completed, and my revelation has been revealed. It remains but to remind you that only our human minds, with their naturally evolved abilities to create and learn and reason, yet abide. Nothing supernatural will ever exist for us, or be available unto us. What can be done by humankind in our new world, where mortals live for this life alone and can look neither to hopes of immortality nor to any power or powers beyond the bounty and boundaries of our natural world, cannot now be known, because such a thing has never yet been fully attempted or truly tried.

We have no choice, it seems, but to live in our world without faith in anything beyond ourselves. For that is all we have. Perhaps it is all that we have ever had. But it is enough.

May the years yet to come unto you bring you peace and joy. And do take heart, for you have this day seen the prophesy fulfilled that there will be Kagin's Columns yet to come.

On Prayer *Pour* Petri

Lord, what fools these mortals be!
—Puck

Be glad you are not a bacterium. If you have an identity crisis, if you don't know who you are, or your place in the universe, and this upsets you, while no one else cares, then be comforted by considering the plight of bacteria. Some authorities consider bacteria plants; others think they are neither plants nor animals, but a completely separate life form. All authorities consulted agree they are not animals. If a choice be forced, they are flora, not fauna. If they were on the ark, they were stowaways. Most people care less about them and their problems than they care about you and your problems.

Divine intercession has been sought for bacteria. It had to happen. Faithful readers perhaps recall that we have, in these pages, considered many events that may seem to us extra-ordinary—visits of the BVM, custody fights over frozen fetuses, satanic plots to stop abortions, public prayer as the cause of social dysfunction, together with diverse other matters too numerous to recount—yet never, for all of our commentary, uncritically perceived by some as blasphemy or religion-bashing, have we had occasion to reflect on so curious an idea as praying over bacteria in petri dishes. We didn't dream this up. We saw it in a TV documentary, so it has to be true. A secular humanist couldn't have concocted a fantasy so funny. The hysterical reality of this event sprang unprompted from the creative energies of certain of those numbered among the righteously saved.

It came about in this wise. Many have long maintained that prayer changes things, and that, upon proper petition, some god will supernaturally intervene in human affairs to alter the course of events that would, without prayer, proceed according to the laws of nature. It is alleged that this divine intercession extends to the healing of sick people. If one prays for the sick, god will heal them or at least make them better. Without the prayers, god will simply let the sick suffer. Many believe this and have offered narrative proofs. There have been 'studies' of questionable reliability done to demonstrate the power

113

of healing prayer. The research results showed, to the satisfaction of the faithful, that people who were prayed over did better than those not so favored. The data were challenged by certain of those cynical, sneering religion-bashing secular humanist skeptical-of-everything godless types that religious faith knows so well and would be so much better off without. These scoffers thought that maybe the mere belief that prayer worked caused the improvements, if any, and that the results sprang from the mind of the believer, not from the intercession of divine providence. Equally effective, claimed the critics, would be any other conviction the stricken might believe would cure them. By way of example of this principle, our household, for some years now, has remained free of the scourge of leprosy by avoiding the eating of possum. [*This was almost certainly in truth more due to the unavailability of possum-pot pies, though Kagin might not admit this. —Editor*]

To prove that prayer, not placebo, worked the miracles, and to eliminate insofar as possible, as religion likes to do anyway, the menace of the mind, it was decided to test the effects of prayer on experimental and control batches of bacteria. Guess what? The occupants of the prayed over petri plates did better (whatever that means) than the prayerless petri plates. Proof positive to shake to their very foundations the demons of doubt.

While this research and its results have not been published, to our knowledge, in any learned journals, nor have we learned of its details, nor heard of its replication, the implications, apart from proving the truth of religious faith, are awesome indeed. We need no longer waste money in secular medical research trying to cure such things as cancer or AIDS. Biological research labs can now close. Departments of microbiology can now become departments of miracles. Imagine if the human race had this knowledge when we were struggling with smallpox, polio, typhoid, malaria, and even the bubonic plague. Think how many innocent rats could have been spared with this new knowledge.

But no use lamenting the mistakes of the past. We must press forward into the new frontiers of faith. To this end, the following is suggested as a petri prayer. You are welcome to use this sword and shield of the spirit, at home in your closet, in the certain trust that it will prove divinely beneficial against anything biological that might prove bothersome.

All mighty and all powerful God, maker of all things visible and invisible, maker of the mighty beast behemoth, and of the bacteria found in the bowels of behemoth, and of all of those least of thy plants that trouble thy creation man, hear, oh Lord, this our prayer of supplication and grant intercession unto us. We most humbly confess we have, in our blindness, followed other gods. We have sinned against thee and forsaken thy path. We have blindly ignored thy eternal truths, and forgotten thy ways that are above our ways, as we have sought to cure the sick through the teachings of the false gods of science. In our weakness and folly, we have followed and whored after the medicine of man. We repent of our error, and ask thy divine forgiveness, as we now reject those idols of the mind that have separated us from our God, the only true source of all good and perfect gifts of healing. Stretch forth thy mighty hand and smite the plants of thy creation that are unseen. Remake, oh God, the bacteria you made. Remold their tiny forms to forms less harmful. In dish, in dessert, in duodenum, they ravage us. Restore to them the innocence they had before the sin of our first parents, before our fall from grace. Render them, we pray, harmless to us, and, in thy infinite mercy, cure us, and protect us from them. We are weak, and they are strong. Nevertheless, oh god our strength and our salvation, not our will but thine be done. Amen.

Please let us know if this works. It should. Can't think of any reason it shouldn't.

Edwin F. Kagin: *Baubles of Blasphemy*

On Restoring Traditional Family Values
(June 1994)

Come, my friends, 'Tis not too late to seek a newer world.

—Tennyson

Say you wanted to destroy civilization. Create a mythology whereby all products of human conception must be born. Punish indiscriminate breeding by insuring that every pregnancy produces a baby. Run slick TV ads showing a neurotic woman lamenting an earlier choice to have an abortion, a lament created by the mythmakers. Show tidy, nicely dressed, scrubbed, well fed little children and convince people their unwanted kid will be that way. Base all of this on the will of God, and decree the authority of scripture over absolutely everything, including evidence and common sense. Ban all sex education, contraception and pregnancy interruption. Deny public funds for abortion, but rather give women free state money for every baby produced. This method will insure that the most useless and uneducated will have the most children. Then those little 'gifts of God,' unwanted, unloved and unparented, can grow up to kill and rob you, and make more kids who will, if the Mother Theresas prevail, accumulate to be seen starving or murdering on the nightly news.

One should then, with civilization in chaos, decide that the most Christian nation on earth is in trouble for drifting from the myths that created the problem. Confident that the myth must win no matter what, create a movement to return to "Traditional Family Values," *i.e.*, a comprehensive mythical control system, based on the Bible, a pre-scientific Bronze and Iron-Age document. If a Trojan horse wrecks your civilization, haul in another one to fix the problem. Our restoration of Traditional Family Values won't be the first time religion has destroyed a culture. Just watch the news. Better yet, read a history book.

To restore these Traditional Family Values, we should have some notion of what they are. What type values? What kind of family? What is traditional? That kind of thing. "Traditional Family Values" means those beliefs held and customs practiced by a white Anglo-Saxon protestant churchgoing married-with-children unit in a small

116

American town between 1946 and 1956. If we live exactly as they did, everything will be fine. That's the goal. Any other vision is a highway to Hell. Now that we've defined them, how do we restore them? Basic to the restoration of Traditional Family Values is the abolition of democracy. Democracy really has no place in Christian thought, is not found anywhere in the Bible, and is a troublesome holdover from pagan systems Christianity destroyed. Democracy permits diversity and invention for individuals and cultures. Expansion of ideas is forbidden by Traditional Family Values, for all we need know is in the Bible. School boards must be controlled so wrong ideas like birth control, evolution, and the solving of problems without supernatural intervention do not get into students' heads or text books. Democracy prohibits this control. Democracy encourages independence of thought and seeking of new ways for believing and doing. New ideas and different ways are bad—democracy must go. Despite attempts by the righteous to establish a government controlled by their religion, our founders gave us a democracy. Democracy has tolerated thoughts and actions that are properly forbidden, and the sooner we get rid of it the faster everyone will get back to right thinking.

In our efforts to restore Traditional Family Values, we should be able to learn from the examples of those who advocate them. Regrettably, some of our finest models are flawed by over-exposure to democracy. His soon-to-be Most Christian Majesty, King of England, Charles, heir apparent, has separated from his wife and children to sport in adultery with a married woman. Our own Ronald and Nancy Reagan married following divorce and after conceiving their daughter Patti. Patti appeared buff naked in *Playboy* (July 1994). She was also on the periodical's cover scantily clad with a Negro standing behind her with his arms about her and his black paws cupping her exposed white breasts. If not for that democracy business, she would be in prison for this pornographic display. And this Reagan daughter was raised by parents who practiced astrology and who want everyone to return to Traditional Family Values.

The example of one Rush Limbaugh, an outspoken, if boorish, advocate for the religious right and Traditional Family Values, may help. He was recently united in holy matrimony with a woman by a

117

member of the U.S. Supreme Court, Mr. Justice Clarence Thomas. Perfect? Hardly. Brother Limbaugh had been twice married and divorced before the wedding, as had been his bride. Further, he and the female had cohabited, and, presumably, fornicated (a crime under Traditional Family Values) by engaging in sex before the church said they could. This behavior deserves the Traditional Family Values Hall of Shame, not emulation. And the marrying judge was civil authority, not church certified. The judge was also a Negro. Under proper Traditional Family Values, he would have been known as a 'nigger.' He could not have sat on a jury, much less the Supreme Court. Indeed, he would have been in jail, for he has a white wife. Othello, on the Supreme Court, would have been unthinkable, and Traditional Family Values prohibited interracial marriage. The crime was called miscegenation. So Traditional Family Values are simply not satisfied by persons married to four other people being married civilly by a nigger who couples lustfully with white women. The evolution of constitutional freedoms has changed all that, but we are seeking Traditional Family Values as they are properly, and undemocratically, understood.

Failing to find, among the powerful and outspoken, proper role modeling for Traditional Family Values, let us attempt to construct a composite of what can be, and must be, if we are to restore what was and live by biblical truths. Consider the ideal, in Francis and Felicity Fundangelical. We meet them on their wedding day, in their bridal suite, alone at last, where Francis says, "Felicity, my darling, do you know what we are going to do tonight?" "No, my beloved husband," she says, "what?"

Felicity knew from her Traditional Family Values training that her duty as a woman and wife was to obey her husband Francis as she had obeyed her father. Men had received the right from God the Father to control women, daughters of Eve who had caused the fall of man from the Garden of Eden. She was Mrs. Felicity Fundangelical and it was her wedding night. Her Norman Rockwell world of Traditional Family Values was fulfilled. She had her MRS degree and would devote her life to her god, her church, her husband, and her children, in that order. It was 1954, in Sperm Bank, Georgia, and all was right with the world.

The marriage of Francis and Felicity Fundangelical had made them one flesh. Divorce was unthinkable—they were mystically joined for life. Neither partner had any idea whatsoever of sexual union, for this nasty little subject was not discussed by anyone, inside or outside of marriage. The couple generally knew that married people had babies (only married people!) but had been told they were "gifts of God" and, for all they knew, occurred through spontaneous generation. Francis had heard boys giggling about naughty things in shop class, but had averted his ears, and Felicity had wondered what her Home Economics teacher meant by the remark that a girl on her wedding night was well advised to think of canning apricots.

The Fundangelicals brought their collective life experiences to their wedding night. They knew they lived, and would live, in a relatively secure world, with little crime, most people employed, and everyone doing and believing much the same, so long as they were just like the Fundangelicals. And everyone they knew was. Life would proceed as it presumably always had. We are studying them as a model of Traditional Family Values to better learn how to restore the Traditional Family Values we've lost because of participatory democracy. Prince Charles, Rush Limbaugh, and Ronald and Nancy Reagan all proved wanting as proper role models.

(Here it must be confessed that an error was made earlier in this treatise, wherein the human male standing naked behind the Reagans' naked daughter Patti, and handling her breasts on the cover of the July 1994 *Playboy*, was incorrectly identified as a Negro. Careful reading of the accompanying text, by Mrs. Lisa Mohnsam, has revealed he was not a Negro but a darkly tanned white dude. However, he does simulate a Negro, mocking the Traditional Family Values we want to restore, mirroring similar pornography offered by *Rolling Stone* and Janet Jackson). [*And your Editor cannot help but note, with pride, this example of startling prescience by your Author, regarding the destruction of Traditional Family Values to be visited later by Ms. Jackson—the Author wrote these words, after all, well before any famous Super Bowl involving revelations from the aforesaid Ms. Jackson.*]

Our goal is to restore Traditional Family Values and to enjoy, in all its fullness, the world of the Fundangelicals. To this end, Mr.

and Mrs. Fundangelical provide a microcosm for explication of an America that tragically recedes before the assaults of godless humanism and democracy. This world was not politically correct; it was religiously correct and grounded on the certainty that everything in contradiction was wrong. There was prayer and Bible reading in schools, and everyone attended religious school plays. There were church camps, potluck dinners, revivals, patriotic parades and minstrel shows. Everybody smoked, even in hospital rooms and the minister's study. All men wore short hair and hats; women wore long dresses and girdles. Library books were censored for right thought. Divorce was illegal, abortion was illegal, birth control was illegal, strip bars and pornography were illegal. Sex education was not taught in school, and certainly not in the home. The *Sears Catalogue* and *National Geographic* were the best sources for that information. Science classes Francis attended were taught by the football coach, who knew evolution wasn't true because it didn't fit the Bible stories of Jehovah's interactions with Adam and Noah. There were no color televisions and no computers, two more things that have destroyed Traditional Family Values. At least television and movies were moral. Married couples were shown sleeping in separate beds, and while murder was okay, physical love was not. It was no more discussed in polite society than cancer, or Uncle Herman passing out in his turkey and cranberries from alcoholism.

When one is right and good he naturally wants to keep himself and his children from people and ideas that are wrong and bad. Traditional Family Values had erected for Francis and Felicity numerous barriers against wrong thinking and interaction. Negroes (known as 'niggers') went to different schools, and had their own restaurants, restrooms, drinking fountains, waiting rooms, and places on public transportation. They could go to the Fundangelicals' church, but they sat apart in the balcony, while whites sat on the main level, fanning themselves with funeral home fans. Interracial dating was unthinkable, and interracial marriages unlawful, except perhaps for Moses, and Captain John Simpson would not now be in trouble. Of course he wouldn't have played football either, at least not with whites. No decent person interacted with the children of slaves as anything other than master to servant. Some debated whether they possessed souls.

All foreigners, their countries, cultures, languages and histories were seen as vastly inferior to those values taught Francis and Felicity, who believed white Christians had "discovered" America. The savages they discovered led to the maxim that the only good Injun was a dead one. The Fundangelicals had learned cute xenophobic slurs for members of other races and of most foreign nations, and would teach them to their children.

Other religions were wrong and were studied, if at all, only to refute them. Jews were Christ killers, greedy, and universally damned; no Traditional Family Values person would have anything to do with this hated race unless absolutely necessary, like borrowing money to finance a war. The modern idea of a Judeo-Christian tradition was unknown. Jews were bad people who refused to accept Christ's offer of salvation and were to be shunned. Catholics were little better. They were Papist pawns and idol worshipers. Francis and Felicity's ancestors had killed many of them in holy wars. A fish sandwich was known as a Catholic hamburger, and Catholics were called mackerel snappers. Such religions as Buddhism, Hinduism, and Islam were understood as heathen beliefs having something to do with flying carpets. All that was known of them was that they needed missionaries, or better yet, the killing of their followers.

Dirty-minded readers probably think that when Felicity asked Francis what they were going to do on their wedding night that something sexual was afoot. Repent! We'll get to it. First, we must consider how to restore the Traditional Family Values of the Fundangelicals and destroy civilization and democracy.

If you want a taste of what those good old days were like, turn off the air conditioner.

Those committed to an early and full restoration of Traditional Family Values should be heartened by recent events. In Florida a religious crazy named Paul Hill shot and killed two gentlemen, a retired doctor who performed abortions and a retired U.S. Air Force Officer volunteering to help women exercise civilized democratic rights. The Colonel's wife, a retired nurse, was wounded.

In Rome, another religious crazy, his Holiness the Pope, John Paul II (J2P2) denounced a United Nations attempt to control the horror of humans destroying their species by over-breeding. J2P2 said abortion

Edwin F. Kagin: *Baubles of Blasphemy*

and artificial contraception deny couples the right to determine the size of their families. And they could, if they didn't want to populate, restrict sex to those days the female is not fertile. This game is called Vatican Roulette and the players are called parents. J2P2 believes limiting population any other way is unethical and immoral.

So we are well on our way to restoring the world of Francis and Felicity Fundangelical, the glorious world of Traditional Family Values. Some who may find murder a bit extreme so early in the restoration process cannot argue with the results. If civilization and democracy are to be destroyed by too many people overrunning a planet under dogmatic religious authority, no means of accomplishment is too extreme.

Prudence, however, dictates a more moderate approach. We should simply repeal the Bill of Rights, and pass an Amendment making the Fundangelicals mythical system the law of the land. Religious repression would then be fully constitutional and 'God,' negligently left out of the constitution by the humanists who wrote it, would be back in control. After all, God's on the money. There will be some resistance from Jews, blacks, liberated women, secular humanists, homosexuals, and probably the nation of Islam whose followers think they should be in control.

That's the problem with democracy—too many different people thinking they're right. God's on the side with the heaviest artillery. Take away the guns of those who disagree with you. Kill (maybe just jail) their lawyers, professors, and judges. Burn their books and write your own. Outlaw computers. If a manual typewriter was good enough for Harry Truman, it's good enough for us. Ban color televisions. The world should be seen in black and white. Democracy will be gone and civilization will soon follow. There will be arguments and tribal warfare over how best to enforce Traditional Family Values and just whose values are required by our Reformed Constitution. But there are ways of handling these disagreements, assuming you are in power and have authority from a god.

We are studying our model of Traditional Family Values, Francis and Felicity Fundangelical on their Traditional Family Values wedding night. The Fundangelicals actually believed their god had invented moral law. To them, Socrates, Buddha, Cato, Euripides, and other

122

pre-christian heathens had nothing to do with the awareness that an honorable life is to be preferred to a dishonorable one. The moral law of Traditional Family Values would have seemed odd to those ancients whose works Christianity destroyed. Particularly tonight.

Francis and Felicity's first night as one flesh shows us the conflict between nature and nurture. Their glands were programmed by nature, their minds by Traditional Family Values. They knew that, now married, they were permitted to do something with each other, something beyond petting. They knew they had their god's okay to go all the way. There was great embarrassment and blushing, much fear, guilt, and fumbling.

To tell just what happened would be a gross violation of the Traditional Family Values we are trying to restore. A description of that night could not lawfully be printed then or in the world we will have when Traditional Family Values are restored, the Constitution is changed, and democracy replaced by dogma. From the later circumstantial evidence of babies, one might conclude they eventually got it right, but it was never discussed. And there is precedent for exceptions. We cannot, therefore, know what happened. Before too long we will forget there was ever a time we could.

When Felicity told Francis she did not know what they were going to do on this night of nights, he took her soft hand. He knew, without his god, he and the wife he was to lead [sic] were incompetent to do anything. He knew he needed guidance from a ready source of all answers. He knew that earth was but a pilgrimage and Heaven was their home. His world had not yet evolved beyond Traditional Family Values. Francis looked at his wife Felicity with the fixed smile and thousand-yard stare characteristic of the Fundangelicals and said, "Let us pray."

And the Fundangelicals turned off the light.

On the Holy Trinity, or
Mysteries of Monotheism

Hear, O Israel: The Lord our God is one Lord...
—Deuteronomy 6:4

...for there is one God; and there is none other but he...
—Mark 12:32

Ye shall not go after other gods, of the gods of the people which are round about you... —Deuteronomy 6:14

...in the name of the Father, and of the Son, and of the Holy Spirit...

—Words of art contained in miscellaneous
Christian blessings, baptisms, benedictions, *etc.*

Unitarians, it is said, believe that at most there is one god. Thomas Jefferson was a Unitarian. He wrote our Declaration of Independence. Various Unitarian churches are named after him, *e.g.*, "Thomas Jefferson Unitarian Church." "Unitarian-ism" is considered a heresy by other Christians who view themselves as "Trinitarians." In that this difference of supernatural opinion has proved at least as important to human progress as the much warred over issue of whether soul-saving baptism is best accomplished by dunking or by sprinkling, and in that this controversy over the nature of the godhead has led to much bloodletting, has caused much human misery, and could well prove useful for secular humanists in surviving the ARCW, the dispute merits some consideration.

Popular mass religious culture holds that monotheism—the belief that there is only one god—was introduced into human thought by the Jews of the Old Testament and was rarified and glorified in the New Testament by Jesus, the Christ. It is widely, and uncritically, believed that the idea of there being only one god was original to the Judeo-Christian tradition (whatever that is) and that this 'monotheism' clearly demarcates Jews and Christians from lesser breeds who hold to the more primitive eschatological (maybe 'ontological,' but certainly metaphysical—it's hard to keep this nonsense straight) view that there are many gods. As with much religious belief, it just ain't so. And kindly refrain from yelling that one who points these things out is engaging in 'religion-bashing.' Your author didn't make the facts. If he had, they would be quite different from what they are.

The sad truth is that the Jews of the Torah, like most people of the time, clearly believed there were many gods. A notable historic exception was the Egyptian heretic pharaoh Ikhnaton (or Akhenaton). His belief in one god got him murdered by priests who made their money from the old time religion—it is comforting to know there are some absolutes. The point of the 'covenant' with Abraham, Moses, *et al.*, was that Yahweh (Jehovah, God, 'I Am That I Am,' or whatever) agreed to be the god of the Hebrew people, and they agreed that he was to be their god. Sort of a contract—one that might read, "Out of the many gods, other people can have their god or gods, but you will be our god, and we will be your people." Thus, in the Ten Commandments (second edition, of course), it is decreed, in the very first commandment, "Thou shalt have no other gods before me." Similarly, the second commandment (the one about not making graven images), states, in pertinent part, "...for I the Lord thy God am a jealous god...."

There is nothing here about this god being the only god. The other gods could stand side by side with him, but should not be before him. Further, he is a "jealous" god. Jealous of what? Of the other gods, of course. And he has reason. Much of the Old Testament involves the children of the covenant worshiping other gods. They were doing it even as Moses was getting the Ten Commandments. If they believed there was only one god, why were they worshiping a golden calf? Because they knew there were lots of gods, that's why, and they were trolling for a better god than the god of their covenant. A great deal of holy ink is spent on god asserting himself as the god of Israel. He has contests with other gods. He is as paranoid about protecting his position as Superman is about protecting his secret identity. None of this competitive zeal would have been necessary if the Hebrews truly believed there was only one god, *i.e.*, him. By the time the stories of the Bible made the Bible, the Jews had no doubt convinced themselves that there is in fact only one god. The Christians were not so sure.

Jews, in general, follow the teachings of the Bible better than Christians. They celebrate the Sabbath on the Sabbath, as god ordered; Christians do not—they celebrate it on Sunday, without a whit of biblical justification for ignoring god's orders. Jews also rather carefully follow the proscription against making or worshipping graven images. Christians apparently don't think this commandment is very important, as they peddle religious statutes of every possible variety (the more offensive ones can be found at any decent redneck truck stop). Roman Catholics deal with the problem by leaving the commandment out of their Catechism. Getting one god out of many took greater creativity.

If there is ever a contest to choose history's worst villain, the award might well go to the emperor Constantine, who made Christianity the official religion of the Roman Empire. In 325 CE, he convened a council at the city of Nicaea to stop Christian squabbling over the nature of god and to establish once and for all, by majority vote, what Christians must believe to be saved.

Seems there was much argument over whether the god under discussion was one person or three.

The council produced a remarkable document known as 'The Nicene Creed.' It remains the official statement of Christian faith recited every Sunday in many Christian churches. Some Protestant churches use a simplified version known as the 'Apostles' Creed.' Both versions reject the idea of one god while claiming to embrace it. Simply put, the doctrine, and 'mystery,' of the 'Holy Tinity' holds that while there is in fact only one god, he consists of three distinct, yet indivisible parts: 'God the Father,' 'God the Son,' and 'God the Holy Spirit.' Or, in choirboy humor, 'Daddy-O, J.C., and Spook.' If it made sense, there would be no need for faith to believe it. This is true of many religious doctrines. After Nicaea, the belief in only one unitary god, instead of the triune god, became a heresy that could get you killed. And we dare call the priests who wasted Ikhnaton heathens. See now why Thomas Jefferson, the Unitarian, didn't want an official religion?

The logical gymnastics of the trinity is but one example of the discomfort Christians experience in trying to believe in one god. They also believe in angels, the Devil (Satan, *etc.*), demons, and all manner of disembodied occupants of the spirit world. There are *legions* of them. Many are prayed to as 'saints' and are asked to intercede with 'God' on behalf of the believer, *e.g.*, "Holy Mary, mother of God, pray for us sinners...."

Now just what is a *god*? A god is any supernatural personage that isn't a living human being. In other words, one is, if not an animal, either a human or a god. Clever attempts at creating subdivisions among immortals, while maintaining there is only one god, simply don't work. While believers want to believe in one god, they really can't. A single god would have to embody contradictory attributes, like good and evil, male and female (does god the father have both male and female DNA?). In that this is impossible, at least in Western thought, believers invent good gods and bad gods, just like the heathen do. If attempts to

Edwin F. Kagin: *Baubles of Blasphemy*

argue this is in fact monotheism prove unbelievably absurd, the problem can be easily corrected by calling any contradiction a "mystery."

The only real mystery is why adults give this matter any serious attention at all.

To Lesser Breeds

We think your theology

Just one more mythology.

But something you must never do

Is teach our theology

As some other mythology!

'Cause the things *we* believe in are true!

128

On the Gospel of Thaddaeus
(June 1996)

But if there be no resurrection of the dead, then is Christ not risen:

And if Christ be not risen, then is our preaching vain, and your faith is also vain

—Saul of Tarsus, a.k.a.,
The Apostle Paul
(1st Corinthians 15: 13–14)

For the protection of persons yet living, the circumstances of the discovery and translation of the following cannot now be revealed. The authenticity of this document, and its accurate rendering into English from first-century CE Greek, is assured. It is presented now, and with some urgency, for fear that it might otherwise be lost through the efforts of persons who are aggressively attempting to suppress forever any evidence of its existence. The very zeal of those who seek to prevent this work from becoming known, when considered together with the tone and content of the writing itself, indicates this is something far different, and perhaps more reliable, than the pseudepigraphical writings of the Canon pronounced holy at Nicaea.

Thaddaeus, a Jew by birth, a Greek by temperament, and a scholar of Alexandria by circumstance and the Peace of Rome, to Marcus Ulpius Trajanus, conqueror of Dacia and Mesopotamia, to the Emperor Trajan, in Rome, greetings. Long life and good health most noble Caesar, and thanks to the gods you worship for keeping you and making you victorious in battle and bringing you safe to your throne as the worthy successor and heir of our late good and just Emperor Marcus Cocceius Nerva.

I write, great sir, as a man who has lived well beyond the four score years that, by reason of strength, are allotted to some men. It therefore comes as no surprise that the most able physicians of Alexandria, and therefore of the world, have assured me I am on my deathbed, and that I will soon be gathered to my fathers by virtue of maladies that, while perhaps not beyond the skills of Aesculapius, cannot be cured by mortal means. This assurance of imminent and certain death has provided a surprising sense of tranquility. I now fear neither the wrath of men nor the whims of gods. Neither have I the slightest concern for debates touching on any aspect of this world or on the hoped for world to come, in that I will soon vacate the former forever, and learn first hand what truths, if any, are to be learned in the latter. Socrates was surely right when he observed that death is either the most peaceful of all sleeps or the opportunity to meet souls who have gone before. Neither option should cause a dying man any concern, and neither concerns me. I can truly say that I am at peace, or, more correctly, I will be at peace when this testament to you is completed. Please forgive me the digressions permitted, and expected, from old men; be assured that my mind is sound and my memory good, and I will explain why my final hours are spent in writing the Emperor of the Romans, the oppressors of my people.

It is said that all manner of shameful things wind up in Rome. In the same wise, all subjects of intellectual curiosity, no matter how obscure, wind up somehow, eventually, in Alexandria. Thus I came to learn that you had inquired, through Pliny the Younger and others, for information on a religious sect that has come to be known of late as Christians. I will not reveal my sources for this information, but assure you that Pliny did not violate your confidence. There are things known to curious scholars that are denied even to kings. I also know that you do not believe the Christians are a serious threat to the security of the state. From my deathbed, great Caesar, I write to tell you that you are wrong. This superstition, if left unchecked, will become a fire upon the earth that will destroy your empire. This irrational movement, that you perceive as a religion of slaves, has the potential to infect even the imperial throne in Rome, to reduce learning to a barbarism that will cause longing for the erudition of the Celts and the logic of Gaul, and to make men wish for the return of the murdered despot Domitian. How do I know these things? Permit me to reveal something of my personal and, until now, secret history.

I was born two years before the death of Caesar Augustus, in the village of Nazareth, in the country of Galilee, north of Judea, north of

Samaria. This land is, or rather was, part of the region you Romans called the province of Palestine before it was destroyed, and its people dispersed, during the reign of the Emperor Vespasian, by the authority of his son, that compassionate idol of the Romans, Titus Flavius Sabinus Vespasianus, later your predecessor, the Emperor Titus. My given name was Judas. My father was Joseph, a carpenter. My mother was Miriam. My older brother was named Joshua, in full Yehoshuah, or in Greek, Jesus, whom some now call Christus, or the Christ, the Messiah, the anointed one, the Son of God. In consequence of his tragic life, and of certain beliefs that arose concerning his final end, the cult of Christianity was born. As your historian Tacitus is no better informed concerning the history of this belief than he is on the history of the Jewish people, and as our own historian Joseph Ben Matthias, better known to you as Flavius Josephus, understood the true history of the Jews too well to give any credence at all to my brother's life and death, and in that widely circulated anonymous tracts have built fantasies around Jesus that many, to the detriment of themselves and the state, believe to be true, so it has fallen to me, an eyewitness to the events of his life, to tell the truth of that life, my reliability and my safety both being assured by the comforting and certain knowledge of my pending death.

My brother was over twice my age when he began his, for want of a better word, ministry. This ministry lasted about three years. I, at his urging, became one of his apostles, whereupon I was given the surname of Thaddaeus. I, who had barely become a man under Jewish law, was the youngest of the apostles, and not on good terms of friendship with any of them, all also relatively young men, save for my best friend, another Judas, given the surname of Iscariot when, out of friendship, he joined me as an apostle. I did not know Jesus well. I do not believe anyone did. He was a man by law when I was born. I admired him, respected him, and loved him. He was my older and wiser brother. But he was a stranger, even to his own family. He kept his distance, and brooded often. He was frequently disrespectful to our mother, did not obey our father, and later even maintained that his followers should leave their families and responsibilities to follow him to live in poverty, without giving any thought to how they might be housed, fed, or clothed. I realize now that my brother Jesus was mad. It is hard to believe that an illiterate peasant from the despised Nazareth, together with twelve equally illiterate peasants as followers, could start a movement, a religion, that could change the world. To appreciate how this could happen, you must understand something of our people and our times.

The Jews, sir, must be the most conquered, despised, and warred against of any people. We are not merely a religion, we are a nation, even now in exile without a country of our own. At the time my brother and his followers started out to do whatever we were doing, there were several competing religious groups seeking to dominate Judaism. Chief among these were the Pharisees, the Sadducees, and the Essenes, each vying to be the most repressive, the most religiously authoritarian, and the most holy. Stir into this mix the fanatical Zealots, those Maccabees imitators who arose during the time of Herod the Great and were slaughtered by their own hands at Masada some two or three years after the destruction of our temple, and you can come to better appreciate the instability and uncertainty of our national spirit. Common to all these groups was a hatred of everything Roman, and the hope for the coming of a deliverer sent from god, a Moses, an Elijah, a David, a Samson, a Judas Maccabe, a Messiah who would lead the Jews in glorious war to drive out the invaders and restore the grandeur of the reign of Solomon.

There was no shortage of pretenders. The ill-fated John the Baptist was one. There was also Judas of Galilee, and Theudas the magician, and many other rivals for the office of Messiah. Some, in the manner of Elijah, were said to be able to raise the dead, walk on water, cure the sick, and perform other miracles, and all had their followers. My brother's message was so unusual, so ill-defined, so incoherent, and so incapable of being articulated or understood, that a few thought he must be the promised one. These shepherdless sheep seemed to believe the more obscure the speech, the more holy the speaker. An analogy might be found among those who find meaning in the unintelligible utterances of the Delphic Oracle. Jesus said such things as his followers were the salt of the earth, and that salt could not be salty if it lost its saltiness. Some found this a brilliant parable. If anyone could explain or demonstrate just how salt could ever cease to be salty, there might be some justification for taking the statements of Jesus seriously. But all religions have their mysteries. This is how priests control fools.

My brother was a harmless madman. He didn't view himself as the Messiah. To my observations, he had no clear definition of himself, or of anything else, at all. Our little band wandered about for three years, attracting attention to ourselves, creating some followers and more enemies. Our mother and father had given up on Jesus long ago, but still held hope that I would eventually come to my senses. From the time we left Nazareth, we never saw our parents, those rather good people, again.

But I digress, and grow tired. Death waits for no man. I must hasten to finish this narrative so you may understand what happened, and appreciate the threat of the irrationality I fear will overcome the world.

Eventually we made our way to Jerusalem. Jesus rode into the city of David on an ass, and was mocked by some who threw palms in his path. I have never been so embarrassed. Few in Jerusalem had heard of Jesus, and, because our religion prohibits the making of images, even fewer knew how he looked. Nevertheless, his activities and small following had managed to attract the attention of the Sanhedrin, the supreme national tribunal of the Jews. One night as we slept, outdoors as usual, agents of the Sanhedrin came upon us with torches and weapons looking for Jesus, who freely identified himself to them. The band of apostles, weary of our way of life, missing their families, uncertain of Jesus and his mission, and unwilling to confront the intruders, fled into the night, never to be reunited again. They were ignored by those who wanted Jesus. Only I, loyal to the safety of my brother, remained, together with Iscariot, who remained from loyalty to me. We asked to be permitted to accompany Jesus, who appeared unaware of all that was happening. This was granted, and we were taken to the meeting chambers of the feared Sanhedrin.

The officials who questioned us were surprisingly reasonable. They attempted to interview Jesus, but when he responded to questions with incoherent answers, for example saying that faith in the kingdom of heaven is a mustard seed, the authorities realized their problem was not political as they had feared. Nevertheless, Jesus had proved an embarrassment to them, and Roman authorities had been disturbed upon learning that Simon, one of the apostles, was a Zealot. The last thing the Sanhedrin wanted was a Jewish movement in revolt against Rome. They had worked with Pontius Pilate, the procurator placed in Jerusalem by Tiberius Caesar, in an effort to maintain safety through an uneasy peace.

Iscariot's talents had been wasted in the wilderness, as he proved a master of sensible compromise. By morning it was agreed that we would remove Jesus from the country forever, and word would be circulated that he had been crucified for treason. This would both explain his sudden disappearance and warn off other potential troublemakers. Judas was provided with thirty pieces of silver to finance our relocation. To make the ruse more effective, the authorities agreed to use their influence to have a wreath of thorns placed on the head of one of three anonymous persons who had been hanging on stakes of execution on Golgotha for several days, and to place a sign above the poor victim's unrecognizable head announcing that this was the King of the Jews. Officials would be instructed to keep the curious at a distance. Finally, the unclaimed body would be placed in a new tomb that could be bought from one Nicodemus, who was suffering financial difficulties. The timing was perfect, as the Sabbath started that evening, and all elements of our departure and the burial of the surrogate could be accomplished while potentially interested parties were in their homes obeying ritual Jewish laws. We were provided a room where Iscariot could wait with Jesus until sunset, the beginning of the Sabbath, while I spent the day in Jerusalem spreading the word of Jesus's death.

I was successful in locating several friends of my brother and wept with them over the story. As a final assurance that everyone would soon learn of the tragedy, I went to the lodgings of Mary Magdalene. Mary was a woman of loose virtue who seemed to know everyone in Judea. She had a face of angelic stupidity, and a body that could have tempted a castrated stoic. Properly bathed and attired, she might have been a courtesan in Rome, were she not so hopelessly ignorant and so subject to fits of dementia. It was said that Mary Magdalene wanted only two mites and a mattress and the wit to fall backwards. I couldn't say. She had a great fondness for Jesus, perhaps because he had no carnal interest in her. Indeed, he seemed to have no carnal interests at all, unless credence be given to a work that has been falsely attributed to the apostle Thomas. The less said of it the better for both their memories. Mary was, in a word, insane, but pleasingly so. She believed Jesus had freed her from seven demons. She was overcome by grief at the story of his death, and feared the demons would now return. I left her just in time to return, before sunset, to the upper room where Jesus and Iscariot waited. Under cover of darkness, we hired passage with a caravan bound for Alexandria.

It is difficult enough to predict the actions of the sane. Mary Magdalene was unpredictable at her best, but no one even wildly could have guessed what she, in her grief and delusions, would do next. What she did may well change the world. The next morning, the first day of the week, by first light, she went to visit the tomb of Jesus. And she went to the wrong tomb. She had somehow gotten the idea, that is now part of the emerging mythology of Christianity, that Jesus had been laid in the tomb of a rich man called Joseph of Arimathea, and he, enjoying the attention, not knowing for sure and not really caring, never denied it. When Mary came to this newly finished unused tomb, she naturally found it open and empty. She immediately concluded Jesus had risen from the dead. She told others who went to the tomb, and, seeing it empty, believed her. Her illness was such that the story changed in every telling, and thus grew stories of angelic visitations, and even visions of Jesus. Those who believed her added their own embellishments, until many accepted the story as too complex and fantastic not to be true. The three of us were with the caravan and learned nothing of these events until it was much too late to attempt a correction, had we had any desire to do so. The story was a more perfect cover for our disappearance than we could have hoped. People either believed Jesus was dead or that he had ascended to his Heaven. In either case we would not be missed. After some days we arrived in Alexandria.

Words cannot convey how overwhelmed we three from a small village felt in that great city. It would be error to say we were out of place, for nothing ever seems out of place in Alexandria. It is the crossroads of the world and gives meaning to the very ideas of city and civilization. But we saw ourselves as out of place, and dislocated from all certainties we had ever known. We rented a room with the silver of the Sanhedrin. After refreshing ourselves with sleep and foreign food, we set out to explore the wonders of this new world. In one of the many markets run by persons of strange race and tongue, Jesus wandered away. At length we found him at the booth of a trader in exotic reptiles. He was gesturing and talking wildly, to people who did not understand Aramaic, about how those with faith in his idea of god could handle poisonous serpents and not be hurt. Before we or any of the shocked onlookers could stop him, he somehow grasped an asp from a closed basket and held it to his bare chest. He was bitten repeatedly in the neck and face before the reptile could be safely removed. My brother Jesus died before our eyes, in the manner of Cleopatra, in her city, in the dust of a foreign market, before horrified gentiles he had hoped to win to his vision of the kingdom of god. He had preached his belief in the virtue of remaining ignorant of the things of this world. In his death he demonstrated the folly of that belief. Iscariot and I had my brother buried privately, in a manner and place I will not even now reveal. This information must die with me. We grieved for Jesus and for a life wasted and ruined by destructive beliefs and religious madness.

Iscariot and I changed our names. I have not used the name by which I now write since we left Jerusalem. We knew our money would soon be gone, and we agreed to part ways. We were grown men who had to claim our own lives. My friend, who had helped save Jesus, had a great love of the sea, and he found employment on a Roman ship going to the seaside resort of Pompeii. He planned to settle there and to seek his fortune as a servant to the wealthy. I never heard from him again, and, if he remained there, he either died before, or in, the great calamity. In either case, all memory or record of him is probably forever lost. I resolved to take advantage of the opportunities to acquire knowledge available in Alexandria. I sought out, and became apprenticed to, that most famous and worthy Jew known to you as Philo of Alexandria. The only time I left Alexandria was when I accompanied him to Rome where he argued in defense of the Jews of Alexandria before your evil predecessor, the Emperor Caligula. I remained Philo's student until his death. I note, with some grim amusement, how his writings on the Logos have been contorted, by some Christian writers, to appear to apply to my poor brother, whose snake bitten body lies dead in an unknown Egyptian grave. I became a scholar and teacher in my own right. Pardon me, and please understand, when I do not reveal even to you the name by which I have been known.

In the many years that have followed our great deception in Judea, I have had occasion to read diverse and contradictory tracts purporting to give truthful accounts of my brother. I am mentioned by name in some of them, but, perhaps because of my unexplained disappearance, nothing else concerning me is reported. I am almost disappointed at this absence of myths about myself when they are so liberally bestowed upon my associates. The stories tell preposterous lies. They usually even start out as lies, with the unknown author falsely claiming to be one of the named apostles of Jesus. This was no doubt done to give credibility to their reports, either invented in whole or borrowed from other fictitious accounts. I will not attempt to recount all of the nonsense, as unhappily it is all too easily available for you, if you are so disposed, to read and believe, or reject, as you choose. To mention but a few of the lies, you will find reports that Jesus was born in Bethlehem where he was worshiped by goatherds and astrologers, that our mother was a virgin, that he was taken as a child to Egypt while Herod the Great killed all the little boys, that angels announced his birth, that the dead came from their graves when he died, and that he was taken to heaven after his promise to return shortly. If any of these things had happened, there would be no doubts, no excuse for disbelief, and no reason for faith. If they had happened, Josephus, you can be assured, would have reported them, as would your own correspondents. You may also note that the promise of my brother's quick return has not been fulfilled. I believe, great Caesar, that this superstition would never have taken root and flowered if it were not for the work of another madman, a Pharisee named Saul of Tarsus. His bizarre life and work are known to you through his writings under the name of Paul, assumed after he saw, in a fit that temporarily blinded him, Jesus arisen from the dead.

I tire, my Emperor, and must end this writing even as the gods end my hours of life. Much more could be told, but I lack the strength, and I hope I have given you enough to cause you to consider my warnings. Much mischief has been spawned by these Christians, and many evils lie ahead, the nature of which can only be seen in dreams. What can be predicted of men whose main religious ceremony involves the belief that they, by consuming bread and wine, are eating the flesh and drinking the blood of my dead brother? One might wonder if they would do this as eagerly if they knew he had died from snake venom. I have informed you as best I can, have cleansed my conscience, and can die in peace. I will never know if you receive this, so there is no need for a reply, even if you knew to whom to write. I have charged my beloved daughter, who I know by our secret name of Kather, with making three copies of this writing. One will be sent to you personally, under seal, through the usual channels. One will be hidden in a safe place known only to ourselves in the Museum, the great library of Alexandria, for if anything of our time and culture survives the intellectual destruction I fear from the Christians it will be the library's priceless repository of the collected knowledge of the world that has survived even the onslaughts of the great Julius Caesar. The third copy will be taken for concealment and protection to a Greek island of Ionia, where knowledge and science will surely continue to exist and flourish despite the mischief of this new superstition. There, my daughter and a fellow scholar will see that these words of mine become known in proper season.

May that measure of peace, justice, harmony and understanding denied religion and its deities be attained by mortals through the use of their minds, and may reason, science, curiosity, and discovery replace the fear, the guilt, the pain, and the ignorance of trembling in terror before capricious gods. *Ecce homo.*

Here the text ends.

On Homosexuality

I don't care what other peoples' sex practices are, so long as they don't practice them in the streets and frighten the horses.

—Oscar Wilde, I think.

[Editor's note: according to the omniscient Internet— en.wikiquote.org/wiki/Mrs_PatrickCamp-bell—it was Beatrice Stella Tanner Campbell (9 February 1865-10 April 1940), a British actress, who said something of the sort, but Kagin's guess is more fun.]

Some years ago, on a camping trip, my friend Joe Ray and I resolved that should one of us be unfortunate enough to be bitten on the penis by a venomous serpent, and oral suction by the other was the only lifesaving measure available, then the afflicted party would simply have to die. My liberated stepdaughter finds this view "homophobic," meaning fear of homosexuality. I don't think so. I am not afraid of homosexuality; I simply find the idea of people of the same sex having sex unaesthetic and curious and do not understand why up to ten percent of the world's population wants to do that.

But there are many things I find annoying, don't understand, don't want to do, and don't know why anyone else would want to do, like being left-handed. Why, I wonder, would anyone choose to be left-handed? They look funny when they write, and their hand moves across what they have written. Also, lots of manufactured artifacts are most unhandy for people electing this deviation. Parents sometimes force their children to be right-handed and normal. In the superstitious past, such maladapted persons were thought blessed or cursed, depending on prevailing local mythology. Kids forced to alter their basic nature became psychologically scarred. *[Editor's note: it is a well-known fact that we're all born left-handed; we become right-handed when we commit our first sin.]*

We are more enlightened now. Left-handed people are accepted and their rights acknowledged. Sports stars and Presidents can be

139

left-handed, as can anyone else, and special goods are manufactured accommodating their variance from the much larger right-handed population. Their condition is seen as a result of the roll of the genetic dice, having no moral or pejorative implications.

Homosexuality appears to have been an aspect of the human condition forever, praised by some societies, condemned by others. Because of the 'Judeo-Christian tradition,' American culture has feared, condemned, and criminalized this left-handedness of human sexual drives. To the followers of Yahweh and St. Paul, sex has been suspect anyway, the source of original sin, and tolerated only to create new believers. Homosexuality was viewed as a practice permitted by the unsaved heathens whose science and culture Christianity destroyed. The Bible specifically condemns same-sex erotic love, but then it also condemns women and gives instructions on repressing them. One might muse darkly on what those twelve apostles did together on long nights in the desert, without women, or why the woman-hating apostle Paul lavished such affectionate words on his young disciple Timothy. Anyway, the religious right wants homosexual acts to stay criminal and sees the practice as a sin, not as the genetically predisposed state of being it appears to be. Because of this sin myth, homosexuals have been banned from the American military, and, if not made criminals elsewhere, have been denied the rights to live together and constitute a lawful family. They may not behave as heterosexuals in love because their sexual orientation is mythologically viewed as immoral and wrong. They appear to be not only loathed but feared.

The fear comes from the belief that homosexuality is voluntary and contagious. Bigots believe gays and lesbians choose to be that way and that they try to convert others to their perversions. As is usual in matters of religious certainty, if the facts contradict the myth, the myth wins. The existence of homosexuals in the military is unsettling to many, proving that the perceived immorality is not confined to the arts and the priesthood. We will not expend space here in prolonged discussion of the obvious hypocrisy of priests practicing that which they condemn as sin and absolving those sinners through the power of God. That many religious leaders do 'unnatural acts' is known from the confessions of nuns who have kicked the habit and from the confessions of priests in open court to the criminal molestation of same-sex children. If gold rusts, what will iron do?

The matter of gays in the military has brought our social myths on sexual orientation into sharper focus. Gays have always been in our military, and in every military since society started resolving their differences through organized violence. The Greek way was not confined to the armies of Alexander and has been accepted, if not condoned, in all ancient and modern land and naval forces, except in those who insist, despite all proof, that the myth is right and reality is wrong. The armed forces can function with homosexuals in their ranks because they have so functioned and continue to function, despite official denial. Gays and lesbians have served with distinction, flying planes, running hospitals, manning artillery batteries, and so on. Many have risen to high command rank without their sexual preferences interfering with duty and good order. A well-disciplined conscientious gay in the military is certainly to be preferred over a sexually misbehaving heterosexual officer harassing female subordinates or a priest molesting choirboys.

If the sexual drives of the homosexual are propelled by forces within put there by his Creator, whose creations are perfect and whose will is unknowable and unknown, then prejudice against him is theologically unsound. If homosexual behavior has a biological basis, then one so predestined did not choose his orientation any more than heterosexuals choose theirs, and the idea that such genetic drives are somehow catching is as absurd as a fear that left-handedness may be acquired by proximity or persuasion. If gays and lesbians voluntarily choose to practice a lifestyle of deviation from mythical standards of proper behavior, they must be severely masochistic individuals.

Imagine *choosing* to be rejected by family members you love, risking shame, imprisonment, loss of career, and being denied the ability to publicly express affection, obtain housing, or serve one's country. Does it seem reasonable that a military person who adheres to rigid standards in rules of conduct and discipline would, in the sexual area of life, elect to destroy all that has been worked for, and risk beatings, private scorn, and public disgrace merely to flaunt freely chosen homosexual behavior condemned by others as repulsive and perverted? Barry Goldwater correctly observed we should be more concerned with whether they can shoot straight. (He probably intended none of the possible puns.)

The notion that homosexuals are seeking special rights is in the same category, and is maintained by the same people, as was the idea that blacks were seeking special rights when they wanted to vote, buy a home, or ride at the front of a bus. What is so special about wanting the same human and civil rights enjoyed by people who have a genetically ordained yearning for the opposite sex? Actually, I am glad I was not born gay. Heterosexuality has caused me quite enough problems, thank you. Sometimes I think the Almighty erred by inventing it. But I can accept that which I cannot understand without fear of being converted. I do not believe my left-handed paralegal, daughter-in-law, or President are likely to cause me to write in their strange way. It seems equally unlikely that I could be persuaded to substitute my excessive fondness for warm, soft, perfumed women for attraction to hairy-legged males.

Oh, yes, I bought a snake-bite kit.

Back in Their Burkas Again

(May be sung to the tune of "Back in the Saddle Again" —
composed with Helen Kagin, based on her idea)

They're back in their burkas again,
Women obeying their men.
No other man should ever see
Her eyebrow or her knee,
They're back in their burkas again.

Women are wrapped up by men,
Protecting their bodies from sin.
Women must comply
And not tempt some lustful eye,
So they're back in their burkas again.

The wrap must be shared with a friend,
With sister and cousin and kin.
It costs far too much
With accessories and such,
But they're back in their burkas again.

A woman can't leave her pen,
While the burka is still out on lend.
So in her house she's trapped,
'Till in that horror she is wrapped,
'Till she's back in her burka again.

The burka's a smothering affair.
No garment can even compare.
It gets so hot in there,
She can barely breathe the air.
They're back in their burkas again.

Covered head and eyes and nose,
Down their thighs right to their toes,
They're back in their burkas again.

But sometimes under there
They wear sexy underwear,
They're back in their burkas again.

Everybody will finally win,
When women aren't wrapped end to end.
Law is a disgrace
When it hides a pretty face,
And puts women in burkas again.

Freedom can only begin
When women can show off some skin.
That law will have to go
When all women just say "No,"
"We'll not wear those burkas again."

And on some happy day
They will put those laws away,
And never wear burkas again.
And on that glorious day
They will throw those rags away,
And never wear burkas again.

On Religion as a Public Health Threat

My own view on religion is that of Lucretius. I regard it as a disease born of fear and as a source of untold misery to the human race.

—Bertrand Russell

The Christian Religion produces in many followers a kind of mass psychosis. Belief in fundamentalist dogma is a contagious, addictive disease that destroys all thought that might challenge the delusional system. The disease is so virulent and destructive to affected believers that it threatens the extinction of the human species through overpopulation, and must also be understood as a threat to the mental health of the public.

Christianity teaches an infantile belief in imaginary places and imaginary friends. Jesus, the Blessed Virgin Mary, Angels, Satan, *et al.* travel from Heaven and Hell to visit Earth, perform miracles, impregnate Earth girls, and teach that we are doomed for eternity if we prefer being alive in this world to being entombed in a scriptural world. Contentment is reserved for those who have died for Christ. Everyone else is cosmic flotsam.

Rather than remain silently smug in the knowledge they are saved and all non-believers are damned, Christians attempt to make all human beings play in their sandbox and to agree with their fantasy world. It really does make an enormous difference in how adults view the world if they were humanistically reared or if they were raised to think like children: to believe that a magical Being magically made everything, including them; that the purpose of their lives is to worship and obey the magical Creator so they can be with the Creator after they die in a magical place called Heaven; and that the Creator raised his magical Son from the dead—after killing him as a blood sacrifice for their otherwise irreversibly shamed and debased nature. This is a message guaranteed to scramble your mind.

145

Edwin F. Kagin: *Baubles of Blasphemy*

Fanatical believers in this system recognize a duty to force others to believe it. This is a threat to the public's psychological health. Of course the First Amendment to the U.S. Constitution permits the free exercise of religion. But the Constitution isn't a suicide pact. If we can, through law, try to protect the public from itself by regulating smoking, alcohol consumption, and sale of firearms, surely we have the constitutional power and duty as Americans to defend the wall between church and state and to protect freedom of conscience from the force of ancient myths.

Fundangelicals are pounding their battering rams at the wall of separation and at the pillars of democracy. They want people to surrender their personal power to them and share their pathological illness. They have seen many changes and have been against every one of them. What a difference it might make if their one life was seen as one to live for growth in relationships and for the discovery of knowledge that permits something beyond groveling before non-existent, capricious gods.

Our species may well be in a transitional evolutionary phase wherein we either use our minds to survive or become extinct in consequence of idiotic religious behavior. Easter Island is a tidy little microcosm. Space was limited. Islands are that way. The people destroyed themselves, their civilization and their environment by over breeding and internecine wars. Religion was their fatal disease. It might be ours.

We might have settled other planets somewhere by now, but we have wasted the lifespace of our species with such nonsense as mythically believing there is a god who wants sex used only for making babies. This defect in rational thought alone has produced tragedy for countless humans.

Despite overwhelming evidence that uncontrolled population growth will destroy the human race as it destroyed Easter Island, certain Christians will kill you if you believe in preventing this through contraception and abortion. That Pope, J2P2, has canceled a visit to the U.S. He is piqued because the U.S. didn't support his deadly doctrine, at the world population control conference in Cairo, that population should be controlled by using no population control. Clearly, religion is a threat to public health.

146

Christians display another dead give-away symptom of an addictive disease—denial. Facts are not facts. Believers have not committed provable crimes. They are afraid of dying, and rather than deal with it, they invent a make-believe world that Pliny described to the Roman Emperor Trajan (1st century, CE) as "an absurd and extravagant superstition." He further observed, "In fact, this contagious superstition is not confined to the cities only, but has spread its infection among the neighboring villages and country." Pliny saw it coming.

The ancient terrors are still here. The disease continues to threaten democracy, personal freedom, and life itself. How can it be controlled? The Chinese have a neat criminal law punishing theft by superstition. That might help. So might taxing religion and using their money for repairing their damages. Religious practices could be limited to certain times and places and be scrupulously kept out of public life. Under no circumstances should impressionable children be exposed to religious beliefs until they no longer believe in Santa Claus. Religion must be rated R. Reason is an effective inoculation.

Religious bigots must be exposed. They don't like being called bigots, but they are. *Bigot* is defined in the *New Little Oxford Dictionary* as an "obstinate and intolerant adherent of creed or view." Yup, that's them. They don't like what they perceive as 'religion bashing,' either. This, in their diseased view, is what occurs when potential victims refuse to consent and fight back.

Would a rational, caring God really endorse what Christians believe? Fundagelicals are right when they say they are at war with secular humanists. If you are fond of freedom, you'd better pray the humanists win.

Edwin F. Kagin: *Baubles of Blasphemy*

Ode to Witch Doctor Laura

Have you heard of that witch Dr. Laura
That ecumenical babeling horror
    Who knows what is right
    In her and God's sight:
That most sex will just lead you to sorrow?

The Ten Commandments must be followed and posted
Those who don't like them are doomed to be roasted
    Though not very bright
    Laura knows what is right
And her right thinking is everywhere hosted.

If a woman lives with a man when unwed
And she sinfully enters his bed
    She's an unpaid, base whore
    Just a slut, nothing more.
Laura knows all the "Shalt Nots" God said.

If a female while single gets pregnant don't think
She can just suck her blessed unborn down a sink.
    Giving birth is her fate,
    So don't consummate.
Laura tells us God's will, for to God she's our link.

Hear Doc Laura opine that all gays
Have deviantly chosen their immoral ways.
    They could all be changed
    And live lives less deranged
If they only saw truth through her biblical haze.

If a baby's adopted, or by other sperm made
Than by that of the husband of a mother who strayed
    The child must never know.
    Dr. Laura's so low
She says both truth and trust simply must be betrayed.

Dr. Laura's advice is as pious as prayer:
Don't send your child off to some godless day care;
    Be your kid's full-time mom
    Drive her safe to the prom
There are bad things, like life, that are waiting out there.

If her words seem quite Christian to you,
Please recall that she's really a Jew:
    One of those killers of Christ
    Who God knows just aren't nice
So what can this Jew say to you that is true?

Once in a lewd and much less holy mood
Ms. Laura adulterously posed in the nude
    See this vicious threat
    Revealed on the net
Hypocritically wanton, and naked, and crude.

Dr. Laura's much hyped PhD
Is not a psychology degree
    It's in physiology
    Yet without an apology
This fraud gives bad counsel for free.

So this tart of those much younger days
Now stars in morality plays;
    Maybe tomorrow
    Witch Dr. Laura
Will be prayed to — a saint we should praise!

Mapplethorpe in Cincinnati

What should Cincinnati say

When told by prosecutor Ney

That the Mapplethorpe display

Doesn't quite do art his way?

    And when art critic Sheriff Leis

    Sends out morality police

    Who will not give an artist peace

    Without a Leis approved release;

And when grand juries will indict

And launch storm troopers in the night

To trample wrong with hobnailed might

To purge all art that is not right;

    When ignorance and dogma rule

    Suppression is the tyrant's tool

    Destruction of thought does not seem cruel

    To the bigot or the fool.

Cincinnati takes its name

From a Roman and the fame

Artistic freedom could proclaim

Once there was glory, now there is shame.

Inauguration

We had seen sights, but this mocked our imaginations.
We had used words, but this defied our metaphors.

We had once been, our heritage proclaimed,
"One Nation Indivisible," and "Out of Many, One,"

Until smallness of soul began to smother dreams.
Then, suddenly, sorely profaned, and wounded, soon to die

Our nation did an unimagined thing:
We rolled away the stone.

We shook the heels of history
Upon retreating wrongs;

We watched as hope,
Long dormant, bloomed,

And, through eyes blurred with tears,
We went outside and raised the flag.

Edwin F. Kagin: *Baubles of Blasphemy*

Two Lines

The future waits in one of two great lines, two endless human queues
And each of us is in one line—there is no other line to choose.
  Our journey as human creatures has fashioned these two lines
  With very different features following very different signs.
Through kingdoms and through ages these lines unbroken run
One line snaking into darkness; one line straining for the sun.
  One line holds shining visions of what humankind can be
  When at last we make decisions free of myth and tyranny.
Our race, our creeds, our sex, and the religions we proclaim
In this line yield to human needs we cannot always name.
  Some careless few within this line may hurt you and make you cry
  But villains in the other line will kill you to watch you die.
Those marching in that other line seek to control, not to achieve,
By trying to deceive our minds with lies that they believe.
  Prizing money over friendship, and power over human need,
  They do not work for kinship, but only for their greed.
Anyone can leave their line, whenever they see fit
If perhaps they change their mind, from facts, or acts, or wit.
  No one must stay within a line where rules are learned by rote
  That dictate how we all must live, and breed, and love, and vote.
In the coming great election, one line will finally decide
If our future takes direction from the bright or evil side.
  Set aside all pious passion of who you are and where you've been
  What now must be in fashion is "Which line are you in?"
How will you answer to the future when a new world starts to dawn?
How will you tell your children which side of history you were on?
  There are but two great questions to be raised when life must end:
  "How did you use your roads and days?"
  And "Which line were you in?"

Religion

On Baptists and Beer

And from thence they went to Beer: that is the well whereof the LORD spake unto Moses, Gather the people together, and I will give them water.   —Numbers 21:16

Drink no longer water, but use a little wine for thy stomach's sake and thine often infirmities.
                    —Paul's 1st Epistle to Timothy

Now it can be told. And it *must* be told. And repeated down the ages until the end of all things, at the picnics of the Daughters of the ARCW, at the gatherings, and repeated unto thy children's children so the story be not forgotten to time nor the legend thereof go unremembered.

It came about in this wise. It was at Camp Quest, the first residential summer camp for the children of secular humanists. We of the Free Inquiry Group, Inc. (FIG) were in Kentucky at camp, in second season, following our wonderfully successful debut the previous year. The world was watching. We had engaged the same facility from the Southern Baptists, and we were viewed by them, most charitably stated, with ambivalence. A few months earlier, FIG, sponsors of Camp Quest, had led a battle in the American Religious Civil War (ARCW) against the creationists in Northern Kentucky, in the self-same county that housed the Baptist camp we rented. Our hosts were sympathetic to the creationist cause, and were very much aware of our activities against them that had stopped a creationist museum from arising to challenge the proofs of evolution displayed at Kentucky's Big Bone Lick State Park.

Were they ever aware! They had earlier informed us in writing that they knew what we had done, and inquired just how their renting to us carried forth their purpose of fulfilling the cause of Christ. We reminded them of the story of the good Samaritan. They let us come back, but they were prepared. Brand new creationism tracts, with the glue of their bindings unbroken, appeared this year in the dining hall, as did The Ten Commandments affixed to the walls of the cabins,

153

Edwin F. Kagin: *Baubles of Blasphemy*

complimenting "Jesus Loves You" newly inscribed on each cabin's mirror. We felt they were trying to tell us something. Indeed, we learned from our spies that many among them had been upset that our kind had been on their hallowed grounds the past year, and were outraged we had been permitted to return. There were rumors that the friendly staff of the camp had their jobs on the line for actually acting in the best sense of Christian charity toward the strangers at their gates. At any rate, the Baptists did not deny us our second year. Maybe it was because we had a signed contract, and the camp director was known to be a lawyer. Who knows. Anyhow, we were there, but, at best, on spiritual probation.

And then unto those hills of the Ohio valley came two high emissaries from the distant state of New York. From the very center of the world they came, from our sponsor, the esteemed Council for Secular Humanism. These fearsome guests from afar were named Anthony and Timothy (their surnames will not be revealed to prevent embarrassment to their families and friends, if any, and to provide new topics for future doctoral research), a.k.a., Tim and Tony. These paragons of our cause, these standard bearers of those values we hold dear, came to see if we were behaving ourselves, if we were acting in the best traditions of secular humanism, if we were managing to peacefully co-exist with folks generally predisposed to hate our guts, if we were doing our sponsors proud, and if we had somehow managed to live in peaceful harmony with those whose values seemed at such unbridgeable variance with our own.

We thought our honored apostles' fears unwarranted, for we, conscious of obvious differences, keenly sensitive to the sensibilities of our hosts, and most mindful of their beliefs, standards, and rules, had taken great pains to insure that no camper or staff of Camp Quest should, by act or omission, trespass on the traditions, beliefs, or principles of our Baptist friends, with whom we had achieved a workable, if uneasy, peace. We knew we need not and could not agree, but we would be rude to mock. We were strangers in a strange land, fed and housed by hosts we dearly sought not to offend.

On the second day of the visit of TnT, apostles of Council, as our entire assembly sat together at table, a message came from the director of the Baptist camp to our camp's registrar, requesting

154

immediate audience in the kitchen on a matter of grave and utmost urgency. Our registrar, a physician, was steeled to crisis. She who started and stopped human hearts on operating tables went bravely to the unknown that awaited. Camp Quest's director stoically waited for news that could not be good. Had some horrible something happened to a family member of one of our assembly? Was the world suddenly at war? Had the messiah arrived at the gates? The director had preached, and tried to practice, grace under pressure, so outwardly he remained calm, attempting to become, as the Zen masters taught, a lotus in a sea of fire.

The registrar returned, ashen and shaken. It was bad; the director knew that. He didn't know it was this bad. "We have a serious problem," she reported. "Beer has been found in the refrigerator. The Baptist chief executive has been called. They are talking of expelling us from the camp." Outwardly unmoved, inside curtained consciousness the director's life and dreams of success for this first secular humanist summer camp cascaded crimson.

Calmly, he surveyed the gathered diners. Campers and staff had all stated in writing, at his request, that they knew alcohol, drugs, and weapons were strictly forbidden, that even tobacco, America's gift to the world, was banned at Camp Quest. They knew this. What could have happened? As his eyes cast about, they passed over, and then returned to focus upon, Tim and Tony, on TnT, the behavorial watchdogs, the unguarded guardians, that had been sent unto them from Council.

Calmly, he went to them and told them of the thing that had come to pass that had been made known unto us. They freely confessed they done it, and wondered whence the fuss. The director patiently explained that the harboring of beer in Baptist halls was, to Baptists, roughly analogous in predictable degree of offense and outrage, to the manner in which orthodox Jews might be expected to regard the roasting of a pig in the holy of holies of their synagogue on Yom Kippur.

We are pleased to report this story ended well. The offending beer was poured, with great disdain and ceremony, down Baptist drains by our forgiving hosts. Our misguided miscreants did much backpedaling and crow eating—groveling, apologizing, and explaining insofar as they could. In the best of Christian charity, realizing we were damned anyway and not expected to know better, the Baptists in the end finally forgave and let us stay out our term of contract. TnT were persuaded not to seek legal redress or compensation for their confiscated goods that had been so scornfully trashed. The Baptist director was told apologetically that we had no idea the offenders would do as they did, and that they were Yankees. She understood, and offered her condolences. We remained friends, but realized, without being told, we would never again be permitted to return. Enough is enough. We were through there, and "that's that," said the grammarian.

So Camp Quest has found other quarters, and will continue. The new facility does not permit beer either, and all within hearing are thus advised and warned.

A postscript. Some weeks after our camp had ended in triumph, we had occasion once again to be visited by Anthony and Timothy. At a seminar on secular humanism, in Northern Kentucky, before those assembled to discuss our future and our cause, TnT had presented unto them in solemn ceremony by the staff of Camp Quest, who were mindful of their sacrifice, a somewhat large brown jug of beer.

It was labeled:

Baptist Beer
Circa 1997
When You Care Enough to Waive the Rules

So we suppose these men of wit, being so disposed, disposed of it, and became indisposed before they quit, and now we've told the truth of it.

156

Pity Little Jack and Jill

Pity little Jack and Jill
And their lives so very tragic:
For everything—both good and ill
These two ascribed to magic.

If times were good, if things went bad
If the kids were well or sick:
On their knees they fell to pray
And God's great boots to lick.

For they only lived to seek
Reward on Judgment Day:
They thought it was God's plan you see
That things were all that way.

Obedience was their only goal
Service their only aim:
Whatever God might will to be
Their faith remained the same.

They lived in groveling platitudes
In whining faith they died—
Not knowing that in living life
They hadn't even tried

To touch the magic life contains
When minds are free to see
That what there is is all there is
Now is eternity.

Edwin F. Kagin: *Baubles of Blasphemy*

Eupraxophy Limerick
(*ca.* 2003)

A female who loved for a fee

Said she was cheap, and really quite free;

So for a few mites,

In just a few nights,

She took me to Eupraxophy!

nota bene: At the discretion of the performer, the verb 'loved'
in the first line of this work may be replaced with an alliterating
Anglo-Saxon synonym.

—Author

On Coping with Christians

cope: *deal effectively or contend with.*
The New Little Oxford Dictionary

There are Christians who will kill you if you don't agree with their understanding of the will of their god. There is nothing new about this. Other Christians think these Christians are nuts who do not understand the Christian religion. The kill-your-neighbor Christians are more dangerous than the love-your-neighbor Christians. There are hundreds of groups, with wildly different beliefs and ends, all calling themselves Christians. The disagreements among these heterogeneous believers over correct interpretations of the supernatural makes coping with them confusing.

In general, Christians share a superstition, believed on faith not evidence (if it could be proved, there would be no need for faith), that human life will continue after death, with rewards from the deity for believers who believe that some twenty centuries ago the son of a god (the Christ) came back to life after dying for their sins. The Christ went to heaven to be with that god. People who die accepting this get to join him. The Bible is the sacred text, the word of a specific god.

A growing number of Christians treasonably want to establish their version of Christianity as the law of the United States, replacing the Constitution and the Bill of Rights that guarantee Americans freedom from having to follow somebody else's religion. These fanatics think the Bible infallibly prohibits abortion, disproves evolution, regulates sexuality, and gives them authority from a god to tell everyone else what they can do, see, read or think. Government by Bible is a scary idea. A literal belief in the Bible mandates that people be stoned to death if they don't follow the religious rules, including rules prohibiting criticizing anything about the religion. The Bible also approves of slavery and encourages the beating of children and the subjugating of women. It presents a violent, vain, bloodthirsty god who continually changes the rules, punishes people for the sins of their ancestors, and has never heard of computers or democracy. Christians who believe the Bible teaches a god of love, mercy and tolerance and who understand that religion can only flourish when there is no official religion are baffled by the fanatics. They had better be afraid—very afraid—they might be stoned for blasphemy along with those secular humanists. The coming civil war over religious freedom will make strange bedfellows indeed. The Fundangelicals are at one with the Pope, Islamic fanatics, and the teachings of Hitler on prohibiting reproductive freedom. More reasonable Christians may join nonbelievers in defending the wall of separation between church and state that gives democracy its vitality.

Christians whose religious addiction has not become terminal can be shown that democracy and fundamentalist Christianity are incompatible. They must choose, in the coming civil war, if they are going to be patriotic Americans and support the cause of constitutional democracy that gives religious freedom to all, or if they will permit themselves to be controlled by a world view that rejects evolution and progress for the beliefs of pre-scientific Bronze Age nomadic tribes.

Neurotics build castles in the air—psychotics move in. Even paranoids can have real enemies, and it is not unreasonable to observe that Christians who take the Bible as an absolute guide to faith and practice and believe it is their god's will that America be made into their idea of a Christian nation are capable of starting a civil war to further these ends. They are already organizing a 'militia' to defend their beliefs against godless humanism in schools, hospitals, libraries, and government. Believers are taught what firearms and ammunition are best suited for winning America for Christ. These people are serious and will not stop. Proof of their intent is readily available in their literature and in their rantings on your local *fun*-damentalist radio talk show. Further proof is seen on the national news as religious crazies commit acts of terrorism—bombing clinics, killing doctors, burning books and generally threatening and intimidating anyone who doesn't consent to being governed by their superstitions. And their leaders urge them on, preaching encouragement to those who know their god wants them to kill those who dare follow a different drummer.

Coping with Christians demands different techniques depending on the degree of progression of the individual believer's addiction. Coping with the lunatics may be a matter of pure survival and armed resistance if the rule of law fails to contain them. This would be pure civil war, a repeat of the dark histories of religious wars that the United

States was established to avoid. Coping with more rational Christians involves understanding that while they do not want to hurt you, they do believe that they are going to heaven and that you are going to hell. This may limit dialogue.

The majority of Christians (you'd better hope) are decent caring folk of the live-let-live variety. They want what nonbelievers want: peace, happiness, meaningful relationships, expansion of knowledge, freedom from fear and hunger and the right to do their thing while permitting their neighbors to do theirs. These Christians generally have only a limited knowledge of the Bible (the feel-good parts) and would be horrified at some of the brutalities it advocates and the absurd contradictions they would have to accept if they were to become true Bible-believing Christians. These cafeteria Christians take what they like and ignore the rest. Nor do they fully understand what is at stake when fanatics want our country to have an official religion. These folks have accepted the faith of their fathers without critical inquiry; they see it as the basis of morality, community, and social order. Some spend their lives in a childlike faith (recommended by the Christ) and mythical fantasy world that prevents them from becoming self-actualizing adults. This is why some Christians grow old without growing up.

So coping with Christians requires strategies ranging from tolerant acceptance and cooperation to self-defense. The human race is constantly evolving and may eventually learn we can get along without a need for belief in the supernatural. But for many people that time is not now and should never come.

Religion is not the answer—it is the problem. Everything considered, we would be better off without it.

Edwin F. Kagin: *Baubles of Blasphemy*

On Public Prayer

The family that prays together stays together.
    —Religious putdown of the families of non-believers.

Prayer is the means whereby humans communicate with the supernatural deity or deities in whom they believe. Most religions accept uncritically the reality of beings who exist outside the laws of nature and who can, upon appropriate application, alter those laws for the benefit of the believer. One makes supplication to the god of choice by silent or vocal praise and the lodging of requests for divine intervention. This practice is known as *prayer*.

Christianity is the dominant — and domin-*ating* — religion of the United States. It is mythically based on the life and teaching of Jesus, the deity made man. Fundamentalists believe every word of the Bible (the sacred texts) to be the word of a god. Here's what that god, through Jesus (also 'God'), said about prayer: And when thou prayest, thou shalt not be as the hypocrites are: for they love to pray standing in the synagogues and in the corners of the streets, that they may be seen of men. Verily I say unto you they have their reward. But thou, when thou prayest, enter into thy closet, and when thou hast shut thy door, pray to thy Father which is in secret; and thy Father which seeth in secret shall reward thee openly (Jesus Christ, Matthew 6:5–6 in a stolen King James Version Gideon Bible). We need not bother with the more recent translations. If the King James Version was good enough for the Apostle Paul, it's good enough for us.

What we have here is the Son of God, the Messiah, the Savior of the World, God Incarnate, the Light of the World giving definitive, authoritative, and unimpeachable information on how to pray if the person praying wants his or her god to pay attention. Preempting all contrary mandates, the One God has given his orders on prayer to all people for all times until the end of the world. The instructions are strict and inflexible. There are no exceptions. When one prays he should go into his closet and shut the door.

This command of the deity on earth in human form was given publicly in the "Sermon on the Mount," wherein the Christ conveyed the will of the Father. The Lamb of God went on to dictate into the

Religion

record an example of how to pray: "Our Father which art in heaven," *etc*. (How Jesus was a god and discussed the will of his father, who was also a god (Yahweh) in heaven is explained fully in the essay, "On the Holy Trinity" —see p. 124.) This is known as "The Lord's Prayer." When one prays it, or any other prayer, one has to do so behind closed doors in one's closet, not publicly. The "Lord's Prayer" was not openly prayed by Jesus, but was taught to be repeated only in private. When Jesus prayed in the Garden of Gethsemane, before being crucified, he prayed privately. He probably didn't have a closet. While hanging on the cross, he prayed with others about, but he really couldn't, under the circumstances, be expected to deliver these final prayers elsewhere. Thus, prayers are to be given from behind closed doors unless you are alone in the mountains or trussed up for execution. In fairness, the orders probably leave room for any silent or quiet prayer that is not rendered in public. All public prayers are forbidden and are a deliberate disobedience to the will of the biblical god.

The Son of Man not only set out the rules for prayer and other matters in the Sermon on the Mountain but concluded with a warning of the dire consequences of disobedience: And every one that heareth these sayings of mine, and doeth them not, shall be likened unto a foolish man, which built his house upon the sand: and the rain descended, and the floods came, and the winds blew, and beat upon that house; and it fell: and great was the fall of it (Matthew 7:26–27).

So there it is. Our world is coming unglued and we suffer crime, violence, and war because of public prayer. The more out-of-the-closet prayer, the more awful things get. Those who yell loudest that "the Bible is the inerrant word of God" are the worst offenders. The more they argue that we must return to the Bible, the more they blasphemously engage in uncloseted prayer. They doom us by their forbidden entreaties to the Almighty whose commands they flaunt. Nowhere is the influence of Satan clearer seen. Satan has deceived the faithful to engage in prayer meetings, prayer breakfasts, and all manner of condemned celestial communications reaching into the very foundations of government. Heaven help us, there are even those who advocate publicly praying in our schools as a solution to the problems directly created by that very disobedience to ultimate authority. There are prayers on radio and on television, in churches, in

163

homes and in auditoriums. The more we publicly pray, the more we become the most violent and crime-infested nation on earth. Is this our American heritage, our family values? Why do we deliberately disobey God? The American civil war was conducted by armies who publicly prayed and believed a god supported their cause and was on their side. Lincoln observed that "both sides may be, and one must be, wrong."

Humanists who wrote our Constitution tried to prevent the problem. God is not mentioned in the Constitution, and church and state are separated in the Bill of Rights. This is probably all that has kept Satan from totally leading us to destruction. Our greatness comes from humanists, our problems from the folly of those who advocate and practice public prayer.

It is all so simple. A believer is not permitted to disregard a direct order from the deity without consequences. Better to be a nonbeliever than one condemned under one's own rules. Examples that impious prayer doesn't work are legion. Every fundamentalist bigot in the country publicly prayed that Mr. Clinton not be elected President of the United States. The prayers failed. God is not mocked.

So if you must be a believer, get it right. Read your Bible. Do you think Jesus was wrong? Obey your God. Stop all forms of public prayer. It's hard to stand on your feet when you're on your knees.

And don't naïvely assume your daughter has religion when she comes home with a Gideon Bible in her suitcase.

HOLIDAZE

Dear Virginia,

No, Virginia, there is no Santa Claus.
It is a myth . . . .

The person who tells you the truth
should never be blamed for the hurt
that comes from learning that others
have lied. . . .

Your friend,

Uncle Edwin

Holidaze

On Christmas, or
"No Virginia, There is No Santa Claus"

If I could work my will, every idiot who goes about with "Merry Christmas" on his lips should be boiled with his own pudding, and buried with a stake of holly through his heart. He should!
—Uncle Ebenezer Scrooge (not to be confused with Uncle Scrooge McDuck)

I can't prove that no ungulate unit of reindeer persuasion can fly, any more than you can prove I don't have two invisible unicorns that frolic in benign innocence at Camp Quest. I can't prove there are no living dinosaurs (as the arkonuts challenge the skeptical to do) anymore than the arkonuts can prove the English text of Genesis they rely on is identical to the original version they hold was dictated, or inspired, by Jehovah. But if one says that all crows are black, there is no need to check every crow to falsify that assertion. All that is needed is to find one white crow, or any crow of a different color. Similarly, Santa skepticism can be soundly silenced by the production of one flying reindeer. Yet Christmasterians insist doubters disprove Santa, sleigh, and such, or keep silent, lest they destroy a child's simple (mindless) faith. This method of proof proves useful later, as children, programmed to believe fantasy is truth, grow to adultery and unquestioningly follow the fantastic follies of faith of their fathers (and mothers—political correctness must not be permitted to fall down a personhole).

To be sure, Plato (not to be confused with Mickey Mouse's dog) argued that, to conceive of something that is real, one must somehow get the perfect idea of that something from the place it really exits, to wit, the world of forms—a place somewhere that no one has ever seen. Reality alone wouldn't do. Thus, everyone but philosophers knows what a horse looks like, and kids know all about Santa without having to survive Philosophy 101.

167

Edwin F. Kagin: *Baubles of Blasphemy*

Can we imagine, or even believe in, something that doesn't exist? Sure we can. Just talk with those who have been abducted by aliens. If some unseen thing is believed in by many, *e.g.*, angels, it is called faith. If a thing is believed in by only one, and is wildly outside the gates of common sense and experience, then the belief, *e.g.*, suddenly realizing that one's guardian angel is made of grape jelly and having him (there are no female angels—check your Bible, you can win bets on this) on toast, it is called psychosis. The problem is that the invisible and the non-existent look much the same. Christmas beliefs fall somewhere between the province of priest and psychiatrist.

Christmas combines two contradictory images of godlike characters: Jesus, the Christ, who taught that to be saved one should sell all of his property and give it to the poor (the church later declared belief in this teaching a heresy), and Claus, the Santa, to whom children are taught to write letters requesting property—believed to be given by Santa, in one night, to those children of the world found worthy—in direct challenge to the counsel of the Christ. One should note, before teaching the latter belief system, that an anagram of 'Santa' is *Satan*.

The day itself, meaning Christ's Mass, is the same day the Romans used to honor their sun god with gift giving and feasting. Christmas is quite pagan. Its secular celebration involves rituals specifically forbidden by holy writ, like hewing down a tree, bringing it inside the house, decorating it, and praising it. (See Jeremiah 10.) This is as clear a violation of divine decree as public prayer, or celebrating the Sabbath on the first day of the week instead of on the seventh day as ordered (Commandment IV). No wonder we are in such trouble these days with crime, inflation, and teenage pregnancies.

Unfortunate cultural consequences flow from the forced frivolity and jejune joy Christmas creates and requires. People get depressed when they don't feel happy as they should, when they do not have their artificial expectations fulfilled, and when they cannot meet the unreasonable artificial seasonal needs of others—like their mercenary relatives, and their materialistic, greedy, spoiled children—and get even deeper in debt by trying to behave as expected. Thanks to Tom Flynn, and his wonderful heresy, *The Trouble With Christmas* (Prometheus Books, 1993), I chucked the whole thing a few years ago, and lived. Try it. You will feel better for it.

168

Holidaze

Should I be granted a Christmas wish, it would be that the holiday be canceled, and that the whole show appertaining to this business of Christmas not be done at all. Please understand that I do not care if others celebrate Christmas if they wish, nor would I suggest that they be prevented from doing so. I just don't want the holiday to be compulsory for me or anyone else—any more than I want other people's prayers, that they have an absolute right to pray, to be forced upon me by public officials or upon children by public schools. One who would rather decline gets somewhat tired of listening to those who absolutely and uncritically assume all good people celebrate Christmas, and that something is horribly wrong with anyone who ignores the invitation to attend their compulsory party. Failing the unlikely event of Christmas being made optional, I would alternatively wish, in seasonal answer to Virginia's famous question, that we might see something in the public press, for innocent children, like:

Dear Virginia,

No, Virginia, there is no Santa Claus. It is a myth that has been cruelly used to deceive children for the pleasure of adults who unwittingly destroy children's sense of basic trust by teaching them that the world is something other than it really is.

I know this news must be a shock to you, and I am truly sorry for your discomfort. But it is not my fault. The person who tells you the truth should never be blamed for the hurt that comes from learning that others have lied.

You should not believe in Santa Claus any more than you should believe in fairies, or in demons waiting around to pull you under the earth, or in angels lurking about to transport you above it. People do not need to believe foolish things to have love and compassion and caring, any more than they need a special season or holiday to be nice to one another.

If things believed prove false, does that mean peace, and sharing, and kindness must dissolve like mist along with the untrue things? Of course not! We don't need magic to have happiness, and wonder, and joy. Our beautiful world is full of these things, and they are very real, and our real world holds more interesting and wonderful people and things than any fairyland anyone could ever even imagine.

Edwin F. Kagin: *Baubles of Blasphemy*

Some adults are afraid of things they don't understand, and they teach children to believe in magic. But the truth is really far more exciting. Wouldn't you rather learn what is on real planets that are millions of miles away than believe reindeer can fly? Have you ever seen the northern lights? I have, and I can tell you they are more beautiful, more mysterious, and more wonderful than any pretend story anyone could ever invent about elves that have workshops at the North Pole.

Is it okay to pretend and to believe things we know are not true? Of course it is! And it can be a lot of fun. Intelligent people love to play. Any time you watch a movie or a play or go to a costume party you are playing and pretending something is so that is not.

We know those aren't real people in the TV—only images of them—but we know we are pretending, and this is fun and much different from believing a falsehood. Would it be wrong to tell a friend of yours, who firmly believed there were really small people inside the television set, that his or her belief was not true? Would it be right for you to be condemned for destroying that friend's childlike faith? What if several of your best friends thought they could fly, and set off for a bridge over a 600-foot deep gorge to prove it? Would it be wrong for you to politely try to convince them that they just might be mistaken, no matter how firmly they believe they are right? Would you be destroying their childhood or saving their future?

Follow the truth, no matter where it may take you. And don't pay any attention to those who think comforting falsehoods are better than understanding the world as it is. If you ever have children, teach them trust by telling them the truth. By the way, just in case you didn't know, the stork didn't bring you. You are here because your parents had sex.

Keep questioning, Virginia, and don't feel it is the least bit wrong to demand correct answers. Asking questions is what makes us human.

Your friend,

Uncle Edwin

170

Cycle of Spring

Today I walk through autumn leaves
Holding the five-year-old girl child's hand
Who, without warning, stops and thrusts
Questions at me I once asked
Questions that were satisfied
By maiden aunts and Sunday saints
Whose answers that I soon forgot
They still believe and can recall.

Questions that were asked again
When thoughts ran like young stallions run
Over hurdles that can't be crossed
And spring back strong like new bent bows
Eager to feel the morning wind
Smooth and stroke their strong hot sides
As they rip holes with their hard hoofs
Into the soft turf of the mind.

But scholars pull the English grass
That plugs the cracks in Roman roads
Pompeii's relics are admired
By cuff-linked men who softly ask
Why such a culture had to fall
Beaks and claws of mocking birds
Can pluck the eyes from a dead king
And so pubescent moderns scorn
Ancestral portraits in the hall
For what good can the dead past bring?

Edwin F. Kagin: *Baubles of Blasphemy*

Questions that will still invade
Twilight thoughts before sleep draws
Unconscious mind to other things
Where logic seldom pushes hard
Whisper softer every year

And tinny answers echo down
The catacombs where childhood lies
So soft the sound had grown by now
It might have vanished in a while
But now it screams at me again
In the smiling questions of a child.

Whatever I might tell her now
Will never do when snow is cold
And summer seems too hot to run
When girl skin sags and breasts break down
As years forget the nipple's thrust
And flesh looks like a bombed out town.

Last winter's dead
And springtime myths can be retold
The tiny hand tugs at my sleeve
It's good to know there's nothing old.

Around first light on March 30, 1997, an odd grouping of unknown pictographs appeared upon my computer screen. After some days of intense cryptographic analysis, the symbols were finally translated as follows:

Easter Greetings from Heaven's Gate

Come my darling children

It's time for you to die

Friends wait behind the comet

In their spaceship in the sky

So eat your tasty pudding

Put a purple shroud upon your head

And don't forget your suitcase

You'll need it when you're dead.

On Easter

The things you are liable / to read in the Bible,
they ain't necessarily so.

—Porgy and Bess

Easter is the High Holy Day of the Christian religion. In its many manifestations, Easter celebrates the myth of the reanimation from death of the god Jesus, a.k.a. the Christ. Like its womb-mate Christmas, Easter is a marvelous blend of Christian and non-Christian nonsense. The Christian side is represented by "Handel's Messiah" and hot cross buns (a seasonal pastry with a sugar cross on it) and the non-Christian nonsense side by "In Your Easter Bonnet..." and hunts for Easter Eggs — dyed boiled eggs in the shell. These have been laid, young minds are taught to believe, by rabbits. Some hold the rabbits don't lay the eggs, only deliver them. What do you think?

To understand the phenomena of Easter, one must understand the Christian 'Gospels.' These four small propagandist tracts, written long after the supernatural 'fact,' by unknown authors who did not know Jesus, contain the only known evidence for the existence of Jesus. Believers will argue other historic proofs, but these are provable forgeries added centuries later by pious priests who copied or translated Jewish, Roman, and Greek texts. If the ancient writers had deliberately omitted Jesus merely because they had never heard of him, this error was often fixed for later Christian editions. The only evidence for Easter beliefs comes from the gospels.

Here's a neat Bible study exercise for nonbelievers. It will help you learn something of the Christian belief system and will prove useful in the American Religious Civil War when believers try to force you to play in their sandbox. Read all four gospels and, including every fact contained within them, write a concise, noncontradictory chronology of what happened between the time Jesus was crucified on a stake (the Greek word *stauros* translates 'stake' not 'cross' — tell that to your preacher and watch him ring them bells) and the moment he went up to Heaven. Then you will know what Christians believe.

174

To make the challenge more exciting, be sure to include facts, for the same time frame, from "The Acts of the Apostles" and from the letters of Paul. Paul really got Christianity going. He claimed to have seen Jesus after Jesus had gone to Heaven. Lots of people believed him. Lots of people believed Joseph Smith too. Joseph Smith wrote *The Book of Mormon* and claimed an angel helped him translate buried gold plates the angel later reburied. At least Paul had honest delusions.

The reason the death of Jesus is of importance to Christians is because if they believe Jesus died for their sins they get to live forever with him when they die. Because Jesus survived death, believers will too. Somehow Jesus' 'sacrifice' doesn't seem like such a big deal, being a god and all, and getting to come alive again after being dead only one day and two nights. Many people have died for others and have *stayed* dead. There should be no shortage of volunteers willing to die to save everyone forever and be worshipped as a god if they could come alive again after being dead between Friday evening and Sunday morning.

Once you finish the Bible stories about Jesus, you may well wonder how anyone could believe this stuff, and you should understand why the events were omitted from every other history of that time. When Jesus died on the stake, the Bible reports that dead people came out of their graves (whether decomposed or not isn't revealed), walked around the city and were recognized by many. This should have provoked some interest by the scandal sheets of the day, but no other reference is found of it. We might wonder if the risen dead sued to get their property back from their useless heirs.

You will note from your Easter biblical studies that the primary witness to the resurrection of the Christ was one Mary Magdalene, a woman thought to be a prostitute who had been possessed by seven demons, *i.e.,* she was nuts. Wouldn't it have been nice if the risen savior of the world had appeared in all his glory to the Roman Senate where literate rational humanists could have recorded an accurate account of this miracle? Why have your immortal soul hang in the balance on less than credible evidence? Should one accept that laws of nature have been broken and that a dead body has come alive again on the word of a deranged hooker? Would a just, rational, compassionate god condemn one to eternal torment for doubting such evidence? Clearly the Senate, or even a meeting of the Aqueduct Committee, would have been a better place to break the good news of salvation.

But we are not dealing with a rational god or even decent moral behavior in the Easter story. The god the myth says was the father of Jesus believed in child sacrifice. Previously content with blood drained from the slashed throats of sheep, goats and such, this god needed more gore to save everyone. He wanted his own kid killed as a blood sacrifice for the sins of the world. This is what little children (kids) are taught in Sunday School (that's where Christians violate the Fourth Commandment by worshipping on the first day of the week instead of the seventh as Yahweh ordered—no wonder we are in such trouble). But if child murder for the sins of others isn't bad enough, consider this. Christians celebrate the death and rebirth of the god Jesus in a grotesque cannibalistic ritual of (symbolically if Protestant; for real if Roman Catholic) eating his flesh and drinking his blood! This bizarre custom is known as *Holy* Communion — dare we call it "swallow the leader?"

If Jesus rose from the dead, and if he went to Heaven, and if Heaven is outside the known universe, and if the laws of nature invented by 'God' apply to his son, then Jesus could not travel faster than the speed of light. If he left for Heaven two thousand years ago, he isn't there yet, and won't be there for some time. Therefore, we really need not concern ourselves at this point about his return to earth. Presumably he will return sometime after he gets there.

So now you know about Easter. You will probably be a happier and better adjusted human being if you stick to the Easter Parade and pass on the eating of human flesh and blood. And please remember that this disgusting rite is practiced in buildings owned by Christian groups who do not have to pay taxes on their property or income.

And the next time some un-American lunatics want to have forced Christian prayer in public schools, tell them you are a spiritual vegetarian.

Happy Easter.

Passover

In the brief yellow of dandelion sin
He preened with Jesus when the morning spoke
Away the need that made his manhood search
Guilty books in pillow-hidden
Thought that wanted more than bread
To live by through the vapid afternoon
That ached to evening.
Wishing the something that was feared
Could pass the placental shield of faith
Or wink in shadows of the dark but real
To the grieving of the meat around the soul.
Man blood strains as did the lamb's
That dries upon the portals that it stains.

CRETINISM or EVILUTION?

Science and Logic versus Religion and Other Forms of Irrationality

On How One Small FIG Figured in the Flowering of the Fruits of Fulfillment of God's Divine Plan, Sank the Arkonuts, and Made Australian Radio

(May, 1997)

But peace, I must not quarrel with the will
Of highest dispensation, which herein
Haply had ends above my reach to know...
—John Milton

You may have heard of the Battle of Big Bone, now part of the history of the American Religious Civil War (ARCW). We won. It should be remembered down the ages at the picnics of the Daughters of the ARCW.

The arkonuts arrived from Australia, California, and Florida. They had triangulated on Boone County, Kentucky, home of Big Bone Lick State Park, for a 'creation museum' and theme park designed to teach 'creation science' (an oxymoron on the order of 'grape nuts') and to counter, with biblical truth, the godless evolution being vended at the fossil finds of Big Bone Lick. The enterprise was targeted for rural land on Highway 42, between Big Bone Lick and the town of Beaver Lick, Kentucky. One wit suggested that "Answers in Genitals" might be more appropriate to the location than the proposed "Answers in Genesis." But I digress, and this is a family-friendly book.

The genesis gambit had been in the planning for some time. Only a small legally mandated announcement of the proposed zoning change and a small sign on the targeted property informed the secular world that a request had been make by the arkonuts to rezone the land from rural to recreational so they could legally do their thing. A sharp eyed member of a local secular humanist outfit, the Free Inquiry Group,

Edwin F. Kagin: *Baubles of Blasphemy*

Inc.—FIG for short—spotted the newspaper post and, in the manner of a true patriot who has seen the signal lights, raised the alarm to be up and to arm.

Some FIG members got the word out. At the standing-room-only public zoning hearing the news item announced, the arkonuts, who had good reason to believe their scheme would survive the legal hoops as slick as goose grease on marble, were stunned to be met with reasoned opposition from both secular and religious neighbors. Their plan, proclaimed as their god's will, was suddenly, plainly, and most unexpectedly, in deep trouble. On national Fundangelical radio stations, and on call-in-your-contribution-cause-God-needs-money 1-800-numbers, the faithful were urged to pray that secular science lose to the truths of Genesis and that Jehovah would bring to Kentucky, and to his glory, a museum of creationism. The prayers failed, because prayer doesn't work. At least not for creationists trying to limit 'God' to their understanding of Bronze Age myths.

Sensing the need to regroup, those who teach children that dinosaurs were on the ark and that the Earth was created six thousand years ago, made the fatal strategic error of requesting more time to polish their presentation before the final hearings. This permitted the quickly formed and disorganized opposition to get organized. Public hearings were held, a TV debate, in which your narrator participated, was conducted, and—most importantly—citizens of the county learned, largely by door-to-door visits, just who, what, and why the arkonuts really are. By the time of the final public hearing, over one thousand voting residents of the county had signed petitions urging a denial of the zoning change. The plan was unanimously defeated. And it went down for zoning reasons, not religious ones, *i.e.*, the requested change to recreational use was a subterfuge for the true commercial use this new international headquarters for nonsense intended. If they had wanted to build a church, even to teach that the earth is flat, or that things fall up if dropped, FIG would have fought for their First Amendment right to preach their thing.

Now to the point. FIG has a membership of around sixty souls, maybe some one hundred on the mailing list. Only two FIG members live in Boone County, and only four FIG members ever opened their mouths at any public hearing. And to what cause did the arkonuts attribute their defeat? Why to those godless secular humanists of FIG, of course. Those thousand good Christians who came together and stopped them were ignored.

So here's how their leader, Ken Ham, described their situation on Australian radio in December, 1996, during Hanukkah, just a few days before his plan sank like an overloaded ark (he doesn't know we have a tape of it, but we do):

*Actually, overwhelmingly, we had the support of the local community. It's really only a small number of people who have stirring up (*sic*) opposition to this museum and most of them belong or associated with (*sic*) a group called "Free Inquiry" which is a local humanist group which of course are against anyone believing at all in the supernatural and actually the Boone County Courthouse, the Fiscal Court, and the Zoning Board have received overwhelming support from local residents. In fact we have a long list of churches, businesses, organizations in Northern Kentucky who support us so really it's got overwhelming support from the community.... There's been a lot of exaggeration about what's gone on here, mainly because there's a very vocal humanist group who are very anti-god and anti-anything to do with the bible and they're the ones that have sort of stirred up the controversy, but actually, as I said, the residents of Northern Kentucky overwhelmingly support someone to come in and give people an opportunity to have a family center...we've been very low key in all this...and certainly there's been a few residents, just a small number who've been stirred up by this vocal minority here...because the local humanist group went to the press...* [sic semper sic].

When the plan was defeated, Ken Ham announced on the Internet that the defeat was clearly "God's will," and revealed unto them that his god had other plans for their ministry.

Guess so.

And now you know the rest of the story.

Edwin F. Kagin: *Baubles of Blasphemy*

Kentucky Ham Song

(May be sung to a sorta combination of "Davy Crockett" &
"The Beverly Hillbillies")

Hear the story of Kenneth Ham
Australian huckster slick as jam
Left the creationists at El Cajon
To try to make a fortune out at old Big Bone.

Kentucky has a state park called Big Bone Lick
Where Ken planned something really sick
Tried to teach 'creation science' near those fossil finds
To get little children not to use their minds.

Here's what Ken says we should believe
Every kind of living thing lived with Adam and Eve
Forget proof and science and believe Ken's news
On the Ark there were dinosaurs and kangaroos.

Ken's creationists are just plain wrong
We know evolution worked hard and long
Until we humans could evolve a brain
That could keep our minds and money out of Ken Ham's drain.

CHORUS:

Science deals with problems it sometimes solves
And sometimes finds new truths such as life evolves.
Creationists have no questions and no need to look
The answer to every question is in Ken Ham's book.

184

OmniMyth of Kentucky
Theme Park Proposal
(January 2005)

Answers in Genesis has led the way with its brand new, soon to be opened, multimillion dollar extravaganza in Kentucky, called the "Creation Museum." This delightful diversion into fantasy could be but the first in a major undertaking to expand the area into a world-class amusement theme park complex in rural Kentucky. Permit me to propose that this pooling of the preposterous be known collectively as "OmniMyth of Kentucky."

This suggested grouping of sites, featuring magical explanations for everything, is an idea whose time has come. OmniMyth could provide genuine creative comedy relief in a world all too weary with the mess created by failed attempts to solve real problems with make-believe. The theme parks could also make their owners a decent profit.

The possible recreational facilities that could be constructed are limited only by the creative imagination of potential designers. The Creation Museum, after all, posits the proposition, which no educated person would hold as true, that the Earth is only a few thousand years old and that it and all life on it were created by magic. The lushly exhibited creationist fantasy rejects, as its central premise, the fact that humans developed from less complex life forms in the process of change over time known as evolution. Instead, the visitor is treated to the myth, presented as true, that humans were magically made from dirt. One can be transported to a time before computers, space stations, and wireless telephones when people wrote on rocks, set broken bones without X-rays, and answered tough questions, like where did people come from, by saying a god did it.

Similar delightful ideas could be represented by similar theme parks grouped in OmniMyth of Kentucky, making the attraction truly international in scope. The diversity of the project might contribute to a lessening of tensions among the world's peoples, who could come to visit and to see and to laugh at our commonality of recognition that we

185

all share primitive pasts in which our ancestors created make-believe stories to explain things not understood. Ancient Greek stories of gods living on a mountain and hurling thunderbolts of lightning. Egyptian stories of preparing the dead for an afterlife by removing the brain. Indian stories of a god who was crucified and arose from the dead. Eskimo stories of a raven who made the sun, moon, stars, the earth, people, and animals.

OmniMyth of Kentucky can put Disney to shame. Thanks to Answers in Genesis, without which this project would not have been birthed, for such creative leadership in education.

Here is a possible advertisement:

Antidotes to thought. Magical reasons for everything. Fantasy is made real and Myths become true. Pretend it is so and it will be so. See models of humans and dinosaurs together—and you can believe they lived at the same time. See a model of a god pulling the sun across the sky in a chariot—and you can believe it is true. Forget reality for a few hours at OmniMyth of Kentucky, where Reality is Fantasy and Fantasy is Reality.

Ode to the Butterfly Mind

The Parliament of Butterflies
Was racked by deep division
Questions of what to teach the young
Demanded their decision.

It had been known and taught and thought
Since butterfly life began
That butterflies in glory rose
From their creator's mighty hand.

Now some few who this truth had mocked
Had attacked faith's very pillars
"All butterflies," these skeptics claimed,
"Came from caterpillars."

This indecent theory spread
Into butterfly education,
Until this "caterpillar cult"
Threatened creation's revelation.

The faithful sought to restore the truth
About the origins of butterflies;
And to build a solid moral base,
To stop the metamorphic lies.

"Believe you descended from some worm
And wormlike you will be!"
Reasoned those who'd seen faith's light
And knew that naught was left to see.

Edwin F. Kagin: *Baubles of Blasphemy*

"We see no proof," some butterflies said
"That we're all come from cocoons—
Unbelievers who would teach this tale
Are all immoral loons."

Some said the metamorphous lie
Was laid by "the enemy" they believed
Had set candle flames and windshields
To destroy butterflies they'd deceived.

The matter was at last resolved—
Both theories must be taught—how fine!
Now youth can just decide the truth,
In each young butterfly's simple mind.

FREEDOM!

Free At Last, Free At Last, Thank Mother Nature and the U.S. Constitution, Free at Last!

Poems and Essays on the Glorious Quality and Abiding Need to be Free

—and, if the truth be told, this is the editor's "miscellaneous" section, since *everything* Edwin Kagin writes about is closely tied to freedom.

Home Do Not Change
(May be sung to the tune of "Home on the Range")

Oh, I want my home
Safe from where bigots roam
Where fanatics are all kept at bay
From courthouse and school
So no pious fool
Can control what I think or I say.

Home, home do not change
Don't let freedom be taken away
From courthouse and school
Let no pious fool
Control what I think or I say.

Some folks think it strange
When they can't rearrange
Me, and I can't get it quite right
To do things their way
And behave as they say
I just want them out of my sight.

Home, home do not change
Don't let freedom be taken away
From courthouse and school
Let no pious fool
Control what I think or I say.

Edwin F. Kagin: *Baubles of Blasphemy*

I want to stay where
I can breathe freedom's air
Safe from the righteous deceived
No invisible friends
No new life when life ends
Far away from pretend things believed.

Home, home do not change
Don't let freedom be taken away
From courthouse and school
Let no pious fool
Control what I think or I say.

My home is my place
If they get in my face
Trying to make me believe
As they want me to do
Telling me what is true
I can just make them all leave.

Home, home do not change
Don't let freedom be taken away
From courthouse and school
Let no pious fool
Control what I think or I say.

On Competentiating Children
(December 31, 1997)

Train up a child in the way he should go: and when he is old, he will not depart from it. —Proverbs 22:6, Holy Bible

Your children are not your children...And though they are with you yet they belong not to you...You may house their bodies but not their souls, For their souls dwell in the house of tomorrow, which you cannot visit, not even in your dreams. You may strive to be like them, but seek not to make them like you, For life goes not backward nor tarries with yesterday...
—Kahlil Gibran

Hoping to one day get it right, your narrator, in his day job, practices law. In this capacity, he, as do others of this too often justly vilified and too often unjustly maligned vocation, sees much others do not want to notice or know. Lawyers, like clerics, prosper on the misery of others. What would lawyers do if everyone became peaceful, honorable, and just? What would the preachers do if the Devil was saved? Among the insights attained in trying to help people get out of their self-made problems is the realization that messed up kids become messed up adults—and that messed up adults create messed up kids.

While the Bible may say the sins of the fathers (in a politically correct world read 'parents') are to be visited upon the children, we can be better than those Bronze Age nomads who thought the earth was flat and that π equals 3. The godless Constitution of the United States forbids "bills of attainder." Look it up—don't have space to explain it—it's some more of that legal mumbo-jumbo that defines our freedoms (if you don't understand it, be thankful someone does and don't glory in your ignorance). It means the sins of the parents are not to be visited on the children, no matter what the Bible says.

So what are children anyway and what does one do with them? The English romantic poet William Wordsworth prosaically opined

193

Edwin F. Kagin: *Baubles of Blasphemy*

"The child is father of the man." This meaningless observation is found in his much overrated poem, tightly titled "Ode on the Intimations of Immortality from Recollections of Earliest Childhood," a name befitting the poet's musings and ramblings on reincarnation and other supernatural nonsense therein contained, and meriting recognition in your author's contemplated "Secular Humanist Anthology of Eupraxophy and Other Plain Speaking." Wordsworth thought children came from 'God' in purity and innocence, uncorrupted by adult thought, and "trailing clouds of glory...," whatever that means. Others of his time thought storks brought them. Wordsworth had not read *Lord of the Flies*. Neither he nor the others had read Dr. Ruth. Either view of human children—arriving in glory or by stork—is a blueprint for architecting screwed up kids. There are ways of thinking about rearing (not raising—one raises horses) children that avoids petty piety, banal barbarism, and pretentious psychobabble.

Children can be taught (shown) the power of inner strength that permits self-control and empathy. They can come to think of themselves as worthwhile human beings who are entitled not to be hurt and who do not wish to hurt others. They can grow up knowing they are loved unconditionally. Young human beings can learn not to be afraid, that life involves taking certain risks, and that the meaning of life is to live it. Children can be taught to be competent.

Children are little people, not possessions. Regrettably, children do not come with instructions. Generally, big people learn how to deal with children from the behavioral examples of those who dealt with them as children. And lawyers and therapists continue to prosper, as faith in biblical teachings cause their professions to thrive as growth industries. If you think beating a kid physically or emotionally hurts you more than your victim, there are ways one could test this theory on you, if such treatment was not considered unlawful when applied to an adult. In blasphemous indifference to the moral teachings of the Bible, humanists have made such violence unlawful when applied to defenseless children—at least in this country. In some countries infected with Mother Teresa morality, surplus kids are shot as vermin. But for the Christian god's sake don't abort them. Keep repeating the mantra "God loves little children." Who are you to let reality get in the way of religious imperatives?

If holy writ says to beat the kid to save his soul, who are you to argue? You could wind up no better than those secular humanists. If the child asks your reason for some unreasonable command, simply say it's because you said so. Questioning is bad. The important thing is to obey. That's Jehovah's way, isn't it? And don't forget to constantly remind the child that in your view he or she is unattractive, burdensome, clumsy, lazy, incompetent, selfish, and stupid. That liberal self-esteem nonsense can come later.

It is said that if you want to make a god laugh, tell him your plans. If you want to make him laugh harder, tell him your plans for your children. You will almost certainly be wrong, and if said child or children follow your dreams for them, they will not follow theirs, and they will probably live miserable, unhappy lives. You can then have a whining pity party for yourself and wonder wherein you failed, and what you did to deserve this, when it was your own neurotic needs that caused you to teach dependency and to foster insecurity. How, you might wonder, did you fail? Bernard Shaw observed that there is no worse villain than the person who tries to mold a child's character. You did not teach your children to be competent.

There is another way—the humanist parenting way. One can teach children they are people of worth and able to make sound decisions, that they are not inherently bad and in need of salvation, that morality is not based on authority or absolutes or decree, that morals are manners and manners are subject to change, and that authority changes its mind. We now learn from Roman Catholic authorities there is no Limbo. Belief grounded in authority must now figure out whence went all those little unbaptized souls that the same authority had for centuries taught were in fact in Limbo. Teach your children to see absurdity and not be destroyed by it. Teach them to laugh.

Tell those whose ideas of proper moral conduct involves the use of the Bible as authority for forcing Christian prayers and other aspects of their private belief systems on public school children to tread carefully. Let them know that intelligent adults trying to rear competent children have read their book and will resist and will teach their children the morality of knowing how to defend themselves with knowledge, weapons, and will. And that such people will know that Jesus forbade public prayer, and that there is no biblical evidence that a single apostle, including Paul, ever prayed at all. Let them know their own weapons can be used against them in defense by those who decline to be their victims. Reading the Bible, Mark Twain noted, gives one a sinfully unfair advantage over those who believe in it.

Righteousness and self-righteousness are different words representing very different things. Teach this to your children. Let them know it is sometimes more moral to waive the rules than to wave the rules. When people tell you they are born-again Christians, thank them for the warning. Such people are often even more distasteful and dangerous the second time around. Teach your children the Bible for their own safety's sake and as inoculation against its venom.

Let your children know that morality did not originate with the Bible or any holy writ, no matter what believers believe. They should understand that the strength of a belief has nothing to do with the correctness of that belief. Morality developed and evolved as human beings learned that the consequences of certain actions are so awful that the behaviors should be avoided, forbidden, and sanctioned. Humans had noticed some good while before the Bible was put together that it is not a good idea for people to murder one another with impunity. Teach your children we have gotten a good deal beyond Bronze Age biblical morality, or your son may worry that, if you find him to be rebellious, biblical morality requires that he be stoned to death as the Bible god ordered. Before becoming moral, people create gods in their own image.

The Bible is the stuff of nightmares, not a work to which children should be exposed. It is filled with depraved behavior and fails to provide examples of moral conduct worthy of emulation. The Bible god was either wrongly quoted or is not a moral god. He sanctions things a just society abhors and punishes with prison. We have a right to expect our teachers of morals to be at least as moral as we are. If you would not drown all the little children of the world in a flood because their parents did things you didn't like, how could you possibly teach your children that a god who did just that should be seen as a good moral compass? Teach them to distinguish between logic and fallacy, between science and superstition, between things believed and things proved. They should learn how to tell the difference between a horse chestnut and a chestnut horse.

Your children will be competent when they can survive, thrive, create, empathize and interact justly with others, free of pain, fear, and guilt—without gods, without religion, and without you. If they can be thus brought to self-reliant adulthood, they will not need the gods or the religion, and they will not miss them. If you have done it right, they won't need you either.

But they will miss you.

January 29, 2000
Editor
Cincinnati Enquirer

Dear Editor:

On January 27, 2000, your paper opined that the current attempt by certain self-righteous modern Pharisees to gain special rights to discriminate against those who do not believe in their god, like the children of Camp Quest, is a good idea that the Kentucky Legislature should pass into law. One might wish that, for this appalling assault on our American freedoms, you would have taken greater care to get your facts, your theology, and your spelling of my name right.

Camp Quest is the first residential summer camp in the history of the United States for the children of secular humanists and other nonbelievers. It is operated by the Free Inquiry Group, Inc. (FIG), of Cincinnati and Northern Kentucky, and is endorsed by the Council for Secular Humanism and by the American Humanist Association. It does not proselytize, but it does attempt to offer safe haven for those bright and beautiful children who may feel themselves diminished in consequence of the incredible prejudices directed against them by those who see themselves as superior to them by virtue of nothing more than their diverse, and contradictory, beliefs in a supernatural world. We teach these children, ages eight to thirteen, that they are not alone, but are rather in the company of giants about whom history has too often lied. One of the reasons Camp Quest was started is because the Boy Scouts do not, in obedience to their views of virtue and Americanism, admit children who are avowed nonbelievers to membership.

For its first two years, 1996 and 1997, Camp Quest was held at a camp facility rented from the Baptists in Boone County, Kentucky. The staff of the camp knew who we were, and we knew who they were. Their staff wore their "Jesus is Lord" tee shirts, and we wore our Camp Quest (Question, Understand, Explore, Search, Test) tee shirts. We got along wonderfully, and we treated each other with mutual respect. One Baptist staff member very kindly conducted a fishing derby for us. One of their children joined us in our pool sessions. We made these most decent hosts of ours an aerial photograph of their campgrounds on one of our plane rides, and we discussed with our campers the Bible quotes the Baptists had posted on their hiking trail. We were told that our campers were more polite, better behaved, and kept the grounds cleaner than many of the religious children to whom they normally rented. Their staff was left, we believe, with a different view of secular humanists than they had previously held, and we left with a better feeling for those Baptists who believe in a god who wants them to be kind to everyone, regardless of their creed.

Now, three years later, some, whose religion appears to consist of views that Jesus condemned in the Sermon on the Mount and in the parable of the Good Samaritan, have asked the Kentucky Legislature, in HB 70, to amend the civil rights laws of Kentucky so that churches can discriminate against those who do not believe in the basic tenets of their religion when they offer their facilities to the public for rental or other public uses. As grounds for this request, they claim that they were forced, by current law, to rent to Camp Quest, and to its parent organization of nonbelievers. This apparently proved unbearably traumatic to those good Christians sponsoring the bill who were never at Camp Quest. Now, they want the civil rights law changed to assure that they will never again have to trespass against their understanding of brotherly love by being forced to acknowledge Samaritans as their neighbors. They of course have, and have always had, the option of not offering their facilities for rent to the public at all.

Their proposed law, HB 70, is an attempt to give special rights, not equal rights, to churches. As such, it appears facially to violate the Constitution of Kentucky. Section 59 prohibits "special legislation," and Section 5 guarantees, as one of our basic freedoms, that "...the civil rights...of no person shall be taken away, or in anywise diminished ...on account of his ...disbelief of any religious tenet, dogma or teaching." In that this is exactly what the proposed legislation seeks to do, it is something our wiser ancestors saw coming. It is the sort of un-American activity they took great pains to prohibit and prevent, should any later day prospective tyrants ever again attempt to make their religion our law, followed by their inquisitions and heresy trials.

Just who, under the proposed law, will decide just what are the basic beliefs of any religious group? The courts? The camp staff

Baptists, who saw their God and their religion as big enough to include the children of Camp Quest ("suffer the little children to come unto me"), or those Baptists who want the Samaritans kept off of their road? Questions of just who shall say what is to be believed have caused no little unpleasantness in the past.

We have separation of church and state in America so the Baptists and the Anabaptists won't have legal excuse to kill each other, so Catholic children do not have to endure forced readings of the Protestant Bible in public schools, and so churches cannot refuse, on what they choose to call religious grounds, to deny facilities offered to the public to atheists, to those who suffer from the last taboo. Under testimony in committee, those pressing the adoption of this law said they would rent to the KKK, for they believe in God. So did Hitler. The motto of the Nazis was "God With Us." The bill's sponsors, and your editorial, apparently find these God-fearing folks less objectionable than the children of Camp Quest.

What Would Jesus Do?

Assuming the correctness of their views on reward and punishment in an afterlife, how will it be with those called before the Blissful Seat, before the great Judge of World, to answer for their deeds of life, when inquiry is made regarding just why they denied use of property dedicated to God to the children of Camp Quest?

Wonder if the reply, "Because they didn't believe in you, Oh God of Love" will prove to be an altogether satisfactory answer?

Edwin Kagin
Camp Director
Camp Quest

On a National Identity Card

" "Who are **YOU**? *' said the Caterpillar.* "
—Alice in Wonderland (Lewis Carroll)

The advances of humanism in the development of civilizations have involved a balancing test between the possible and the prohibited. Does the end ever justify the means? Of course it does, sophomoric philosophy notwithstanding.

Thus, a loving mother may bash out her infant's brains to stop its crying that would otherwise bring certain death to the entire tribe hiding from enemies. To stop an enemy submarine from sinking an entire ship, irreplaceable human beings who have fallen off the ship into the sea may be killed if it is necessary to drop depth charges before they can be rescued.

For a more palatable analogy, consider the moral issue of lying, *i.e.*, of stating as true something that is not true. Not lying is generally held as a moral virtue, and we teach our children not to lie, and reprove them when they do. Yet what person of decent human sensibilities would tell the truth about the whereabouts of a child to a maniac you knew would murder the child upon discovery. When asked, "Where is the kid," the more moral answer would be the lie, "I do not know," rather than "Hiding in the closet on the left." Under these conditions, the person disclosing the child would be considered a monster and a complicitous actor in any injury to that child. Here lying would be good, and telling the truth would be unthinkable.

These, of course, are examples of "situational morality," the tough stuff of true ethics and decision making, condemned by those, usually of an immature religious bent, who seek absolute, final, and unchangeable answers in commandments or rules from a deity. You've seen the bumper stickers, "God said it, I believe it, that settles it," or something similar. Yet such, if Christians, generally do not sell all that they own to give to the poor, turn the other cheek, pray only in their closets, go to church on Saturday, not covet, abjure statutes and photographs, never kill, honor abusive parents, leave their families to do their god's work, or live lives of poverty and self denial, all

201

as directly commanded in holy writ. Such Cafeteria Christians take only those rules they like of the teachings, advocate them, make laws encompassing them, punish those who do not obey them, and ignore the rest. Thus, they practice situational ethics. Other religions do the same; they just do it with different rules. That's why we have a First Amendment.

No matter how many ethics seminars are conducted on why we should prohibit the doing of something, if that something can be done, it will be done. Get used to it. If someone can build a small nuclear device, it will be built. If smallpox can be used as a weapon, it will be so used. If humans can be cloned, humans will be cloned.

If it is possible to highjack a passenger plane and crash it into the World Trade Center, someone will do it, no matter how unthinkable you might find such an idea. The idea was obviously thinkable to someone.

What do you really want? At what price do you want it? What are you willing to pay or to give up? Having trouble losing weight on all available diets? Don't worry. I guarantee I can make you lose weight despite past failures. But you might not like how I do it. There were no overweight prisoners in Auschwitz. Want to stop drunk drivers—*really* stop drunk drivers? Make a law that you cannot drink and drive, period. No nonsense about .08, or whatever, permissible blood alcohol. Anything over .00 and you go to jail for sure for a long time. Then you stop drunk driving. But our society doesn't really want to stop drunk driving badly enough to do that, or we would.

Now, after zero nine one one two zero zero one, we are—and this is new to us in America—we are afraid.

Do you want absolute safety? I can give it to you. But you must not object to me having viewing and listening gadgets installed in every room of your house, as well as in all public places, and you must not object to the instant, no delay, no trial, remote control execution of anyone who violates any of the rules you must permit me to set up for your safety. Would you accept having an electronic receiver painlessly placed in everyone's brain to punish or kill rule breakers? Yes? Then I can keep you safe. No? Then you must take some chances and not be fully safe. Less freedom, more safety. More freedom, less safety. Simple. You cannot have both. How would you care to compromise?

What is your safety worth? What is your freedom worth? Some people were willing to die to be able to crash a passenger plane into the World Trade Center. They are willing to die to do other things to kill you as well. How much do you want to prevent them from doing that? How much are you willing to give up to be safe? Are you ready for a much different, but safer, world?

Now that you know how it works, let's talk about the proposed idea of a national identity card.

I don't like clerks in stores asking me for my zip code. And I won't give it to them. I point out that my contract with them to purchase their widget offered for sale has nothing to do with my zip code. I want to protect my privacy whenever I can, I want to resist having my privacy further invaded, and I will invoke the law to protect it. But I also don't want to be the victim of drivers who are not licensed, or who borrow or steal someone else's driver's license. So I will tolerate some loss of privacy by submitting to a photo I.D. driver's license. Similarly, I do not want a terrorist, dedicated to dying for his cause in the act of killing me, to have a fake passport so he can come into my country and steal an airplane to use as a kamikaze guided missile against me or my fellow citizens. Am I, are you, willing to let the government put your retina print on a national identity card? Do you want to be required to carry a license to move about in our free land? If such be required, is our land still free?

People give up a certain amount of privacy by agreement, and of necessity, when they join a society. Every society has its rules. Laws require that your very birth and death be registered. Your society tells you who you can or cannot marry and where or where-not you can lawfully travel. Your society can jail you if you don't file or pay your taxes. These rules are part of the consensus *ad idem* of a culture, if it is in any way a democratic or representative government, and these are different things. Such rules are something your national unit, or a majority thereof, has, directly or indirectly agreed upon for its governance; something the people governed have said may or may not be done.

Illegal aliens don't want a national I.D. Nor do criminals trying to change identities. Or maybe they do. Could a dishonest type steal another person's card and assume that identity? Guess it depends on the information on it, and the guarantees thereon for proof of identity. And therein lie the great questions. Remember, if it can be done, we must assume it will be done and guard against it. What will be on the card? If not now, then later, maybe under a government less compatible with your beliefs than was the government in place when you, or your representatives, voted for the card. Will the card record your credit history? Your employment record? What an ex-spouse said about you in a divorce? Your income? Your buying habits? Whether you own a gun? Your hobbies? Your tastes in reading, movies, clothing, cars, food, drink, or sex? Certain Internet sites record this kind of thing right now, whether you know it or not or like it or not. Your political activities and associations? Your membership in controversial groups, like maybe the Masons or Humanist organizations? Your church affiliation or lack thereof? Your psychological profile?

What if some government, now or later, says you cannot be a good American if you do not attend church? And a later government defines the right church? It has happened before. Ask the English Catholics under Oliver Cromwell.

When, and why, will presentation of such a card be required? And who can require its production? Would you need it every time you tried to buy gas or groceries, so "Big Brother," for your own good, can know where you are at any given time and what you eat? Who is to say who cannot require presentation of the card? And who can change the rules?

Why should you object to a national I.D. card if you are a law-abiding and loyal American? For the same reason that you should object to an unlawful warrantless search of your home or person, even if you have nothing to hide. To *not* object to an unlawful search is to invite, or condone, tyranny. The same rules that limit freedom of movement for bad people can limit freedom for you.

Why should you welcome such a card? So you can be safe, and so people trying to kill you can be identified and stopped from doing so? That's not a bad reason. And to gain this safety, you must trust your government to use the information on the card only to protect your safety and to not use that same information in a wrongful diminution of those rights that fashion us a free people.

There has been a paradigm shift. And the Attorney General of the United States, who enforces the laws, is having Bible Study Classes in his office, paid for by We the People.

Truly, there is reason to be afraid.

Edwin F. Kagin: *Baubles of Blasphemy*

A Welcome Clarification on the Second Amendment and That Militia Business
(June 2000)

If, as the gun grabbers would have it, the Second Amendment does in fact only bestow upon military forces they perceive to define the "militia" the exclusive right to bear arms, and denies this basic and vital guarantee of freedom to individual citizens, then our Constitution is even more unique than previously understood. Our Bill of Rights must be remarkable among the autographs defining nations by numbering among those ten rights therein contained, that are given directly to the people as shields against the power of the state, a grant to the nation's military of the right to own weapons.

One might have naïvely thought, absent this welcome clarification, that the right of a nation's armies to possess arms was assumed. Who would have thought that a Bill of Rights was needed to permit an army to have guns? Imagine the foresight of our ancestors, who sought a Bill of Rights to guarantee "the people" of the United States protection against the power of the government they created, to have so memorialized the mandate of their intent that the government in power at any given time be forever assured the right to ownership of weapons that would, by the same words, be forever denied to the very people who had demanded that a Bill of Rights be placed in writing for their protection before agreeing to form a nation.

Hanging Gardens

Nebuchadnezzar jabbed his seal

In wax that Icarus used for wings

And helped melt Alexandria down

With Papal Bulls in German towns.

Let the concave mirrors flame

Papyrus ships that float the dead

Down Lethean sands as words gush red

And staffs squirm as snakes again.

Paste a mummy with the scraps

Grecian scribes threw out, or

Hid in caves where goats played round

The lettered skins of ancient sires.

Unless some boy throw a rock

And find a few old scrolls to hock

That wear all inquisitions out

Scoring rock with acid doubt

Until holes dug with Aaron's rod

Are smoothed to cover King and God.

On Self-Righteousness

self-righteous: *confident of one's own righteousness, esp. when smugly moralistic and intolerant of the opinions and behavior of others.*

—Webster's New Universal Unabridged Dictionary

Pretty soon I wanted to smoke, and asked the widow to let me. But she wouldn't. She said it was a mean practice and wasn't clean, and I must try not to do it anymore....And she took snuff too; of course that was all right, because she done it herself.

—Huckleberry Finn

The self-righteous are everywhere, trying to control our lives. With the zeal of reformed nymphomaniacs peddling AmWay, they freely vend their negative judgments on the behavior and opinions of others. Unable or unwilling to control themselves and their unhappy lives of frustration, insecurity, and despair, these petty dictators seek solace in desperately attempting to control others. For they are right. Those who disagree with their toxic tyranny are clearly and obviously wrong, if not evil. And they do attract followers, persons easily led, seeking certainty, and willing to praise, to flatter, and to sing unto them, How great thou art. Self-righteous leaders reward fidelity and elevate select obedient disciples, especially worshipful ones who are confused but shamelessly self-righteous, to CULT (Counseled Until Learned Truth) status.

The existence of such personalities is not new. Jesus is reported to have said, "And why beholdest thou the mote that is in thy brother's eye, but considerest not the beam that is in thine own eye?" There are similar references, for self-righteousness is justly and frequently condemned in the Bible, a work that, for all its many and obvious faults, is not without certain merit. Indeed, we recommend you read it. The book is much better than the movie.

Self-righteousness and hypocrisy may be joined, as in the widow's views on tobacco reported by Huck. But they are quite different concepts. Hypocrites, like the widow, do themselves that which they so freely condemn in others. Most hypocrites are self-righteous, but self-righteous persons are not necessarily hypocrites and may in fact practice what they preach. A priest who rapes little boys, and preaches against homosexuality and violence, is clearly both, while a practicing virgin, who moralistically urges this unhappy fate on others, is not. It's all in how you study it. Many have rejected religion largely because it is home to lots of goodie-two-shoes type persons of self-righteous or hypocritical persuasion. Sometimes, in their attempt to live justly in an unjust world, the disillusioned seek solace from religion in the perceived rationality of secular humanism. And guess what?

This may come as a shock to some secular humanist readers, but the self-righteous are also to be found among the ranks of the supposedly rational, among those who look for meaning apart from the supernatural, among those who decry the artificial goodness of the godly. Bummer, ain't it? Thus, instead of holier-than-thou, we have those who feel rationaler-than-thou, or skepticaler-than-thou, and who demean, abjure, reject, and avoid those they feel don't quite measure up to their standards. Such are no less self-righteous than the widow.

Whether religious or secular, the self-righteous and the con-artist are sisters under the skin. Both become outraged if they don't get their way. The slightest reasoned refusal to consent to manipulation or control is punished. The uncooperative mark may witness a presumably well-meaning, but terminally self-righteous, friend go into an inexplicable rage, answering disobedience with irrational and unpleasant emotions, until the victim seems, as best worded by Shakespeare, "beyond reason hated." To further complicate matters, the person deluded by self-righteousness cannot understand when others are disinclined to share their hostility and fail to concede the justness of their attitudes and actions. The world as one conspires.

The self-righteous are troubled by democracy. Why debate or vote on any matter of behavior or morality when truth is available by decree, and when correct answers may be so readily had from those who know the answers beyond any need for question or discussion? To challenge such persons is, in their view, *malum in se*—in the vernacular, reprehensible, wicked, and wrong in itself—denoting a defect of character revealed in the very act of rebellion against ultimate authority. Thereafter, every action or motive of the errant sinner will be understood and punished as an indisputably vile thing—another example of evil attacking good. The psychological mechanism of projection, and the transparent narcissism of the self-righteous, are beyond the scope of this digression. The analogies to theology are scary. If afflicted leaders possess small power, they are

Edwin F. Kagin: *Baubles of Blasphemy*

merely annoying, comical, or pathetic. If they hold real power over nations or ideologies, the graveyards of history harbor their heritage.

The sad part is that they don't have to be like this. The self-righteous prigs can get over it, or get therapy for it. They don't have to expose themselves to the misery. Misery is optional, for predators as well as prey, even if they think they have no free will. Rational beings don't have to live with sustained rage, or with the chronic paranoia of waiting for some other imaginary shoe to drop. Those who live to control others could, using the power of reason they mock, come to realize that compromise and resolution of disagreements can be something more than capitulation or appeasement, and that, in some things at least, they just might be—as impossible as it seems—wrong. One is entitled to be smug, arrogant, and self-righteous only if one has figured out how not to die. The outcast may well be the better person. That's what the Bible story of the Good Samaritan is all about.

If we can't avoid the self-satisfied—the better option—we can laugh at them. A healthy person loves to see the pompous taken down a peg or two, and delights in mocking their phony goodness and proper ways. This is why the common folk laugh when a stuffed shirt slips on a banana skin. But what about self-righteous secular humanists who, in hardening their hearts and softening their minds, do real harm to those who actually favor free inquiry? Maybe we should create a Secular Humanist Hall of Shame. Here could be enrolled and acknowledged those whose actions have earned them the herein proposed SHAME (Secular Humanist Arrogantly Making Enemies) Award.

As adolescent fantasies are best left to adolescents, so childish needs to have one's own way are best left to children, who will outgrow them. Adults should, to borrow again from the Bible, "put away childish things." It would be sad to die without growing up.

For everything there is a season,
For every act there is a reason;
As a garden reflects its seeds,
Deeds of life tell that life's needs.

—Edwin Kagin

210

Camp Director's Opening Night Remarks at the First Camp Quest

The following remarks to the Campers and Staff of Camp Quest were given by Edwin Kagin, Camp Director, on August 11, 1996, the historic first night of the first year of Camp Quest, the nation's first residential secular humanist summer camp.

Hello you all. Welcome to Kentucky and to Camp Quest. My name is Edwin. I am the Director of Camp Quest. You may call me Edwin, or Boss, or Sir, or Your Grace, or Mr. Director, or whatever else you like, but Edwin will do just fine. In fact, you can call all of the adults here by their first names. We were all your age once, we think, and someday you may be our age. The only difference between us and you is that we are older. We have learned some things, and may have some things we can teach you, but we believe you can teach us some things too. We are all equal, because we are all human beings. We are all learning all the time.

I would like to tell you a little bit about Camp Quest, and about why we are here, and why we think you are here, and then maybe you can tell us about why you think you are here. At least we all know we are all here, because everybody has to be somewhere, I think, and we are all here right now to have a wonderful week together.

This is a camp run by secular humanists for the kids, grandkids, and so forth, of secular humanists. It is the first camp for secular humanist kids in the history of the United States, we think, and that is really neat, because we will probably all be in the history books, and you can tell your own kids and grandkids that you went to the very first camp for secular humanist kids.

What in the world are secular humanists anyway? We are going to try to figure that out this week. Maybe you already have some ideas about this that you will want to share with us. We might even come up with some brand new ideas about being a secular humanist that no one has ever thought of before.

211

Edwin F. Kagin: *Baubles of Blasphemy*

That's one thing that's really neat about being a kid—you have a whole lifetime to think up things no one on earth has ever thought of before. Why if someone hadn't thought up the idea of a light bulb, we might all have to watch TV by candlelight. Oh, by the way, we aren't going to watch any TV here at Camp Quest. There are too many other really wonderful things to do. Can you believe there was once a time when there was no TV, or radio, or automobiles, or airplanes, or computers? Why, I didn't see a TV until I was twelve years old. Can you believe that? When my mother was your age, cars seemed strange and new and most people got around using horses, and almost no one had a telephone, and the telephones they did have didn't have a dial or buttons, and when you picked up the part called the receiver and held it to your ear, an operator said, "number please" and connected you to the person you wanted. I remember that. When my father was a little boy, there were no electric lights in his house. There were gas lights and oil lamps. His family's Christmas tree had lit candles on it, just like everyone else's did. Sometimes the candles set the tree on fire. Sometimes they burned down people's houses.

Science has made a lot of things a lot safer, and science has helped make many wonderful and amazing new things possible. Computers are really new. They are so new that a lot of adults don't have the slightest idea how they work or how to work them at all. When my son Steve here was in school there were no computers. He has to ask his little sisters about them. They know about them because they were everywhere when they went to school. If grownups want to know something about computers, they can ask a kid. When you are grown, there will probably be things so new that if you want to know about them *you* will have to ask a kid.

New things can seem like magic. They really are magic if you don't know what they are or how they work. Let's say some people who had lived in caves all of their lives and had never been to school or to a city, and who knew nothing about science, suddenly saw an airplane fly over them for the very first time. What would they think? They might think it was magic, or maybe they might think it was a god. They might be very afraid of it. They might even worship the airplane and pray to it. They might make up a whole religion about the airplane, and they might have priests who could teach people to pray

212

to the airplane, and to beg the airplane not to hurt them, and to ask the airplane to do good things for them. They might believe that people could not be good people unless they believed the airplane was a god. They might believe that if people did not believe the airplane was a god, that the airplane god would punish them and cause disease, and cause the crops not to grow, and cause fires to burn down the forests, and cause wars, and cause all sorts of bad things.

Of course they didn't know that bad things were not really caused by the airplane flying over them, but if they didn't know what the airplane really was, and if they were afraid of something they didn't know anything about, they might make up a religion about the airplane. They might teach their children about the airplane god, and their children might believe it was true, and they might worship the airplane and teach their children to worship that airplane.

If there were any secular humanists around, the secular humanists would probably say that things should be proved before people believed them. The secular humanists would want to know what the airplane really was, and they would want to find out what was really causing the bad things to happen. The secular humanists would say the airplane was not a god, and that it was only something in the real world that people didn't understand. The secular humanists would say that if people kept on worshiping the airplane as a god that they could never find out what the airplane really was, or how it worked, or why the bad things happened and how people could keep the bad things from happening. The secular humanists would understand that the belief in the airplane god was a superstition that was harming people and that their belief in the airplane god was wrong and that their wrong belief was keeping them from finding out true things that would make them happier and less afraid of things they did not understand.

Many of you probably have parents and friends who are secular humanists. Secular humanists are people who practice secular humanism. Secular humanism sounds awfully complicated, doesn't it? But it really isn't. Humanism just means believing in human beings, which we all are, doing human things, which we all do. Human beings do human things. Isn't that simple? Secular means believing in this world, and in the real things that are in our real world, and not believing in some imaginary pretend world that no one can prove is real. So a secular humanist is a person who believes that human beings live in a real world, not a make-believe one. Secular humanists believe that people have to take care of themselves and that people have to use their minds to make things better for themselves, because no god is going to help them, and that all the praying in the world won't do any good.

Secular humanists believe the real world and the universe the world is in is all there is. But that is quite a bit, really. It is enough to keep human beings very busy. So busy that they shouldn't waste their time and their lives believing in things that are not true and in worshiping something that does not exist.

Secular humanists do not try to make people think like them. Secular humanists think everyone should make up their own minds about what is real and what is not real, and about what is true and what is not true. But not everyone thinks like secular humanists. In fact most people don't.

That's why there are not as many secular humanists as there are people who believe in this religion or in that religion and who think that their religion is right and that everyone else's religion is wrong. Because there aren't that many secular humanists, the ones there are can feel a little lonely sometimes and they may feel that no one else thinks the way they do. That's why we started this camp. Here you can meet others who may think the same way you do, but who will not try to make you or anyone else think like them.

At Camp Quest we are going to look at the wonderful world we live in. We are going to see how amazing it is, and how wonderful the living things in it are. We are going to look at the stars and wonder and imagine what human beings are and what they can do and what they can become.

We want you to know that it is okay to be a secular humanist. It is alright not to believe in any gods, or angels, or devils, or heavens or hells. It is okay to be a human being living in a real world that can be understood by people and that can be made better by people for people to live in. Not everyone believes this. Some people think that nothing can be done without a god's help. Some people think there is something wrong with people who don't believe the same things they believe. This is as silly as saying the secular humanists were wrong who didn't believe in the airplane god. But some people say it is wrong not to believe in their religion, and that you must be a bad person if you don't believe in their religion. Some people try to force people to believe in their religion. They even try to force kids to pray their prayers in public schools. This is against the law in America, but these people think the law is wrong and that they and their religion are right. They think they have the right to control your minds and to tell you what you must believe.

The Boy Scouts have said that they won't let anyone be a Boy Scout who doesn't believe in a god. I am an Eagle Scout, and I know that this is a bad thing for the Boy Scouts to do. That is why I agreed to be the Director of Camp Quest. There are some folks who say that human beings can't possibly be good, honest, decent people if they don't believe in their religion. This is not true, and we are going to show those people that this is not true. I bet you were sent to this camp by loving people who know it is not true and who want you to know it is not true. There are a lot of church camps where kids are taught religion. As a matter of fact we are at a camp owned by a church. We are renting it for the week. It is usually a church camp, but it isn't a church camp this week. There have not been any camps for secular humanist kids until now. We are the first. We are making history. We want this first camp for secular humanist kids to be a big success. And it will be a big success if you enjoy yourselves and have a wonderful time. Think you can manage that?

If this camp is a success, we can probably have even better camps with more campers in the future. A lot of people will be watching to see if we can make this camp work. You know what? We think we can.

We are all here to have fun and to learn new things and to make new friends. Now I want you to meet the counselors and staff here at camp. They have all come here without pay to help you have a wonderful week. They are all here for you, so don't be afraid to talk with them and to ask them questions. That is why they are here. And we want to meet you, and we want you to meet each other.

After you learn about our activities at Camp Quest, I am going to give each cabin a little problem for you to work on all week. You are to work on the problem yourselves and tell all of us your answers on the last night of camp. Your counselors may answer some questions for you, but they will not give you any answers to the problem. This is for you to give us.

Each cabin has a different problem, and will give the whole camp their answers. I am really eager to hear your answers.

Now let me introduce the counselors, who will introduce the campers in their cabins. When they are finished, I will introduce the staff who will tell you about our activities.

Don't be afraid to ask any questions you have as we go along. Questioning is why we are here.

Kagin's Second Coming

or

Second Comings from Kagin

Lest We Forget...

Today, February 17th, we should pause and remember a hero of freethought, Giordano Bruno.

On February 17, 1600 Giordano Bruno was murdered by the Christian Inquisition.

(His murderers would protest this statement, claiming that he was lawfully executed.)

His crimes were as follows:

1. Holding opinions contrary to the Catholic Faith and speaking against it and its ministers.

2. Holding erroneous opinions about the Trinity, about Christ's divinity and Incarnation.

3. Holding erroneous opinions about Christ.

4. Holding erroneous opinions about Transubstantiation and the Mass.

5. Claiming the existence of a plurality of worlds and their eternity.

6. Believing in metempsychosis and in the transmigration of the human soul into brutes.

7. Dealing in magics and divination.

8. Denying the Virginity of Mary.

What he was *really* murdered for was for saying the Earth moved around the Sun.

Edwin F. Kagin: *Baubles of Blasphemy*

He was burned alive at the stake.

Before the fire was lit, his tongue was nailed to the roof of his mouth so he could not utter further blasphemies as he painfully died.

You can learn more about this great hero here:

http://en.wikipedia.org/wiki/Giordano_Bruno
http://www.infidels.org/library/historical/john_kessler/giordano_bruno.html

Many think such things could not happen today.

You don't really believe in evolution do you?

And you don't think the Earth goes around the Sun, do you…….?

Edwin.

**UNITED STATES DISTRICT COURT
EASTERN DISTRICT OF MICHIGAN, NORTHERN
DIVISION
CASE NO. 01-CV-10385**

ANONKA JOCHAM and TAMMRA JOCHAM, Plaintiffs,

v

COUNTY OF TUSCOLA, Defendant.

* *

An excerpt of proceedings had …. in the above-entitled matter before the Honorable David M. Lawson, United States District Judge, at Bay City, Michigan on the 24th day of February, 2003.

JEAN MARIE HANSEN, Esq. and EDWIN KAGIN, Esq. Appearing on behalf of the Plaintiffs.

* *

OPENING STATEMENT

MR. KAGIN: May it please the court, opposing counsel, ladies and gentlemen of the jury: This is an opening statement, it's not evidence, so anything I say to you, no matter how persuasive I think it might be, is just that.

It is my honor and duty to open the case and to present you with the first knowledge you will have of the claims of our clients sitting here before you. My daddy, a minister, told a story about a preacher who took his watch out and said here's a time limit. I said: Daddy, why is the preacher putting the watch down on the pulpit, what's that for? The preacher said it doesn't mean a thing, son. But you're here in this courtroom and it does.

I would like to give you some advice, one of which is how to be persuasive in a sermon. I recollect an old fella said first you tell them what you're going to tell them. Then you tell them. Then you tell them what you told them. That's what we're going to do, right now we're going to tell you what I think we're going to tell you.

Then the evidence from the witness stand is going to tell you. And then I'm going to summarize and tell you what I told you. I'm going to ask you to make a verdict for our clients. If you don't think we have proved it, hold for the defendants. It's easy, okay.

Now unlike a criminal case where one side has to prove the guilt of the accused beyond a reasonable doubt, that's where the scales shift like that, in a civil case it's a much lighter burden. You merely have to show more evidence on one side than the other, what is known as a preponderance of evidence, which I believe the judge will instruct you on.

Remember what I say isn't evidence, what opposing counsel says isn't evidence. Actually, with all due respect, what the judge says isn't evidence. His Honor acts as a referee, as it were, in this trial. And if we make objections, one side or the other, it's, we hope, not an attempt to conceal truth but really to insure that the trial follows in a way as it should. And you do have the right to make notes as his Honor told you.

Okay. Now here's what this is about. These are two citizens of the United States. Anonka and — no, that was not always her real name, she had another name, Nancy Ann Hamilton, and she had it legally changed a few years ago to Anonka. It is our honor to have her sitting here. And Tammra. And they run a witch museum in the city of Caro, Michigan, and this witch museum is quite a nice place, I recommend everyone go to it. Not during the trial.

In that witch museum they try to dissuade people of certain, maybe, deeply held prejudices such as witches fly around on broomsticks and have black cats and familiar {familiars and} things like that. It's an educational thing for the kind of people who want to be in {burn} the Harry Potter novels, you know.

You know, I think maybe the reason people want to read {burn} the Harry Potter books is because they think they're true, they really believe there *are* witch-type things going on.

Anyway, these ladies are certainly not witches, there are no witches. There may be people who laugh about them, but there are certainly no supernatural beings, at least not that we know of.

At any rate, the two plaintiffs are not Christians. They do not follow the Christian belief of the majority, and that's why the judge asked you about that.

Now we are very simply asking you to find for two American citizens who were exercising, or attempting to exercise, the kind of thing this country was built on, the constitutional right to freedom of expression, speech, and so on; and who, by the actions of the defendants in this case, were denied the equal protection of the laws guaranteed them by the 14th amendment to the Constitution of the United States.

Now that amendment, by the way, was the one that was passed after slavery was abolished back in the Civil War. Down south they call it the War of Northern Aggression, but it's generally known as the American Civil War where certain minority groups were freed from slavery and given the rights of citizens. It was put into law that no state, or the officials of that state, could deprive citizens of the United States of the equal protection of the laws given to other citizens.

And that's what plaintiffs say happened in Caro, Michigan, that good Christians — and it is a majority of Christians in the community, and there is no problem with that, no one is challenging that right, but they didn't like Anonka and Tammra there and they wanted to drag them out of town. We're going to prove that to you.

And one thing here, specifically around Christmas of the year 2001, there was a crèche, a manger scene, put onto the county courthouse as had been the custom. Now we are not here — let me tell you a little bit about what this case is *not* about. It's not about the legality of the crèche, it's not about whether it was right or wrong, it's not about what they said about the crèche. Really, it was what happened to them as a result of attempting to exercise their rights as Americans. The ABCs of the case is it was Appalling, Baffling and Cruel what happened to them.

Anonka calls and tries to register a protest about the crèche, and she did that around December 8. She spoke to one Norma Bates who was the long-time head of the counsel, the chair. Ms. Bates told her: Why don't you come to the commission meeting on December 11 and express your view. She says okay.

Well she and her daughter go to the council meeting on December 11 and it was as if someone had been laying for them; they were set up, we think the evidence will show, as if someone dug a hole and put some polyurethane {palm fronds} across it and —

MR. KOCHIS: Your Honor, I object {to} is {this} argument.

MR. KAGIN: — then took —

THE COURT: Counsel, when there's an objection, stop so we can hear it and so the court reporter can record it. Thank you, Mr. Kochis. Response to the objection?

MR. KAGIN: This is opening statement, your Honor, it is an overview of what we're attempting to prove.

THE COURT: I believe in this case the objection is overruled, you may proceed.

MR. KAGIN: We're trying to show an improper motive. Now when they got to the council meeting, first there was a prayer and she challenged that. Then there was a challenge to the flag pledge, which is to be argued on March 24 before the U.S. Supreme Court, concerning the phrase "under God" in it, which was put in in 1954 during the Communist McCarthy scare.

At any rate, when it came her turn to talk, she barely got anything out of her mouth when the council started to attack her for being a non-Christian. She'll tell you about it, if she can do so without emotion. I hope she can. They attacked her for being non-Christian.

Miss Bates, the head of the council, read a letter that appeared a few days before in the paper supporting the view of the crèche and the Christ child. And the article, by the way, came up the next day, or a few days later — I think was the next day — said no room for the Christ child again. No room again for the Christ child, you know, similar to no room at the inn.

Rather than the headlines saying citizen denied the right to speak in Caro, there was and has continued to be, a totally pro-Christian and anti-anybody who isn't a Christian diatribe in the city of Caro.

One counsel member took out a dollar bill, held it up and said: "What does this say here? In God we trust. Do you spend this money?"

This kind of attack, without offering where they might get other money that doesn't have that phrase on there. And the attack went on and on, she will tell you about it. As the inquisition of Caro went on, the council attempted to steal these ladies' lives because they have different opinions.

They told Anonka she had no rights because she was not a Christian. That's when she called the lawyer. She will say to you, we believe, how dare they tell me I have no rights. At the hearing, which was a public hearing, where the council says Robert's Rules of Order apply, council members were not recognized by the chair but got up and attacked these women and continued to attack them.

Anonka got to speak less than a minute to a minute and a half, she's not sure. She couldn't go on. Her daughter wasn't permitted to speak at all, was shouted down and yelled at.

In other words, it was wrong not to believe in Christianity. That's what we're suing for. And the damages, they will describe. Damages of this sort, ladies and gentlemen, are difficult to prove, as is the case and the motive itself, but we think we can do that.

There are several types of evidence acceptable at law. One type of evidence is direct evidence, that is which you perceive through your senses: you see, you hear, you taste, touch it. It smelled like vanilla, it was raining out.

Another type is documentary evidence, things that are written, and we have some of that. We have preserved the words of some of the council members that we will show you that were reproduced in the newspaper.

Another type is the physical evidence. A little while after, a campaign of crosses started —

MR. KOCHIS: Your Honor, I again object. This is inadmissible evidence and is well over a year later and has nothing to do with the lawsuit that's before the court.

MR. KAGIN: I certainly —

THE COURT: Members of the jury, understand, as I said before, an opening statement is an opportunity for counsel to present what he thinks the evidence will show. It's up to the court to rule on what is legally admissible evidence, and counsel's statements, as he has acknowledged, are not evidence before you. I'll overrule the objection. If counsel makes a representation — if either side makes a representation — in opening statement that is not borne out by the evidence, of course, it's not something that you would consider in deciding the case. You may proceed.

MR. KAGIN: Thank you, your Honor. That is an example of physical evidence. And we will show you through testimony that Anonka, came to understand that the purpose of the cross campaign was to get her out of town. The crosses to this day are in the Christian businesses, and they are circular, like garlic in the window sills or blood of the lamb on the window sill. In short, the very kind of thing that Anonka and her witch museum is lamenting, the history of the human race and the kinds of things we used to do to each other.

And that's generally, folks, what the case is about.

Tammra wasn't even acknowledged. She tried to speak, she couldn't. They wouldn't let her. They left in a state of shock. They went home, cried. Their children had been abused at school.

The argument, the discussion, hit the Internet talking about "the witches of Caro." And you can decide for yourselves if the opinions and the say so of officials in power in a community have any effect on the public opinion of that community or not. Or are those just nothing opinions when the council is saying to them: We don't need people like you in our town.

It went to a population of well over 8,000. It went beyond the county, it went into the Internet where it can be read in China, anywhere in the world, free or not.

They were condemning these women. The crosses are still there.

Various arguments have been made that the courthouse was a public forum. And, as I say, we're not litigating the crèche, but there are going to be, if you'll pardon me, lies that were told by people in power. One such is that there was a Klu Klux Klan rally, an unpopular group that they let demonstrate —

MR. KOCHIS: Your Honor?

THE COURT: Excuse me, Mr. Kagin.

MR. KOCHIS: Your Honor, I object. This is inadmissible. The court has ruled on this matter and it has nothing to do with the present lawsuit in front of this court.

THE COURT: Mr. Kagin, how does that have anything to do with the offense of December 11?

MR. KAGIN: It has to do with the credibility of the council, your Honor, is the only reason for which it is offered. They said that the Klu Klux Klan rally occurred at the *situs* of the crèche, but we can prove it occurred across the street, a few blocks away.

THE COURT: I think that's collateral, I'll instruct you to move on.

MR. KAGIN: Very well, I'll move on. We're going to show you the newspaper articles, we're going to introduce witnesses who sent letters to the newspaper that was supportive of the two ladies, American citizens, the plaintiffs and these letters were not published. In the face of a statement from the editor, they got no letters of support for the women, only letters favoring the counsel.

We have one witness who was told by a member of the executive staff of the press that they received over 30 letters supporting the women and against the council, but they weren't printed. We'll attempt to show you why those things came about.

We will introduce newspaper articles quoting the commissioner, the chairman of the council. We will introduce business persons of the community who will testify and tell you that pressure was put upon them to accept one of the crosses and put it in their windows so they can get rid of the evil in their midst, the witches.

Basically, we're going to try to show that the city government, the county government, of Caro, Michigan was trying to establish a religion, that being the Christian religion and a certain aspect of the Christian religion.

By the way, when your council's prayer ends with "in the name of Jesus, Amen," you are at a certain level of religiosity that is quite clear. What does that say to the Jewish members of your community, the Muslims, the Atheists, the Buddhists, people who all approach the table on equal footing? What does it say about things being biased, biased against them?

That's going to be our case. Basically we think that the council is attempting to follow the ancient Biblical statement of Exodus 22:18 that you shall not suffer a witch to live. Maybe not literally they didn't mean that, but the women's business has been spat upon, there have been death threats to them, they've been demeaned. Their business has dropped off. They have been publicly humiliated, and all of this a direct and proximate cause of people who define themselves as good Christians.

You'll hear that from the witnesses themselves, we will then hear from the defendants and their witnesses. If the plaintiffs don't prove it — if you don't believe that's what happened — hold for the defendants. Thank you.

Rally for Reason:
Which Line Are You In?
(July 16, 2007)

"All that is necessary for the triumph of evil is that good men do nothing."

—Edmund Burke

*"The best lack all conviction, while the worst
Are full of passionate intensity."*

—William ButlerYeats

There have been seminal events in human history, that, save for knowledge, guts, and skill, or sometimes even caprice, might have gone other than they did, and all we know could now be different.

What if Charles Martel had lost the Battle of Tours? Or Napoleon had prevailed at Waterloo? Or Cleopatra and Mark Antony at the Battle of Actium? Or the Confederate States at Gettysburg? What if William, not Harold, had died in the Battle of Hastings?

These climactic events were preceded by extended foreplay. Other results that changed everything followed protracted, if less orgasmic, human interactions. What if Christianity had not become the official religion of the Roman Empire? What if Christendom had actually won the Crusades? What if religion had succeeded in shutting down the Renaissance and the Enlightenment? What if the Protestant Reformation had been stillborn?

If any of these events had occurred, we might now be speaking Egyptian, or French, or German. If those who think our country is based on the Bible had prevailed in setting up our laws, we, like the biblical characters in Sunday school stories, might be living in a land without democracy, a concept not mentioned or practiced in the Bible.

What if Charles Darwin had stuck to his religious studies at Cambridge and not signed on to sail to the Galapagos on HMS Beagle?

Edwin F. Kagin: *Baubles of Blasphemy*

If science and critical thinking had not replaced Bronze Age mythical explanations for the origin of things, religious Fundangelicals might not now be building museums of nonsense. There would be no need to attempt to prove that evolution is wrong, that religious mythology is science, that the Earth is only six thousand years old, that dinosaurs lived in vegetarian harmony with humans, and that humans were created from dirt. Everyone would believe that. There would be no reason not to.

We might now still be in the dark ages, not opposing a return to them, and there would be no need to oppose the terrorism of this ignorance, and the child abuse of teaching children that science is wrong and that faith and dogma trump truth.

But things happened as they did, at least in the only universe we know. And things are happening now that could change all that is. Because we know history, we can avoid mistakes of the past. And therefore we must once again defend civilization against its traditional enemies. The usual suspects are at the gates.

If the American Religious Civil War is lost, everyone will believe those things that our martyrs to truth rejected. Or they will be dead, in jail, or in hiding.

Those who would impose a theocracy upon us will not, as yet anyway, make a visible frontal assault. The plan appears to be a "Wedge Strategy." A wedge looks like this: ▼. The idea is to get the little end into the piece of wood and then to tap, or to hammer, the wedge in, as in splitting a log, until the gap made grows wider and wider as the wedge is forced in and the unity of the item into which it is forced is lost.

An axe is a wedge. A guillotine is a wedge. Creationism and Intelligent Design (ID) are wedges. Get the edge in a little bit, and you can then get in more and more, wider and deeper, until the wedge has gone all the way through the log, or the society, dividing, separating, destroying, and prevailing.

Thus, things urgently pressed by Fundangelicals, things seemingly harmless alone, are neither harmless nor alone.

Well meaning people have said, often with great passion, that it is wrong to oppose those who hold a Creationist world view. Ideas are sacred, the argument goes, and it is not right for those who accept

230

evolution and scientific laws to ridicule and mock those who believe in creation by a deity. Both sides are part of what such folks understand as 'cultural wars.'

It is impossible to describe, or even imagine, just how dangerous this attitude can be. The seeds of Post-Modernism have fallen upon naïve and fertile ground.

All ideas are *not* of equal value or merit. They simply *are not*. Things cannot be made foolproof, because fools are so ingenious. Imagine for a moment a school in which all ideas have equal purchase. A precious godly child's certainties that the Baby Jesus and Santa Clause are real, and that storks bring babies, should be given equal consideration in politically correct public schools as the views of some Camp Quest-infected secular child who has other explanations for Christmas, for the disappearance of the milk and cookies, and for the appearance of baby sister.

The ultimate aim of the wedge of Creationism is *not* to promulgate an alternative scientific theory to Evolution. The aim of the proponents is to promulgate their understanding of the Christian religion and to establish a theocracy: to "Win America for Christ." Lying when the truth will do is no problem. Knowingly disregarding, distorting, or destroying evidence is also fine, because, in their world view, if the facts contradict the dogma, the facts lose. Reason is seen as something harmful that should be avoided. As Martin Luther is said to have observed, "Whoever wants to be a Christian should tear the eyes out of his Reason."

On Memorial Day, May 28, 2007, "Answers in Genesis" opened a sideshow called "Creation Museum" in Northern Kentucky. It cost 27 million dollars and was paid for by the faithful who want the myth taught — to the exclusion of scientific facts — that the earth is about 6,000 years old, that dinosaurs and humans lived at the same time, that the myth of Noah's Ark is literally true, that all animals were vegetarians prior to the magically created Adam and Eve gaining knowledge of good and evil, and that accepting science instead of this fairy tale leads to all of the perceived evils of the world, including abortion, homosexuality, and, worst of all, Atheism.

People from many different organizations and orientations, believers and non-believers, came from many different places to stand with one mind outside of the gates of the Creation Museum to let

Edwin F. Kagin: *Baubles of Blasphemy*

the world know that the childish world views being therein vended are not shared by all good people, as the creationists would have the world believe. And the world was there. The press from many nations took note that many people, of many differing views, had, at their own expense, come together to bring a message that wrongheaded and dangerous religious nonsense, while lawful to present, is not something that cannot be lawfully endorsed by the state and that faith in absurd things is not only sad, it is dangerous. "Rally for Reason" let the world know that everyone was not playing in the sandbox of the Arkonuts. See: www.rallyforreason.com

Ignorance is a form of terrorism. Teaching children to accept magical ways of explaining reality is child abuse. Persons so conditioned might, in some future Katrina, spend their time praying that the levees hold rather than getting off of their knees and repairing the levees. Such persons will then see themselves as victims. Not victims of their deadly doctrines, but perhaps of some god displeased because they had not killed off the Atheists within their midst.

Belief can create a kind of filter across the stream of information that enters the mind. Imagine that articles of faith are the size of BBs and that scientific facts are the size of marbles. A Fundangelical filter is set to stop anything larger than the BBs. Therefore, the filter automatically permits the BBs to enter the mind but stops the marbles. They simply do not get through. Dare we say that Creationism causes believers to lose their marbles?

The Rally for Reason was wildly successful, far beyond the expectations of the organizers. There was of course criticism and mocking from some who did not think the Rally was a good idea. "Well," someone said, "why didn't you go out and protest against the anniversary party for the alien spaceship crashing at Roswell?" "Isn't creationism so self evidently wrong that you only advertise it by protesting against this museum?"

Yes, of course the idea of aliens at Roswell is dumb. But such is not based on religious doctrine that the proponents want taught in public schools. And the errors of creationism have already persuaded a huge proportion of Americans to reject science for faith, for belief in things hoped for and for the assurance of things not seen. If no

232

objection is made, the faithful can correctly say, to people who make laws, that no one seems to object.

If those who are peddling the snake oil of Creationism, or its womb mate Intelligent Design, have their way, the foundations upon which the Enlightenment, and hence the modern world, are built and sustained will be weakened and perhaps destroyed. The attempt to replace science with superstition endangers the very underpinnings of knowledge. Unchecked and unchallenged, ignorance could wash over us with a fury greater than that of any mere physical tsunami. Our race could, within a generation, be once again in a dark age, gaining 'knowledge' from priests and supernatural revelations. In such a world, as in the past darkness of our species, reason and critical thinking could be punished in most barbaric ways.

All of human history can be seen as people standing in one of two great lines, two queues. In one line are those who, regardless of race, sex, nation, or religious belief, seek progress, exploration, rationality, and knowledge, those who accept objective truths, and who seek to improve the situation of creatures occupying our world. In the other line are those who hold that faith and magic are more important than science and reason, those who seek to repress any contradictions to their beliefs, those who have tried, and who are now trying, to impose their religious views on the people in the other line. They have been successful in the past. They can be successful again.

Creationism is, in a very real sense, ground zero in the American Religious Civil War. This is not simply a cultural war. This is a war for the survival of a way of life and for a view of the universe that can yet take us to the stars. If the Wedge works, if Creationism is accepted by the state as something that can be properly taught as science, then the ARCW will be lost. Everything else that is needed to create a complete theocracy will follow. Truly a 'domino theory.' The Fundangelicals realize this.

The battle is not over. It has only been joined. Quite literally, the fate of civilization awaits the outcome.

Which line are you in?

Baby Jesus Meets
the
Three-Reindeer Rule

Presented December 17, 2005
American Atheists Solstice Bash
Clark, New Jersey

Thank you your Glory, and good afternoon sinners!

The body count in the American Religious Civil War is mounting. Her Glory has succeeded, in conspiracy with the Chief Homosexual, in joining the Atheist Agenda with the Homosexual Agenda to drive god, like a whipped dog, from the classrooms and from the public squares of our land. An apparent clear victory for the Atheiosexual Agenda!

But the forces of tyranny neither slumber nor sleep, and even now, at this solstice season, are intent on imposing their mythology on the conspirators of the irreligious, on those aided by godless activist judges who, intent on forcing upon a free people the radical doctrine of "Separation of State and Church," have ordered that the idols of the whipped dog god not be displayed on public property unless the sacred be modulated and debased by myths of the secular.

And thus we arrive at our message for today, "Baby Jesus Meets the Three-Reindeer Rule."

What is a Baby Jesus? It is a fable. A precious little story set out in the bible about an imaginary son of god whose father god conceived him in the body of an unwed underage teenager, the goddess Virgin Mary. Maybe a god, like a man, is only as old as the woman he feels. God thus made the Baby Jesus so he could grow up and be killed as a child sacrifice to his god father for *your* sins. B.J.'s birthday is celebrated by Christians as "Christ's Mass," or Christmas, an odd holiday that is at once both completely Christian and completely secular, and the only religious celebration officially recognized by the U.S. Government as a legal holiday.

Kagin's Second Coming

Pious Christians think we have always celebrated Christmas. Not so. Those cute Pilgrims little kids color in Sunday School, while there parents are in the sanctuary learning to be more judgmental, banned Christmas. Congress met on December 25th. It was a regular business day. Until Queen Victoria hauled a tree into her palace, Charles Dickens wrote about Scrooge and delicate little Tiny Tim whining "God bless us every one," Reverend Clement Moore wrote "A Visit From St. Nicholas," incorrectly called "The Night Before Christmas," and Frank Church lied to a child in his letter "Yes, Virginia, there is a Santa Claus." Add the Thomas Nash drawings in *Harper's Weekly*, and a few more things, and the modern Christmas, made to look ancient, was up and snorting.

Among the new fake ancient symbols of a Christmas heritage that never was is the beloved crèche, or manger scene. This is a manufact of three-dimensional, living or fake figures representing the Baby Jesus in a feed trough, surrounded by his mother the teenage goddess Virgin Mary, his cuckolded wannabe father, Joseph, sheep, shepherds, lambs, sheep crooks in the shape of candy canes, a star, angels, a cow, a jackass, some straw, and three terrorists with camels bearing gifts to the 'Christ Child.' Point of grammar. The terrorists are bearing the *gifts*. The *camels* are bearing the terrorists. A creationist version of the sacred scene includes a stegosaurus. This godly diorama is often offered on public property in open violation of the First Amendment.

The problems, legal, historical, and theological, with such displays are many and varied, and beyond the ken of many believers. 'Traditional' manger scenes are not correct even from the text of the holy mythology. The Second Commandment prohibits the making or worshiping of graven images or likenesses of living things. Roman Catholics, who like to worship graven images, are exempt because they simply delete the Second Commandment, thereby sidestepping that little problem. Others ignore it, as well as the contradictory images presented in the display that impossibly merge the biblical gospels of Luke and Matthew.

In the book of Luke, the pregnant teenager and the cuckold travel from their home in Nazareth, in Galilee, to Bethlehem, in Judah, where the child of the god is born and laid in a food trough, and angels appear to sheep herders who go to the food trough to worship the god

235

child. One of the angels was named *Herald*. You know, "Hark, the Herald angel sings." After this, the "Holy Family" goes back home to Nazareth and we hear nothing more about B.J. for the next twelve years or so. In the book of Matthew, the teenager and the cuckold and the Baby Jesus live in Bethlehem all along, and the terrorists get to their house when B.J. is no longer a baby but a child about two years old. The terrorists have been following a star that comes to rest above the B.J.'s house, apparently visible to everyone but King Herod who asks the terrorists where the kid is, and when they don't tell him evil King Herod kills all the two year old little boys in Bethlehem, except B.J., who has fled in the company of the teenager and the cuckold to Egypt until Herod is dead and then they relocate in Nazareth, where we hear nothing more about B.J. for the next twelve years or so. That's what the bible says. And it doesn't say there were three terrorists, just that there were terrorists "from the East."

Moving right along in this educational adventure, a Christmas reindeer is a phantasmagorical volitant ungulate. Sort of a Pegasus with a rack and no wings, like my ex-wife. Eight of them, excluding the pretender Rudolph, pull the flying sleigh of one *Santa*, an anagram for 'Satan,' around the world to provide reward and gifts to proper children, and shame and ashes to evil ones, before the dawn of Christmas morn. We should note that according to Rev. Clement Moore, Santa is a smoker. This pagan myth is set out more fully in my monograph "On Christmas, or, No, Virginia, There Is No Santa Claus," contained in my book *Baubles of Blasphemy*, available at a most reasonable price in this very room for those lucky enough to be able to obtain one of the limited copies now available. Disappointed seekers can obtain one on my Web-site www.edwinkagin.com. What good is it to speak for no pay if one cannot engage in some small bit of shameless self-promotion?

But I digress. It is just plain not lawful for the state to display religious symbols, like a crèche, no matter what the Fundangelicals think and what they would like to change our history to reflect. But it *is* lawful to display secular symbols like Santa and reindeer, which have nothing whatsoever to do with the Baby Jesus. So, for a number of years, city officials, desiring to unlawfully promote the Christian religion on public property with public funds, have put a plaster or plastic Baby Jesus and other Christmas religious images on public squares and have gotten sued by humorless outfits like us and the ACLU. This occurred in Cincinnati. The city put up a display of Baby Jesus and company on Fountain Square in the middle of downtown. Some Jews then got city permission to put up a menorah. The Ku Klux Klan then wanted to put up a KKK cross, got denied the right to do so by the city, sued, and won. They put up a cross. The cross got trashed. There was a lot of ugliness, and so the Free Inquiry Group put up a 'Wall of Separation,' with that quote from Tom Jefferson. To settle the squabble, the constitutional methodology developed that public forums have to either keep it all out or let it all in. Rather than save much time and money by the most reasonable solution of keeping it all out of the public square, and letting people do whatever they were big enough to do on their own property, most communities decided to waste the little money they had on lawyers to try to continue to promote religion in public with public funds. Thus developed the compromise in the law, created by those activist judges, that has come to be known as 'The Three Reindeer Rule.' Basically put, this means that if there are enough secular images of Christmas in public displays at Christmas time, like three plastic reindeer, then you can add the Baby Jesus without doing violence to the Constitution or running afoul of the law. Put another way, Baby Jesus is religious but reindeer are not.

For the intellectually curious or compulsive, the U.S. Supreme Court case that created the rule is *Lynch v. Donnelley,* 465 U.S. 668 (1984). The legal term for the test, known informally as the three reindeer rule, is the 'endorsement test.' In a concurring opinion, and as the controlling swing vote, Justice O'Conner stated that, as she saw it, the "central issue" in the *Lynch* case was whether the city "endorsed Christianity by its display of the crèche." This legal reasoning is in line with the earlier three-prong *Lemon* test, of *Lemon v. Kurtzman,* 42 U.S. 602 (1971). Mr. Lemon has spoken to American Atheists. Under the *Lemon* test, courts should determine "whether the challenged law or conduct has a secular purpose, whether its principal or primary effect is to advance or inhibit religion, and whether it creates an excessive entanglement of government with religion." In *Lynch,* Justice O'Connor found that the crèche, set up by the city, was

Edwin F. Kagin: *Baubles of Blasphemy*

placed among enough other objects that were secular in nature, like a Santa Claus House, reindeer, a Christmas tree, colored lights, *etc.* to get around the obvious fact that the city was trying to establish a religion. Baby Jesus a secular display indeed! And thus doth the Baby Jesus meet the Three Reindeer Rule. And that, beloved, is how your city government can legally put Christ back into Christmas. After all, the law has to kinda act like it is trying to be fair, doesn't it?

A real test of whether some city is trying to establish a religion or not, by their public property displays of Baby Jesus and company around the Winter Solstice, would be to see if the city would be willing to put up everything but the Jesus part. Suggest that to your preacher and watch him ring them bells.

If you think this explanation of current controlling law does not make sense, you are of course correct. It does not make sense, any more than the recent twin rulings of the Supreme Court make sense that you can't put up the Ten Commandments in public places in Kentucky but you can display them publicly on a monument in Texas. Yes, there are distinctions. But these may well be distinctions without differences. At least the legal rule is easier to understand than the doctrine of the Trinity.

This year Christmas falls on a Sunday. But even Christians know the *real* reason for the season. That's why churches will be closed this Christmas, so people can be at home celebrating the gifts of Santa the Claus and his reindeer. What a delightful way to put Christ back into Christmas. After all, the family that plays together stays together. That's how it goes, isn't it?

Reply to My Son

Dad,

Someone sent me this. I would be curious to know your opinion on the statement below. Do you think it is accurate?

Stephen

* * *

How Long Do We Have? About the time our original thirteen states adopted their new constitution in 1787, Alexander Tyler, a Scottish history professor at the University of Edinburgh, had this to say about the fall of the Athenian Republic some 2,000 years earlier: "A democracy is always temporary in nature; it simply cannot exist as a permanent form of government." A democracy will continue to exist up until the time that voters discover they can vote themselves generous gifts from the public treasury. "From that moment on, the majority always vote for the candidates who promise the most benefits from the public treasury, with the result that every democracy will finally collapse due to loose fiscal policy, which is always followed by a dictatorship." The average age of the world's greatest civilizations from the beginning of history, has been about 200 years." During those 200 years, those nations always progressed through the following sequence: 1. From bondage to spiritual faith; 2. From spiritual faith to great courage; 3. From courage to liberty; 4. From liberty to abundance; 5. From abundance to complacency; 6. From complacency to apathy; 7. From apathy to dependence; 8. From dependence back into bondage.

Edwin F. Kagin: *Baubles of Blasphemy*

Professor Joseph Olson of Hemline University School of Law, St. Paul, Minnesota [*Editor's note: 'Hemline University' does not exist, but there is a Hamline University*], points out some interesting facts concerning the 2000 Presidential election: Number of States won by: Gore: 19; Bush: 29. Square miles of land won by: Gore: 580,000; Bush: 2,427,000 Population of counties won by: Gore: 127 million; Bush: 143 million. Murder rate per 100,000 residents in counties won by: Gore: 13.2; Bush: 2.1 Professor Olson adds: 'In aggregate, the map of the territory Bush won was mostly the land owned by the taxpaying citizens of this great country. Gore's territory mostly encompassed those citizens living in government-owned tenements and living off various forms of government welfare...' Olson believes the United States is now somewhere between the 'complacency and apathy' phase of Professor Tyler's definition of democracy, with some forty percent of the nation's population already having reached the 'governmental dependency' phase. If Congress grants amnesty and citizenship to twenty million criminal invaders called illegal and they vote, then we can say goodbye to the USA in fewer than five years. If you are in favor of this then delete this message. If you are not then pass this along to help everyone realize just how much is at stake, knowing that apathy is the greatest danger to our freedom.

Thanks for reading.

* * *

Stephen,

Thank you for sending me this. I have seen it in various forms before and, with a critical election just a few days away, I would like to attempt to reply.

The writing is so inherently illogical, and indeed stupid, that it is somewhat difficult to formulate a reply. But I shall try.

The basic assumption appears to be that civilizations rise on the basis of "spiritual faith" and that they then lose such faith and decline into the "bondage" from which they came. This comes about because the citizens of the democracy become apathetic and vote benefits for themselves that they have not won through the "great courage" that comes from their former "spiritual faith." As voters elect people who will vote them more goodies they do not deserve, the democracy will collapse because of "loose fiscal policy," and a "dictatorship" will follow. Good hard working people, presumably of "spiritual faith," who pay taxes and built our country, voted for Bush. Lazy, useless people who want to spend money on the people of the country, and are concerned about such nonsense as safe air, food, and water, overpopulation, and the earth overheating and dying, voted for Gore. To make things much worse, those living in 'governmental dependency' want to grant citizenship to illegal aliens who will then be able to vote. As a result of this, the USA will be gone within five years.

There, I think that is about what the writer is saying, isn't it? Bottom line, of course, is that voters should vote for a Bush type person rather than for a Gore-type person if they want to save the country.

The only thing in the writing with which I agree is that civilizations have an average life span of about 200 years. Ours is on the verge of collapse. But not for the reasons the writer asserts. The real reasons are much the same as those that have caused earlier civilizations to fail. Among these things are:

1)   Like other civilizations that have fallen, the present leaders of our country vote benefits for themselves and their friends while cutting off those things that have made us a great nation, such as funds for scientific research, keeping our roads and bridges repaired, and maintaining quality public schools and education.

2)   Like other civilizations that have fallen, the present leaders of our country have engaged in wars of aggression in far away places that deplete our treasury and other resources, weaken us in the eyes of other nations, make us wide-spread enemies, and spread our armies too thin to defend our homeland.

3)   Friends of the present leaders, who have large incomes and great fortunes, have had their taxes cut, while those least able to pay have had their taxes raised and are denied a fair minimum wage. Programs that help people, such as medical care for sick children, are cut out to make more money for the friends of those in power.

4)   All government expenditures and actives are directed toward making money for friends of the people in power, thereby weakening our country overall. Friends of the government profit, through things like "Blackwater," a private mercenary company, that has more people in Iraq guarding our army for high pay than we have real army personnel in Iraq dying for low pay. All persons in this project are required to sign an unconstitutional loyalty oath accepting fundamentalist Christian values as a condition of employment. Private business friends of the people in power grow ever richer on our country's wars. This is essentially treason.

5)   The constitutional separation between state and church that has led to our country's greatness has been eroded at every opportunity. As things get worse, the louder the leaders yell "God" and assert they are acting under orders from God. Somehow, our nation managed to get thought two world wars without "God" on the money or in the Pledge. The corrupt leaders send out the message, believed by fools, that to be against them and their treasonous practices is to be against God.

6)   The illegal aliens about which the friends of the current leadership complain were unlawfully brought into our country by the friends of the current leadership to unlawfully work at unlawful wages on which the friends of the current leadership did not have to pay taxes or pay for benefits of which they now complain.

7)   Dissent is cut off. Protests can only occur in approved "Free Speech Zones," when our entire country should be a free speech zone. Criticism of traitors in power is defined by the traitors in power as helping our enemies. Prosecutors who prosecute officials who abuse power and break the law are fired. News sources are threatened. People are not permitted to see news coverage of the war the corrupt leaders started to make money for their friends, nor are people allowed to see the bodies of the dead being returned to be buried. The needs of injured veterans of the illegal war are ignored to make more money for the friends of those in power.

8)   As things get ever worse, in order to maintain power and control, blame for the problems is placed everywhere except on the leaders who have sent much of our nation's business to China and to other countries to make money for the friends of those in power, who have caused our children to be killed in unlawful wars so they can make money, who do not pay taxes on money made in other countries and who have the taxes they do pay cut. The money that should go to workers in our country has gone to other countries so the friends of those in power can make more money by paying less in wages and benefits, while the citizens of our country lose their jobs, their homes, their security, and their lives.

9)   As people in our country have fewer jobs and less money, to make money for the friends of the people in power, gasoline prices are raised, insurance costs go up while the insurance companies are permitted to pay less and less on legitimate claims. Those who insist that they receive benefits

they have earned, and that their government has promised them, are dismissed as "liberals," and money they seek, that is theirs by right and by law, is scorned by those in power as "entitlements."

10) Regulations that once provided for clearer air, purer food, safer trucks, keeping bridges in repair, etc. are repealed or ignored, and so people are killed, bridges collapse and millions will suffer poverty in their old age. All of this is so that the friends of those in power can make more money, despite things they see as unimportant, like global warming, ignorant children, lack of health care, and lack of provision for an aging population.

And thus will our society in fact self destruct. The people in power will blame the fall not on themselves, but on a lack of religion as defined by them. The fault will be some god's punishment, rather than a failure to build adequate levees, bridges, or whatever else is coming unglued.

VOTE ON ELECTION DAY.
DON'T VOTE FOR THE BEST PERSON.
VOTE FOR THE LEAST UNDESIRABLE PERSON WHO CAN BE ELECTED.

Perhaps, just perhaps, it is not too late.

Love,

Dad.

In Re: Dead Pope
April 2, 2005

That pope, who assumed the name of John Paul II (J2P2 for the sarcastically inclined), avoiding April Fool's Day died today — April 2, 2005 — right on schedule, in time for the nightly news and Sunday sermons, with an audience waiting outside his window, and the press waiting at their delivery systems. Today, prior to his death, the electronic news, and even the morning newspapers, were speaking of him in the past tense. If he had not died today, there would have been inconveniences.

Opposed to birth control. Opposed to the rights of gays. Opposed to the rights of women. Opposed to the right to have an abortion. He made a virtue of human suffering, rather than working for meaningful ways to prevent human suffering. He sought ways to deal with the persistent problem of so many priests of his church raping children—mostly same-sex children. Perhaps he could have suggested that they obey the law. He exonerated Galileo, and he apologized to Jewish people for his church having not condemned, and maybe even having helped, their un-excommunicated communicant Adolph Hitler.

Many of the faithful thought he was correct in all things. And they obeyed him. Except when he condemned capital punishment and the war in Iraq. The pope, they figured, got it wrong on those—that abortion is god-prohibited murder, but that killing people in prisons and on battlefields is fine no matter what the Vicar of Christ had to say on such matters. The just-today-dead Supreme Pontiff also thought the teaching of evolution was okay. Many think he was wrong on that too, and that they are more qualified to decide where people came from than the chief primate.

The President of the United States is lowering the flag of our country to half staff for this foreign religious leader who is also the head of a foreign state. Our American President said his god sent this person as a "hero for the ages." There is talk of making him a saint. He made more people saints than any other previous pope.

245

Edwin F. Kagin: *Baubles of Blasphemy*

He reinstituted, after a lapse of some centuries, teachings on how to perform exorcisms. Apparently, demon possession is on the upswing.

At least the news put the aftermath of the Terri Schiavo death on the back burner.

Vatican Hill in Rome had been the headquarters of the religion of Mithraism prior to Christianity being made the official religion of the Roman Empire in 325 C.E. Now you know why the home of the pope is called "The Vatican."

One might muse just why the Vatican has not been required to register as a foreign lobby when its leaders are attempting to force their views into American laws and to force our lawmakers to vote as the Vatican thinks they should. And just why the representatives of the Holy See are not charged with a crime when they try to intimidate voters into voting for persons thought acceptable to the faith.

Did you know that before a Pope is pronounced dead, he is smashed in the head with a silver hammer to make sure? My Helen, the doctor, says, "Why didn't they use a stethoscope?"

Why didn't they do a lot of things differently? If they had, we might inhabit the stars by now.

A replacement Pope will be selected soon. Watch for the white smoke. If you don't know what that means, you are about to find out.

Edwin

On Five Deaths and a Wedding

It has been a good fortnight for death.

Lots of people other than those herein discussed—people the T.V.-watching public has never heard of and care nothing about—doubtless died during this past fortnight. People like Saul Bellow, Noble Prize-winning author, who died Tuesday, April 5, 2005 at age 89. But those dead folks are not the subject of this blasphemy. Someone may care about them and someone else may even write about them. Everyone can be written about when they die if someone is willing to pay for it.

At the beginning of the fortnight of dying, my Helen and I traveled to the American Atheists convention in Philadelphia. The convention, complete with demonstrators against us, magnificently graced the home of American freedom the weekend of March 25–27, 2005. From the time we left our Kentucky home, all of the news seemed to be about people dying. The famous and those made famous without their consent. As we discussed Atheism that Easter weekend, others used the law and the politics of power to force the faith of their fathers on others. To violate our Constitution. To use the death of others to force a theocracy on a free people.

We loved the convention. I signed copies of my book "Baubles of Blasphemy," which was being sold in the bookroom. We met many new people and saw old friends. I was on a panel discussion Friday afternoon, March 25, 2005. Afterwards, I had an appointment to finally meet a lovely and brilliant 17 year old girl named Emily Blaine in the lobby of the hotel at 5:00 pm. We had engaged in correspondence on matters involving Atheists and Atheism. She seemed wise far beyond her years, and she had registered at the convention. In anticipation of the opportunity of encountering a young Elizabeth Cady Stanton or a young Margaret Sanger, my Helen and I went to the lobby at the agreed upon time, but Emily was a no-show. This is not unusual in our world. That evening, Helen and I were awarded the American Atheist's award of Atheists of the Year. We were surprised, honored, and delighted. This great honor was totally unexpected.

Edwin F. Kagin: *Baubles of Blasphemy*

But the larger outside world seemed obsessed with other things, things far less Atheist friendly. A woman named Terri Shiavo lay dying in Florida, after her feeding tube had been removed. Her brain no longer existed. Her body, deprived of what makes us human, continued to live with artificial assistance from science. A judge found that she would not want to continue to live that way, with no hope of ever again being the aware person she had been fifteen years ago.

The Fundangelicals who want to govern our lives in all details went into a feeding frenzy. They passed breathtakingly unconstitutional legislation to make a Federal Court judge review the decision of the Florida trial and appeals court because they didn't like the well reasoned rulings of lawfully established courts. The Federal Judge disagreed with the Fundangelicals and refused to order the feeding tube reinserted into the hapless woman's abdomen. The United States Court of Appeals also refused to modify the law, humanity, and common sense to suit the ignorance and arrogance of religious fanatics. Those who had crawled out from under the rocks of history to attempt to dominate us, in a manner rejected some years ago in Philadelphia, thereupon announced that "we need judicial reform." This means that religious fanatics thought it necessary to get rid of judges who follow the law. That is so the fanatics can set ways to forge into law for all of us that which they say should be the law for all of us.

Terri Shiavo, age 41, died Thursday, March 31, 2005.

D. James Kennedy, of Coral Ridge Ministries, Ft. Lauderdale, Florida, a known liar for god, said that Ms. Shiavo should have been sent home with her parents and that they could have fed her. Because, said Rev. Liar, she could chew and swallow. If she could have done that, the case would never have seen a courtroom.

Pope John Paul II, died on Saturday, April 2, 2005 at the age of 84. He was the leader of a branch of the Christian religion called 'Roman Catholic.' This is a religion that replaced other religions in Rome in 325 C.E. The headquarters of the religion is in a place called Vatican City, an enclave within the city of Rome, Italy, and the site of the headquarters of the religion of Mithraism which it replaced.

Millions of humans prayed prayers for the Pope both before and after he was dead. It is unclear just why. Did they pray that, as in the case of Terri Shiavo, the will of their god be thwarted and that that god not call his servant home? Or were the prayers to entreat the god to welcome John Paul II into Heaven? If J2P2 is not welcome, then who is? And what about predestination? Never mind, that is a Protestant thing—like the Second Commandment forbidding graven images (not guns).

The dead pontiff doomed millions to pain and starvation by solidly condemning any attempts to initiate, in any country on Earth, birth control or family planning. A Catholic hospital would doubtless have ignored, for perceived moral reasons, Terri Shiavo's wish to not be kept alive by artificial means in a manner clearly contrary to Jehovah's plan that she die some fifteen years previously. His deceased holiness also condemned those humans of gay orientation. Yet the rules were somewhat less stringent when applied to homosexual rape of children by priests of his church. If gold rusts, what will iron do?

The departed Vicar of Christ was a mystic. He was a follower of St. John of the Cross. This means he thought suffering was good for you. Maybe that explains his tolerance for the plight of buggered little boys and sunken-eyed starving children. St. John of the Cross was a buddy of the original St. Teresa and a follower of a much earlier mystic named Origen who castrated himself because Jesus had suggested it would be a good idea to do so if one could bear (not bare) it. Admiration of this practice seems confined to celibate clerics, and is not generally extended as a meaningful option elsewhere.

American flags are, by Presidential decree, to be flown at half staff for this religious leader whose underlings told Americans what laws to pass and what lawmakers to vote for, under proscribed punitive supernatural proscriptions.

A million people were in the viewing line when the doors were barred to further traffic. Those lucky enough to be still in line at closing time had about a 24 hour wait to see the corpse of the Pontiff.

His Holiness was a good person in the worst sense of the word. And the President of the United States is going to attend his long-procrastinated funeral, along with lots of other important people in the government of our country. This is the same President who flew back to Washington to sign the special legislation passed by the faithful to interfere with the Catholic god's plan, and with the rule of law, and with the separation of powers mandated by the Constitution of the United States, in trying to keep Terri Shiavo alive for base motives. Our President called the dead pope, "one of history's great moral leaders." Guess it takes one to know one.

Johnnie L. Cochran, Jr. died Tuesday, March 29, 2005 at age 67. He was a lawyer who successfully defended O.J. Simpson in a double murder charge. Everyone but the jury seems to know that his client was guilty. Johnnie Cochran made lots of money. He died of a brain tumor. O.J. is still looking on golf courses for the true murderers.

Prince Rainier III, the sovereign prince of Monaco, died Wednesday, April 6, 2005 at age 81. He had been married to Grace Kelly, an American actress. Lots of people, including the Prince, thought she was the most beautiful woman in the world. She was killed in a car wreck on September 14, 1982 at age 52.

Sic transit gloria mundi.

Now please don't get hysterical and think that everybody is dying. Because they aren't. There are a lot of people still left to die.

The wedding? Prince Charles, future king of England and Defender of the Faith, was scheduled to marry his mistress on Friday, March 8, 2005. He was divorced from his last wife, Princess Diana, in August of 1996. Princess Diana died in a car crash in Paris, France on August 31, 1997 at age 36. Prince Charles was at a castle in Scotland when he heard the news. My Helen and I were at a nudist camp in Indiana when we heard the news.

The last king of England who married a divorced woman, King Edward VIII, had to abdicate his throne. Maybe the rules have changed. But then the abdicating king was marrying not only a divorcee but an American. And remember that Charles ain't king yet. Defender of the Faith indeed!

But this connubial celebration to repair certain Seventh Commandment lapses by the parties thereto has now been delayed for yet a little while in consequence of that pope's funeral which, while not scheduled for nearly as long in advance—at least not in this world— has taken over top billing. Despite certain most public deviations in the pointer on the moral compass, Jesus ordained rules, as interpreted by those who claim accurate knowledge, dictating abstinence until marriage will no doubt prevail. In that such codes are so shiningly successful for teenagers and priests, surely they should work as well as cold showers for future kings. Never mind those cynics who say that there will be plenty of time for that abstinence stuff after marriage. I never met any of these people. But then they didn't meet me either.

Oh, yes! The fifth death.

On Saturday, March 26, 2005, I received an email via laptop in our hotel room in Philadelphia from Emily Blaine's father. Emily had died in a car wreck on Thursday, March 24, 2005, the day before we were to meet her.

Her's was the only death I mourned.

Have a beautiful day.

Edwin

Edwin F. Kagin: *Baubles of Blasphemy*

ARCW Field Report

Subject: URGENT. New Treasonous Assault on Separation of State and Church.

Field Report
Battle of Kentucky
American Religious Civil War (ARCW)
April 27, 2000

To those undisclosed recipients who still believe in religious freedom:

I have given my word not to reveal the sources for this information, but I assure you that it is true.

In Boone County, Kentucky, county officials have entered into a treasonous conspiracy to exempt "ordained ministers," living and working in Boone County, Kentucky, from paying the Boone County Occupational Tax. This is the county where the chief executive officer hangs on a cross at Easter time.

The stated purpose of their conspiracy to violate our constitution, and to put the favored group above the law, is to "protect First Amendment rights to freedom of religious expression." This is the same reason given for the passage of that previously reported unconstitutional special rights religious favoritism legislation, the "Camp Quest Law," HB 70.

The planned special rights exemption from the tax laws--that all others must obey--applies only to "ordained" ministers, thereby excluding all other religious leaders, like any Jewish Rabbi, or any non-ordained minister or priest of any religion that does not require "ordination." Also excluded will be anyone else who earns a living in the county who is not an ordained minister.

252

Under this latest brazen attempt to more quickly establish the theocracy they seek to impose upon us, everyone but ordained ministers will have to act like citizens and pay the county occupational tax. Only ordained ministers may, with impunity, keep all of their income. Only ordained ministers will not be required by the law to render unto Caesar that which is Caesar's.

This is being done quietly, with no fuss. Those believed to be setting up this system, like the County Judge Executive, and the County Administrator, don't even seem to be changing the written law--they just won't be collecting the occupational tax (used for the benefit of public schools) from the treasonably favored group.

It is believed, if it is not already being done, that this proposed First Amendment violation is to be implemented soon in Boone County, Kentucky.

It is further believed that a similar un-American violation of our laws and of our American way of life has already been implemented in Kenton County, Kentucky.

People get the kind of government they deserve. If we elect religious fanatics to public office, we get religious fanatics in public office.

Respectfully submitted:

Edwin F. Kagin
Kentucky Colonel
ARCW

Edwin F. Kagin: *Baubles of Blasphemy*

Kentucky Legislature Battlefield

Editor
The Kentucky Post
Covington, Kentucky
February 4, 2000

Dear Editor,

The American Religious Civil War (ARCW) appears to have chosen the floor of the Kentucky Legislature for its most recent battlefield. The un-American forces at work to destroy our freedoms must be defeated if the future Daughters of the ARCW are to celebrate victory for democracy over the theocracy that threatens our liberties on several fronts.

Already certain of our Kentucky legislators, who appear appallingly ignorant of history, of theology, and of constitutional principles, have passed laws giving special rights to religious sects that are unreasonable, unconscionable, and unconstitutional. More unjust laws await their treasonous approval, to be followed in due course by the inquisitions and heresy trials that will inevitably be required to insure their implementation.

Those who do not know history are dooming Kentucky to repeat its mistakes. Those who do not know theology are making a mockery of the Sermon on the Mount, the Parable of the Good Samaritan, and the very idea of a God of love. Those who do not know constitutional principles are acting as if Section 5 of the Kentucky Constitution does not say that no person's civil rights shall be diminished because of disbelief in any religious dogma. Whether through ignorance or disloyalty to their oaths, they tread with impiety on the graves of our martyrs.

How dare they declare religion exempt from laws others must obey? How dare they define religion to suit themselves? How dare they give special rights to religion and make religious rules the laws for We the People?

A lot of blood was shed to stop their kind from doing that in the past. Don't forget this. We have far too many important things to do than to go through it all again.

Edwin F. Kagin

Restoring Freedom to Kentucky's Churches

Editor, The Kentucky Post
Covington, Kentucky
March 15, 2000

Dear Editor,

One might well ponder just how the Kentucky Legislature might actually attempt to pass an unconstitutional law to establish a religion in our Commonwealth, and just how such an unconstitutional law would look.

For have not our legislators—those sworn to uphold our Constitution and our American way of life—told us it is not religious discrimination to let churches exclude children who do not share their beliefs from renting camp property otherwise available for rent by the public? This is merely to "restore freedom to Kentucky's churches" we are told—it is not to discriminate on the basis of religion. If that were so, then language has no meaning. How would a bill look if its purpose *were* to discriminate? If no person or organization ever discriminated, we would have no need for a civil rights law, for everyone who wants to discriminate against others wants the 'freedom' to do so, much as criminals want the freedom to commit crimes. The very reason we have laws is to prevent this twisted moral and linguistic thinking from being recognized as lawful, accepted social behavior.

We are further informed by our elected lawmakers that posting the Ten Commandments in public schools is not an act in furtherance of the unlawful establishment of a religion, but is rather an attempt to teach public school children the historical role of religion in American public life. If we were to post along with this "non-religious Decalogue" — that tells us what god to

256

worship and when and how to worship that god — the unanimous declaration of the U.S. Senate, in Treaty with Tripoli, signed by President John Adams on June 10, 1797 — stating that "...the government of the United States of America is not in any sense founded on the Christian Religion" — then such an assertion might not appear the lying self-righteous attempt to establish a religion that it clearly is.

Those legislators who are unable to name the Ten Commandments, but who seem to think that this code of Bronze Age nomads will work as a magic talisman to prevent violence and foster morality, might well inform us how teaching children by example that it is perfectly all right to flout the Constitution of the United States and the Supreme Court of the United States—that have expressly forbidden what they are treasonably attempting—will further a general respect for the rule of law in our Commonwealth.

And let them tell us what the prohibition against establishing a religion means to them?

Edwin F. Kagin

Is Black Slavery a Myth?
April 1, 2006

Noted historian Dr. Felix von Krautschimer has determined that the notion taught in history classes that black slavery once existed in the American South is a myth. "Yankee liberals invented the whole lying thing," Krautschimer said at a recent talk at the Moore Centre for Clear Thinking in Sperm Bank, Georgia where he presented his controversiant antecaesarian artatype.

The conundrumian revisional theory has aroused some obliquity against its creator from the usual suspects. But the Reverent Guilder Smelt, of the Mail Me More Money Miracle Mission Movement's "7 Ms Club," conversely said Krautschimer is a "great American" who has "corrected bad history," claiming "the detractors are just in it for the money and are in cahoots with evilness people and scum who like to agitate against those who love God and recognize the fallacy of the hyperbola." According to Rev. Smelt, "They have faked the evidence, going far enough to build fake chains and cabins and stuff along the river to make it look like there was something that we know wasn't and couldn't have been."

It is expected that the controversy will not be settled early, in that schools have invested a lot of money in textbooks that make it look like white people once owned black people. However, given the fact that science books are soon to be changed to conform to other more revealed truths, it has been proposed that perhaps just one textbook would do that covered all things students really need to know. "We don't need revised books," said Smelt. "We need a reborn book. We need a whole new textbook that tells the truth for once."

Stay tuned.

Letter to Legislators as Proposed by Edwin
on
Student Expression of Religious Viewpoints Bill

Dear (insert title and name),

I cannot tell you how delighted we were to learn of the STUDENT EXPRESSION OF RELIGIOUS VIEWPOINTS bill now under consideration by the Texas legislature. Let me tell you why.

For some years now there has existed in the State of Texas a "by invitation only" highly secret society composed of students in the public schools who are within the top 1% of the student population as measured by intelligence and school achievement. We are fully aware that none of our members are in the Texas legislature. This is as expected. As would also be expected, persons of the required intelligence and achievement level necessary for membership in our society (which must remain unnamed) universally reject the primitive mythology of the Christian religion.

The proposed bill will permit these splendid and brilliant young people, in the words of the new law, to "express their beliefs about religion in homework, artwork, and other written and oral assignments free from discrimination based on the religious content of their submissions." Further, this remarkable piece of legislation will protect the expression of "the student's perspective on purpose, achievement, life, school, graduation, and looking forward to the future."

Thank you from all of us. We support and praise this legislation that we had doubted would ever even be proposed, much less passed. Already, some of our members and alumni are preparing discussion topics and graduation speeches in reliance upon this outstanding law. Overwhelmingly, you can expect to hear from our members as they speak and produce art from positions of leadership and achievement within their respective schools. Here are just a few of their topics:

Edwin F. Kagin: *Baubles of Blasphemy*

"Masturbation Techniques for Boys Not Dating Catholic girls."

"The Flying Spaghetti Monster—The Twin Meatballs of his Pastafarian Noodleness."

"Clitoral Resection as a Means to Female Holiness."

"Burkas for Men—A Plea for Gender Equality."

"Homoeroticism and Gratification thru Sexual Pain in the Cinematography of Mel Gibson."

"Free Love and Eroticism in Primates as a Model for Teenage Sexuality."

"Religious Crime as a Viable Career Option."

"In Praise of Pedophilia within a Celibate Priesthood."

"Cannibalism and Child Sacrifice as Foundational Sacraments of Christian Perversions."

These few samples represent only a few of the less controversial topics we can look forward to in our schools once your protective legislation has been passed into law.

Now, if you would only reconsider the age of consent. Just joking.

Thank you.

(Signed)

ON THE DONDER SOCIETY

What is truth?   —Pontius Pilate

Of the great theological disputes that surround the Christmas season, none is more pressing than the generally unknown problem presented by "The Donder Society." For the first time anywhere, critical manuscripts are here presented for public consideration and debate. The Donder papers are reproduced with the gracious permission of Mr. Donald M. Heavrin, the society's founder and president. Mr. Heavrin may be contacted at Suite One, 717 West Market Street, Louisville, Kentucky 40202. He would welcome readers' contributions to this dialogue.

December 15, 1989

This year I have organized the Donder Society. There are no meetings, there are no dues and there are no officers in the Society. In order to be a member of the Donder Society, you must remind your friends and acquaintances that the seventh reindeer's proper name is "Donder."

When Gene Autry sang "Rudolph the Red-Nosed Reindeer," he mispronounced the name and called the reindeer "Donner." Since that time, the error has been repeated in many places, including children's books, but alas, the correct name is "Donder."

You might be wondering why someone would bother with such a trivial matter, and, frankly, I was wondering the same thing myself. I am sure this will be used against me at the commitment proceedings.

Don

Edwin F. Kagin: *Baubles of Blasphemy*

December 26, 1989

Dear Mr. Heavrin:

This is in regard to your new organization, the Donder Society. Thank you for creating a problem I did not previously have. I must respectfully decline membership in the society at this time. I certainly want to do all I can to support this worthy reindeer, but I have serious misgivings that the philosophic basis of your concept may be defective.

From the prospective of this student, the reindeer "Donder and Blitzen" should be understood as a unit. The names of this brace of reindeer translates from the German as "thunder and lightning," A few moments with a good German-English Dictionary will reveal that "Donner" translates to "thunder" and "Blitzen" translates to "lightning." "Donder" does not translate to anything in any known language. All eight reindeer obviously were meant to have names that meant something, excluding, of course, that non-existent pretender, Rudolph.

If indeed, as I suspect, these reindeer are meant to represent "thunder and lightning," then "Donner" is indeed the correct spelling of the name of this noble animal.

It may be that the Rev. Clement Moore, or his printer, misspelled "Donner" as "Donder." Such an error would not be unknown to a cleric, as such people are not generally given to rational thought.

Edwin

March 9, 1990

Dear Mr. Kagin:

Thank you for your letter of December 26, 1989, and in response, I offer the following observations.

1. The Reverend Moore was an English writer, he did not own a German dictionary and he did not speak German. Do you always read English literature with a German dictionary in hand?...

2. The Reverend Moore's mother's maiden name was Sarah Donder and I have always assumed he named the reindeer after his mother.

3. The pre-Gene Autry version (Exhibit A) contains the correct spelling of the name. The post-Gene Autry version contains the incorrect spelling (Exhibit B). However, you will note on Exhibit B I have corrected the name so my children will know right from wrong.

Don

Edwin F. Kagin: *Baubles of Blasphemy*

October 3, 1990

Dear Mr. Heavrin:

From time to time, in a futile attempt to maintain a tidy desk, I go through the accumulation of materials to file the relevant and dispose of the irrelevant. Among those items destined for the paper shredder, I encountered again your letter of March 9, 1990, regarding your continued attempts to distort the correct and good name of the reindeer "Donner."

I will concede your exhibits do in fact refer to this avian mammal as "Donder." I further concede that the book "101 Famous Poems" is an excellent volume for introducing poetry to people, such as yourself, who probably were unaware that there were that many.

Having undertaken yet again an analysis of your evidence, I now perceive the basic philosophic assumption that underlies your fallacious thinking. You have assumed that the Rev. Clement Moore was correct! You should understand that the mere fact that Rev. Moore had a wife whose maiden name was Donder and erroneously placed this corruption of the true name of the reindeer in the poem in no way gives authenticity to that denomination.

As I have previously attempted to explain to you, the reindeer's correct name is "Donner." To argue otherwise is to argue that the careless cleric Moore invented the names of the reindeer, and is therefore entitled to authoritative credibility. I am certain you would not want your children or other children to believe that you would promote such an unspeakable blasphemy.

264

I can only assume that you intend to further this delusion with subsequent releases to the Donder Society this coming Christmas Season. If you elect to do so, I trust that you will provide copies of my reasoned refutations, as an addendum, to counter the whimsical belief of the gullible.

Edwin

* * * * *

On December 7, 1992, Mr. Heavrin wrote that he had discovered, to his dismay, that in 1888 and 1902 editions of the poem, the name was spelled "Dunder." Nevertheless, he has elected "to arbitrarily and capriciously declare that the correct name of the reindeer is Donder." We may never know for sure.

Grammatical Order

I once saw a mongoose and thought it quite fine
So I found a store that such beasts could consign
And resolved to order a pair of the creatures
But knew not the plural for two with such features.
So here is the message that I finally writ;
I hope they ascertain the meaning of it:
"Please enter my order for one fine mongoose
And since they seem to be of such wonderful use
Will you, while you're at it, and there is no rush,
Please send along with it another one such."

Edwin Kagin.

January 2, 2006.

Ode to Congressman Foley

A Traditional Family Values Fill-in-the-Blanks Poem
The following is provided in the interest of preserving our sacred values,
and in the interest of promoting greater poetic knowledge and skills.
Instructions: In each blank, insert one or more words to complete the stanza.
There are no correct answers.

Here's to Congressman Foley
Who for traditional values rages
While doing things unholy
With the congressional _____

It seems that this good moral man
A paragon of the righteous class
Has sought in every way he can
To take little boys up _____

Born again and sanctified
Condemning others as really sick
How many foul ways has he tried
To get some child to touch his _____

While Republicans attempt to blame
His deeds on alcohol or bad luck
"Evil" better defines the name
Of one who seeks children to _____

Where are those Christians in this hour
Who gave him the right to strut
And granted him the power
To assault a young boy's _____

Where is Rev. Phelps the godly
Who would put all gays in fear
The one who rants and acts so oddly
To prove he isn't _____

We need cleansing absolution
For our land these perverts vex
We must be freed from their delusion
That the worst moral crime is _____

ON THE PRIESTHOOD

"Fight the real enemy."

—

Sinead O'Conner, while ripping up, on national television, a color photo of His Holiness the Pope, an as yet unprohibited splendid example of the exercise of both protected speech and symbolic speech, an act roughly analogous, in public outrage, to flag burning.

Someone (who, I can't remember and apologize) observed that the priesthood originated when the first con artist met the first fool. Con artist, Priest, tells Fool what to do because Fool believes the world is run by gods, and Priest says he speaks to one or more gods who tell him what to communicate to Fool. All Fool has to do is obey the gods, *i.e.* Priest, and Fool will have better fortune, go to a pleasant immortality or indulge whatever fantasies Fool thinks can only be satisfied by Priest, acting *in loco deo*. Fool is happy, and Priest has the roast sheep, wine, treasure or whatever Fool offers to the gods through Priest.

When this scenario first began is uncertain, both in religion involved and location. It doesn't really matter. All Priesthoods work roughly the same. Certain absolutist views are held by a group of people. The Priests teach, spread, and reinforce the given myth. Every religion has its priesthood, persons learned in the often highly complex system of belief and practice that, long repeated, become the creed and ritual of the faith. Priests acquire specialized knowledge in the secrets or 'mysteries' of their religion, and in manipulation of the believers through cultic magic presented and accepted as coming from the gods.

Understandably, this power is enormous and the priesthood knows it. 'Priesthood' means a collection of priests, the females sometimes called *priestesses*. No matter how humble a priest may be, the ability to

268

instruct on the thoughts of gods and deliver the will of the supernatural carries a lot of clout.

In some societies, religions have been, and still are, one with the civil government of nations. That means the priesthood runs the country and controls people's lives. The law is the religious law, revealed to, and enforced by the priesthood. Disbelief is a crime that can get one jailed or killed. Such a government is called a *theocracy*. That's what some religious nuts want established in our country, and that's why we have the First Amendment in our Bill of Rights to stop them.

It is probably comforting to many to have on their side a select group of the elite who communicate with the deity. The system is so transparently paternalistic that some practitioners of religion actually address their priest as "father" or "mother" and a priest may respond "my children," "my son," *etc.* This artificial family may be necessary to satisfy the yearnings for family of priests, many of whom are celibate, and the need of their flock for the authority of religion and for faith in something beyond the natural world. Maybe some people are born to lead and control others; maybe some are born to follow. The con artist and the fool are found in different forms in all human interaction. The inability of the sheep to be sure which shepherd to follow leads to thousands of contradictory enclaves of religious thought. Wouldn't it be nice if any gods that be were to give a clear sign of their existence and will, like a message written on the moon, or the sky indisputably filled with angelic hosts singing hosannas? Maybe the gods enjoy watching the confusion of mortals.

At any rate, why choose any priesthood at all? What true leadership can these folks who claim to talk for gods really provide? Is there evidence of moral superiority in any priesthood that makes its members better qualified to advise on earthly and eternal matters? Actually, the behavior of many priests ranges from laughable to criminal. What claim can a religion have to any ethical high ground when its leaders are hauled off to jail for everything from fraud to rape? How can religious leaders who suppress the human search for knowledge and repress the human spirit really claim to represent the best within us?

Of course there are priests who are decent, caring human beings. But such persons are not confined to any one religion, so these individuals are not proof of the correctness of a particular belief system. Further, there are plenty of non-believers who, in their private and public lives, better exemplify the humanistic principles found in a given religion than do the acknowledged priests of that religion.

Living with uncertainty can be tough, but may be better than following a mythical system that is demonstratively absurd. Priests certainly have a legal right to do their thing, but don't hold them up as models of correctness and virtue, and don't give them the power to control what you do with your life and your body. There are worse things than ripping up pictures of popes. These worse things include religious authorities ripping up lives.

Be your own person. Don't be an *-ite* following an *-ism*.

ON THE RAPTURE:
SEVEN YEARS AFTER

Not every one that saith unto me, Lord, Lord, shall enter into the kingdom of heaven; but he that doeth the will of my Father which is in heaven. Many will say to me in that day, Lord, Lord, have we not prophesied in thy name? and in thy name have cast out devils? and in thy name done many wonderful works? And then will I profess unto them, I never knew you: depart from me, ye that work iniquity.
　　　　—Matthew 7:21–23. Holy Bible (KJV, of course).

Many kind and compassionate Atheists are concerned about a now-available-in-stores video game in which self-proclaimed good, believing Christians obtain points by killing off other Christians, and members of lesser breeds who are not as godly as they, as the best Christians seek to be taken up into the sky to a make-believe place, a supernatural realm, to there be joined or reunited with invisible friends, both those forever immortal and those heretofore dead. This shoot-thy-neighbor game, this harmless representation of Christian caring, this faith-filled electronic exemplar of a god's love, is said to be being vended by Wal-Mart and other Fundangelical Friendly Facilities (FFFs) throughout the United States. This writing is to suggest that the reactions of both players and critics may be somewhat overdone, although, in general theological reasoning, those who condemn such a deviate departure from decent demeanor are far more correct and 'moral' and have better 'values' than do those who would, even in pretend play, practice the sociopathic acts represented by the game and who would transmit such treasonous terroristic teachings unto their children.

Given the progress of secularism in elevating human behavior over the past several centuries, amazed Atheistic condemnation of the approbation of this activity by the godly is quite understandable. Yet we should perhaps have some sympathy for the hurt, outrage, and fear

271

Edwin F. Kagin: *Baubles of Blasphemy*

these Fundangelical folks must feel, and perhaps we can find some small room for a measure of sympathy for their need to sublimate their despair at having not made the cut. If they are pathetically still awaiting The Rapture, we cannot but feel some pain, as for wounded children, for their hostile striking out, for their projection of passion poignantly presented in this game, where they, the clear losers, can be made to feel empowered and still somehow seemingly worthy of some sort of salvation.

At the stroke of midnight, December 31st, 2006, seven years will have passed since The Rapture. Yeah, I know some readers are now thinking that this is only six years. But figure it out. When a kid becomes 'One Year Old,' said child has lived one year and is starting the second year of life. At child's seventh birthday, child has then lived seven years and is beginning to live the eighth year of life. This is, of course, why many were mistaken in thinking the new millennium began at the beginning of the year '2000,' when it actually began at the beginning of '2001.' They were applying the rule for birthdays. But dates for years don't work like birthdays. Let us say a babe is born in the year 'One,' as some say someone of some importance was. The whole year of the child's birth would be the year One. And at the end of that year, the child would be 'one year old,' but it would also be the beginning of the year 'Two.' Thus, the second millennium was not over until the end of the year 2000, when 2000 years had been completed. But this did not prevent The Rapture from coming as foretold that terrible day seven years ago! And nothing will change that fact. No matter how many video games are vended with the theme of the joy of killing others on one's way to being taken up into the skies to be with the Lord and to enjoy the Wedding Feast of the Lamb. And now, after those seven years, we might pause and reflect on how we are doing. More on point for this rant, how the godly unsaved, the blessed condemned, are doing.

Seven (7) years is, after all, a somewhat magical number in their delusional system, a number recurring throughout their holy writings and prophetic texts, works viewed by them as future history. And seven years is a fairly long time. A person can go through college and Law School in seven years. Seven years is the traditional time after which a missing person is presumed dead. Seven is a magical holy

272

number. It is the trinity plus the four gospels. It is the most perfect of numbers. And it has been that long since The Rapture.

All good and literate persons now know full well what happened. Even little children have read and have been taught that which hath been writ in, "ON THE TRANSUBSTANTIATION OF THE WORLD: THE REVELATION TO EDWIN." This seminal document for our age may be found in electronic form here: http://www. edwinkagin.com/columns/transubstantiation.htm. It can also be found included in the banned book, *Baubles of Blasphemy*, created by your narrator. A few copies from the first printing of this classic may still be available. Check www.edwinkagin.com for information on this and other ultimate realities.

But I digress. The point is that The Rapture has happened, is gone, done, and over. If you are still here, you missed it. You had your chance. You will not be raptured, though you may yet still be ruptured. No one will ever be saved again. End of story. Get used to it.

Most readers who are of age remember that day seven years ago well, even if they were unaware of the happening of The Rapture. It was called "Y2K" (meaning "Year 2000"—for those doing their dissertations on this era), and people were getting ready for every computer on Earth to crash, and for banks, and therefore civilization as we have come to know it, to fail, and for marauding bands of brigands from here or wherever to try to invade their homes to get their stuff, so they hid their gold coins, laid in provisions, and locked their doors to await the end of the world, surrounded by survival equipment and weapons.

And nothing happened. Many credited it to the intervention of a god, totally ignoring all of the efforts of many computer geeks who had worked hard the entire previous year to fix the problems in the nation's computers that would cause them to do dog knows what when they hit the next hour after midnight on December 31, 1999, in that the year had been expressed in computer-speak in only double digits, like "98," "99," *etc.* After all, who could have predicted at the dawn of the computer age that a new thousand year period would one day come— sorta like being in college in the '60s (see how it works—doesn't tell you if it is 1760s or 1960s does it?) and reading George Orwell's "1984," and thinking it was an impossibly long time away. But 1984 came, and is still with us, and 2000 came, and it was not really special in any way at all. After all, dates on the calendar don't really mean anything more than does the line on a map between Kentucky and Tennessee. They are not real things. There are not really lines on the ground between states or nations. Such things only mean what people agree that they mean.

After Y2K, clever shoppers could get great bargains on unused generators, still in their boxes, and on such delicacies as mung beans. Some frightened folks who bravely stayed in bomb shelters may still be there.

The simple truth is that we are all doomed pennies on the track.

Moral persons who incorrectly, but nevertheless sincerely, believe that The Rapture is yet to come should, in consistent good faith, insist that airplanes in flight, hospital rooms doing surgeries, and other highly intensive life preserving industries be required by law to hire Atheist pilots, operating room staffs, *etc.*, thus insuring that persons keeping their charges alive by narrow behavioral decisions do not abandon them when such saved professionals are chosen to go frolic in the phantasmagorical fields of divine dispensations. Those in the air or under the knife, although left behind, should not be left alone. But this is not really necessary, as no rapturing is in their, or anyone's, future, for the reasons heretofore revealed. In any case, it might be nice if they decently suggested making some provisions for those of us they think will in fact be "left behind." Maybe their failure to do so shows just why they didn't make the Jesus Team.

To summarize, at the stroke of midnight on New Year's Eve, seven years ago, all persons ever to be raptured off to Heaven went as had been foretold, and as reported in the revelation to Edwin above referenced. This is a fact beyond dispute. It is simply not open to further discussion. The Rapture is now, and has been for the past seven years, part of our human history. People still awaiting the coming of The Rapture are pathetically deluded, or criminally fraudulent, in waiting for it or in trying to get money and converts for causes that no longer have any meaning. The almighty power is through with the dregs that were left behind. The only thing remaining of theological significance is the final culmination of all things, the end of the world, in which all of us are….. Never mind. It's too awful, and this is a family friendly publication.

As to the game, and its electronic exegesis, that provided the initial excuse for this blasphemy, and the impetus of the exegetes to indulge in such diversions, one can only ironically wonder, "What would Jesus do?"

Anyhow, don't take life too seriously. You won't get out of it alive anyway.

HAPPY NEW YEAR.

Edwin, by dog

December 30, 2006

Edwin F. Kagin: *Baubles of Blasphemy*

JESUS CHRIST HAS RETURNED

by Edwin Kagin, Special Reporter, April 1, 2007.
All Rights Reserved. Permission to Reproduce is Granted.

April 01, 2007. Independence, Missouri, U.S.A,

Jesus Christ has returned to Earth!

The Son of God, the Messiah, the Savior of the World, the Alpha and the Omega, the Beginning and the End, the Great I Am, has returned to our suffering world as He promised to do quickly over 2,000 years ago.

In God's stunning surprise move, this greatest event in the history of the modern world occurred just after Midnight on Sunday, April 1st, 2007. The Christ returned to a sacred spot in Independence, Missouri, U.S.A., as correctly predicted by the Mormon leader Joseph Smith. Believers expecting His return to occur on Temple Mount in Jerusalem were shocked, but red heifers were much relieved.

Religious leaders worldwide were taken completely by surprise, even though the sacred writings had said no one knew the date or the hour of the divine reappearance. But every knee was bowed and every tongue confessed that the Lord Jesus had come. Those few, in Independence, Missouri and elsewhere, who denied the obvious, the "Second Coming Deniers," were classed as persons so caught up in sin that they could not see truth made manifest before them.

The timing, while unpredicted, does fit a pattern.

The Rapture occurred just over seven years ago. For a full report, see:

http://www.edwinkagin.com/columns/transubstantiation.htm .

It is uncertain just what will happen next. God, being God, is fully capable of changing His mind, and then stating that He did not change His mind, and that we, who are but mortals, did not understand Him the first time. And He is of course right. Whatever He says is right.

276

Maybe we are not all condemned as we were told after The Rapture of 2000 C.E. Maybe we just misunderstood.

Those who have long asked, "What Would Jesus Do?" are rapidly finding out.

The Messiah has ordered all churches, of whatever persuasion or denomination, to immediately liquidate their assets, ordering them, as he had the first time around, to "sell all that you have and give to the poor." The Church of Jesus Christ of Latter-day Saints, both reorganized and un-reorganized, has begun to comply, as have Protestant and other denominations. The Roman Catholic Church has issued directives that all of its worldwide holdings are to be given to the poor, after satisfying judgments for damages rendered against them for their priests abusing children.

The Pope in Rome has abandoned his golden throne and offered it to the Christ, who simply said, "Sell it, and all that you have, and give to the poor." Worldwide, gold is being removed from tabernacles, temples, and mosques, and bank accounts are being emptied to provide food and housing for the poor, as the divine directive becomes realized.

Church property worldwide is being liquidated. It appears that all poverty will be abolished virtually overnight.

Ministers preparing to preach Palm Sunday sermons, celebrating the triumphant entry of Jesus into Jerusalem on his previous visit, quickly changed their messages to proclaim the good news of his entry into Independence.

Everywhere, the strains of "Handel's Messiah" are heard in the streets.

All war on Earth has ceased.

American Atheists has disbanded and cancelled their Easter Convention.

Thoughtful people are wondering just how it is possible to know the truth.

But the truth will set us free.

Details on the nightly news, immediately following the latest on the Anna Nicole story.

Edwin F. Kagin: *Baubles of Blasphemy*

Tsunamicy Theodicy

Letter to the Editor, Lexington Herald-Leader:

Tom Schaefer is quite correct in his New Year's Day column "Tsunami has us wondering about evil." Religion cannot explain why there is 'evil' in the world.

'Evil' is awful things done by humans, the ones who define evil.

It would be evil if certain *humans* had destroyed reefs, trees, and other natural barriers to tsunamis to make money. 'Evil' would be if certain humans did not notify other humans of pending danger from a tsunami because they feared they would lose money if they did so.

But a tsunami is not evil. It is the result of natural forces that can be explained, avoided, and, to an ever increasing measure, controlled by human minds and actions. It is a horrible thing with horrible results, but it does not *deliberately* cause harm. Only *purposeful* behavior is 'evil.'

Religion cannot explain earthquakes and volcanoes in the ocean because natural forces are subject to neither faith nor prayer.

Making up fancy theological words like 'theodicy' to define a non-issue won't help either.

Evil is the blasphemous arrogance of those who think their prayers worked, and that a god saved them while murdering tens of thousands of their fellow humans who were not as worthy as they.

Rather than ask if the god prayed to was powerless to prevent the tsunami, or simply didn't care to do so, one can do as some suggest and hope that the god doesn't hurt them even more, and pacify them, like Job, with the assurance that they really should not ask such a question.

Or recognize, as Tom said one theologian expressed it, the truth that "…evil and suffering are 'evidence for the atheist.'"

Edwin F. Kagin
Kentucky State Director
American Atheists, Inc.

Light Shining Through Muddy Windows

God moves in a mysterious way
His followers to confute;
There's nothing in his word today
That they cannot dispute.

The times are past when man was led
By wisdom from on high;
Now water sprinkled on his head
Tells if his soul must fry.

Interpretation must outweigh
Truths of greater good—
To learn what says of Judgement Day
Your sect or brotherhood.

Consider all the mighty mire
One must believe or sin—
How many of the Heavenly Choir
Can dance upon a pin?

Millennium here, millennium there
Millennium pre or post—
Millennium which would surely dare
Confuse the Holy Ghost.

Religion is just one mad ball;
These men so wise and fat
Digest a camel, hump and all
While choking on a gnat.

Edwin F. Kagin, Jr. (such it was at that time)
circa 1958 (really)

Edwin F. Kagin: *Baubles of Blasphemy*

The Seuss Watchmaker's Intelligent Design

Now most people know that watches in pockets,

Are made of different stuff than eyes in eye sockets.

A watch doesn't have wings, or flippers, or feet,

A watch isn't something another watch might just eat.

A watch doesn't live in a nest, cave, or hive,

And that is because a watch isn't alive.

If you can get that small detail resolved,

You can see why it's dumb to say life hasn't evolved.

And pretend that making a watch for a wrist,

Is just like making an arm or a fist.

And pretend people were made and clearly designed,

Because life is complex and sometimes refined.

Life didn't happen by magic or plan,

Like thinking some dirt was turned into a man.

And some folks believe, and this is no fib,

That the first woman was made from first dirt man's rib.

Evolution happened and it isn't true,

That people were made by some god from some goo.

Let's say that you took about ten quillion rabbits,

All alike in their looks, and their hops, and their habits.

And that about half were colored bright snerfell,

And that about half were colored dark murfell.

And if they made babies those snerfells and murfells,

Some of those babies would be colored snerfell.

And some of those babies would be colored murfell,

And some of those babies would be in between.

In some brand new colors no rabbit had seen,

Maybe some would be colored a pleasing snerplean.

Or maybe some awful disgusting murgreen,

And some might be lovely and some quite obscene.

And if the rabbits thus colored should make some more rabbits,

With only those rabbits with their color habits.

A new color for rabbits would finally evolve,

And the colors they started out with would dissolve.

And be completely replaced after enough time,

With snerplean or murgreen not made out of slime.

And enough time and enough rabbit ranges,

Could make in those rabbits amazing new changes.

Until they perhaps were no longer rabbits,

But maybe some new type of postrabbitodabits.

Edwin F. Kagin: *Baubles of Blasphemy*

A new kind of life we could not invent in our mind,

As new as a timepiece some watchmaker might wind.

But made from the life force creationists mock,

Who think life is something as dead as a clock.

So don't be confused by people who lie,

Who think truth is found in a book from the sky.

If it weren't for science we wish they could see,

We would all have to use candles to watch the T.V.

March 24, 2007

Christmas Letter

Dearest Beloved of Our Family in Christ,

There have been many changes this year for our family. Our beloved 17 year old daughter suffered blindness and paralysis after being struck by a drunk driver on her way home from Wednesday night church services. Aunt Polly died of liver cancer, following a long and painful illness. The family cat was smashed by a UPS truck. Mabel's M.S. is getting worse and she can hardly do anything much anymore. Father had to have a triple bypass operation, and now uses a breathing tube. The house was burned down by sparks from the burning of Harry Potter books in our yard. Little Marvin got a chicken bone stuck in his throat at a church picnic and was rushed to the hospital where doctors had to remove his voice box, so he can never talk again, but God miraculously saved him. Miranda is now being home schooled after she left eighth grade to become a single mother. An abortion was out of the question, and we know God has given us a hydrocephalic grandchild for his own good and perfect reasons. Our oldest son had his left foot blown off in an ambush in Iraq while helping to bring Christ and Democracy to those poor heathens. We rejoice in the wisdom of our God, in His gifts, and in His plan for our lives. We bear grateful witness to all that our great and merciful God has done for us in the past year, and we praise the works of His hand. Oh, almost forgot. The dog died.

In His Holy Name,

The Fundangelical Family

(by Edwin Kagin. December, 2006. Permission to reproduce without profit is given. If you make money on it, I want some of it. Edwin)

283

Antimiscegenation Law

Never let the Church and State
Get close enough to meet and mate;
For the safety of our nation
Prohibit this miscegenation;
Keep Church far from the bed of State;
Separate their greed and hate;

Abstinence is what they need

Or the monsters they will breed
Will mongrelize both law and creed.
Never let Church marry State—
Do not even let them date.

April 17, 2005

Edwin F. Kagin

Edwin Frederick Kagin, J.D., was born in Greenville, South Carolina, on November 26, 1940. He is an attorney in Union, Kentucky.

Kagin is the son of a Presbyterian minister born in Kentucky and a Daughters of the American Revolution mother born in South Carolina. His ancestry is Scottish (Stewart) Presbyterian on his mother's side, and Calvinistic German on his father's side. He attended The College of Wooster in Wooster, Ohio; Park College in Parkville, Missouri; the University of Missouri at Kansas City in Kansas City, Missouri; and the School of Law of the University of Louisville in Louisville, Kentucky. He is married to Helen McGregor Kagin, a Canadian of Scottish descent and a retired physician. Kagin is an Eagle Scout, a former college English Instructor, a U.S. Air Force veteran, a National Rifle Association Certified Handgun Instructor, and an Honorary Black Belt in Kenpo Karate, and a Freemason. He was editor of the American Association of Mental Deficiency and National Institute for Mental Health project that created the Adaptive Behavior Scale, an instrument for assessment of mental retardation.

Kagin is a founding member, former Vice President, and board member of FIG, the Free Inquiry Group, Inc., of Cincinnati and Northern Kentucky and is a published writer of poetry and prose that appears regularly in *FIG Leaves*

Edwin F. Kagin: *Baubles of Blasphemy*

(newsletter of FIG) and elsewhere, as "Kagin's Column." He is a co-author of the book *The Fundamentals of Extremism; The Christian Right in America* (Kimberly Blaker, ed.; New Boston Books, 2003), available in English and Arabic. He is a founding board member of Recovery Resources Center, which provides alternatives to Alcoholics Anonymous for addiction recovery, and a member of the Secular Student Alliance national Advisory Board and its speakers' bureau. Collections of his works can be found on his Web-site, www.edwinkagin.com and on his blog, http://edwinkagin.blogspot.com. A collection of his writings is available in his book *Baubles of Blasphemy* (Edward Buckner, ed.; Freethought Press, 2005) now available in the present 2nd revised edition.

Kagin is the originator and Director of Camp Quest, the nation's first residential secular summer camp for children of Atheists and other freethinkers (www.Camp-Quest.com), started in 1996 by FIG. He was an incorporator and is a founding board member of Camp Quest, Inc., a national non-profit corporation established in 2002 to operate Camp Quest. In 2005, following ten successful years, he and his wife Helen reired from this venture, after transferring control and management of Camp Quest to other hands.

Kagin has run unsuccessfully as "the candidate without a prayer" for the Kentucky Supreme Court and for the Kentucky State Senate. He has four children, Stephen, Eric, Heather, and Kathryn, a stepdaughter, Caroline, three granddaughters Maren, Kennedy, and Abby; and two grandsons, Ethan and Quin. Kagin, an ouspoken public citic of attemped religious intrusions into secular life by government, is a frequent speaker and debater on national radio, T.V., and at regional and national freethought meetings. He is the National Legal Director and Kentucky State Director for American Atheists and is on its speaker's bureau. Edwin and Helen were awarded the "Atheists of the Year" award for 2008. He is listed in *Who's Who in Hell* (Warren Allen Smith, ed.; Barricade Books, New York, 2000).